D1452626

Culture

AND

History

IN EASTERN EUROPE

Also by Dennis P. Hupchick

THE BULGARIANS IN THE SEVENTEENTH CENTURY:
Slavic Orthodox Society and Culture under Ottoman Rule

THE PEN AND THE SWORD:
Studies in Bulgarian History by James F. Clarke (editor)

CONFLICT AND CHAOS IN EASTERN EUROPE

Culture

AND

History

IN EASTERN EUROPE

Dennis P. Hupchick

St. Martin's Press
New York

First published in the United States of America 1994
Printed in the United States of America

0-312-12115-6

Library of Congress Cataloging-in-Publication Data

Hupchick, Dennis P.
  Culture and history in Eastern Europe / Dennis P. Hupchick
      p.   cm.
    ISBN 0-312-12115-6
    1. Europe, Eastern--Civilization. 2. Former Soviet republics—
Civilization. I. Title.
DJK24.H86   1994
947—dc20   93-48998
                                                 CIP

Interior design by Digital Type & Design

For My Dearest Wife,
❧ ANNE-MARIE ❧

⬛ Contents ⬛

▣ PREFACE ▣

The collection of essays that follows attempts to provide the general reader with a modicum of in-depth historical and cultural perspective that can help illuminate the human forces driving events in Eastern Europe and in Eurasia. My hope is that they will help clear some of the confusion often unintentionally generated by our news coverage, as well as help in pointing out areas where new developments are likely to occur in the future, and why. The reader should realize, however, that no attempt has been made to play the role of fortune-teller in these essays, despite the currently acceptable fashion for prediction. After the surprising events of late 1989 in Berlin and elsewhere caught most specialists off guard, it should be common knowledge that soothsaying analysts and academics tend to be great "foot gourmets." Instead of predictions, the essays themselves contain certain of my personal conclusions but leave the reader to form her or his own.

The essays take a general, one might say sweeping, approach to the region and field of Eastern Europe. They attempt to provide a broad cultural context for understanding the peoples and the events currently helping to shape the new, postcold war Europe, which differs somewhat from the more narrow political and economic approaches taken by most current analysts. Since the essays are individual entities collected together under one cover, some repetition of ideas and information can be expected. Both the scope and the repetition are intended to aid the informational purpose of this publication.

For the most part, these essays are expanded versions of various public and classroom remarks whose publication have been urged by a number of individuals. Normally, one would accept such reaction as polite response to stimulating and enjoyable intellectual exercises, but when the suggestions come from university presidents, public figures, and journalists, they cannot be taken lightly. So the idea for this collection was born.

Since the avowed goal of this work is to reach an intelligent general reader interested in knowing more about the forces behind the news emanating from Eastern Europe and Eurasia, an effort has been made to avoid the impression of staid academe. The essays that follow have been intentionally placed in a popular format, with their conceptual images painted in broad strokes and without "intimidating" footnotes and "awkward" academic jargon. The ideas and observations contained in the essays are the results of years of extensive reading and research in the fields of East European, Byzantine, Ottoman, and Russian history and of extended periods of firsthand experience in many of the regions discussed. Most specialists will find in these essays little altogether new, though they may disagree with some of my general interpretations. Many of the concepts are unoriginal; however, the interpretations and the conclusions drawn from the works of others most likely would not be those of the original authors. To aid the general reader of this collection, an essay on further readings, containing these sources and other works in English dealing with concepts and topics raised by the essays, has been included instead of a formal bibliography.

I wish to extend my sincere thanks to Tom Bigler, a living legend in the Wilkes-Barre area's journalistic community, for the many hours he spent reading and criticizing the drafts of the essays. He performed wonders in ensuring that the text did not lapse into too academic a realm. Robert Heaman, dean of liberal arts at Wilkes University and professor of English composition, provided invaluable stylistic criticism of the draft texts. Harold Cox, historian and Wilkes University's resident cartographer, electronically prepared the maps supplementing the essays and provided assorted additional assistance in preparing the manuscript for publication, for which I am extremely grateful. Also deserving acknowledgment was the active encouragement to undertake this writing project in the first place lent by Christopher Breiseth, president of Wilkes University, and by Anne-Marie Hupchick, my wife.

Wilkes-Barre, 1993
Dennis P. Hupchick

◼ NOTE ON PRONUNCIATION ◼

In the texts of the following essays, an attempt has been made to retain the native spelling of most proper names and foreign terms, except in the case of languages using non-Latin alphabets, when either a phonetic transliteration of the phonics (for Arabic, Bulgarian, and Russian) or the Latin-based Croat form (for Serbian) are used. Some more well-known proper names (for example, Prague and Belgrade) are given in their common forms rather than in their native spellings. A guide to the simple phonetic pronunciation of certain foreign spellings is as follows:

á (Hungarian): ....as **a** in *a*h

c (in all cases except Turkish): ....as **ts** in bea*ts*

ch (Polish, Czech, Slovak), h (Bulgarian,
    Serb, Croat, Turkish): ....as **ch** in Ba*ch*

cz (Polish), č (Serb, Croat, Czech, Slovak),
    ć (Serb, Croat, Polish), cs (Hungarian), ç (Turkish) ....as **ch** in *ch*ur*ch*

é (Hungarian): ....as **a** in b*a*y

ĕ (Czech): ....as **ye** in *ye*t

ğ (Turkish): ....as **silent h** in o*h*

i (in all cases): ....as **ee** in sw*ee*t

j (in all cases except Arabic): ....as **y** in *y*et

j (Arabic), dj (Serb, Croat), gy (Hungarian), c (Turkish): .....as **dzh** in ba*dge*

ł (Polish): ....as **w** in *w*on

ń (Polish): ....as **n** in *kn*ew

sz (Polish), š (Serb, Croat, Czech, Slovak),
    s (Hungarian), ş (Romanian and Turkish): ....as **sh** in *sh*eet

ü (Turkish, Hungarian): ....as **yoo** in mil*ieu*

ŭ (Bulgarian): ....as **short a** in b*u*t

w (Polish, German): ....as **v** in *v*ery

y (Polish, Russian, Czech, Slovak): ....as **i** in *i*t

ž (Serb, Croat), ř (Czech, Slovak), zs (Hungarian),
    j (Romanian): ....as **zh** in mea*s*ure

CIVILIZATIONAL FAULT LINES
IN EASTERN EUROPE — 1994

Cox 1293

MAJOR NATIONALITY FRACTURES IN EASTERN EUROPE

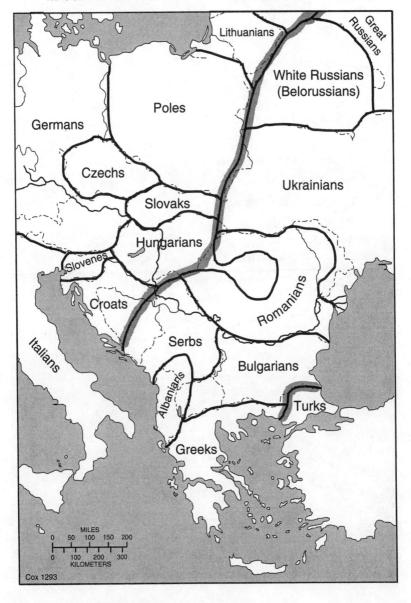

PHYSICAL GEOGRAPHY OF EASTERN EUROPE

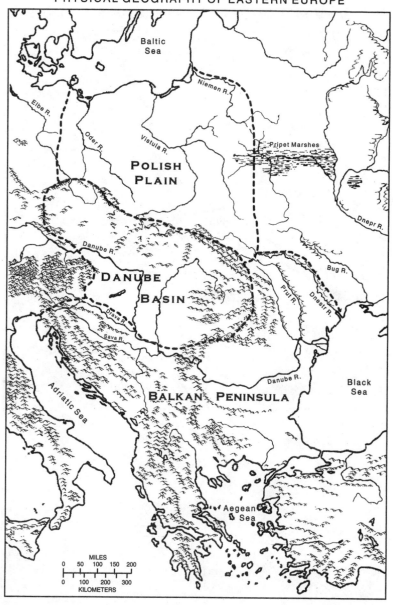

POLITICAL DIVISIONS
EASTERN EUROPE — 1994

BYZANTINE EMPIRE AND EASTERN EUROPE IN 1000

APEX OF THE OTTOMAN EMPIRE IN EUROPE
MID-16TH CENTURY

PERSPECTIVES AND DEFINITIONS

● ○ ●

The dramatic events that have occurred in Eastern Europe and the former Soviet Union since 1989 have elicited a flood of media analysis and commentary in the West. Yet for all the effort expended in trying to explain and analyze events in Eastern Europe and the Commonwealth of Independent States (CIS), most Westerners remain perplexed when it comes to understanding the motivating forces that drive them. Such a situation begs the question: Why is this the case?

The answer might lie in the fact that our framework for analysis is not broad enough to encompass all the forces at play in shaping developments in Eastern Europe and the CIS. We generally have limited ourselves to considering only current political and economic factors. The demise of communism and the failure of central planning dominate our public discussions. In effect, Westerners seem to believe that if only liberal–democratic governments and capitalist economies are installed in Eastern Europe and the CIS all will be well. These criteria alone appear to serve as the ultimate contexts for understanding events occurring in those regions.

Important as political and economic factors undoubtedly are, however, they fail to explain some of the crucial developments in Eastern Europe and the CIS. This is so for a combination of reasons: partly because politics and economics are restatements of concepts held over from the cold war years; and partly because of a human propensity for seeking simple, quick explanations and solutions regarding complex situations and problems. By using politics and economics as our primary parameters of analysis, we are conveniently papering over a real ignorance of realities in Eastern Europe and the CIS. And yet, an informed public will be needed if the new global challenges posed by a post–cold war environment are to be met successfully.

The devastating turns of events that took place in the disintegrating Yugoslavia and the dying Soviet Union in 1991 demonstrated just how limited our perspective has been. Neither the deadly conflict among Serbs, Croats, and Muslims in the former Yugoslavia nor the divisive tensions among the peoples of the former Soviet republics can be explained purely by our political-economic model born of the cold war. For a number of reasons, until the eruption of large-scale ethnic fighting, and despite spiraling currency inflation, many Western analysts commonly considered the former Yugoslavia somehow better off than its Warsaw Pact neighbors. Under Tito, Yugoslavia had broken with the Stalinist Soviet Union in 1948; a seemingly more democratic form of Communist leadership had been created by means of a collegial presidency in 1980; and a mixed centrally planned market economic system had been instituted. As for the Soviet Union, until the failed coup attempt of 1991 resulted in the dismantling of the country into independent states along ethnic-nationalist lines, our view of the central issues exclusively tended to focus on Gorbachev's demonstrating how far and how quickly he was willing to move toward democracy and market economics and on his ability to impose his will upon what we considered an essentially monolithic and subservient "Russia." (Americans and West Europeans continue to hold this view regarding Boris Yeltsin.) Events in both former countries have belied our standard preconceptions.

Before the beginning of the bloodbath in the former Yugoslavia and the Moscow coup attempt, serious public discussions of the potential explosiveness for the regions posed by unresolved nationalistic tensions and the innate dangers of possible cultural conflicts could rarely be read or heard outside the walls of universities and colleges. Lest a false impression be made, however, it is important to note that, in many respects, higher education suffered from the same ideological and perceptual shortcomings that afflicted the media and the political pundits.

When centers for studying the Soviet Union and Eastern Europe were first founded at some major universities in the early 1950s, they were staffed primarily by former World War II military intelligence officers and political emigrés, who brought their cold war mentalities and old world nationalist antagonisms into the academic arena. Much of what they produced smacked of political and nationalist propaganda disguised as objective scholarship. The academic image of the Communist world that emerged was that of a monolithic socialist entity—the East Bloc. That being the case, little specialized investigation of the component peoples who inhabited its territory was demanded because all true national divergences from the Soviet model were considered to have been eliminated. As a result, scholarly specialization in the various areas and peoples of Eastern Europe and Eurasia was stifled. Graduates of doctoral programs in the 1970s and 1980s who attempted to specialize in the East European and non-Russian Eurasian fields outside that specifically of the Soviet Union found it increasingly difficult to find academic positions. Most colleges and universities considered having a Russian or Soviet specialist on the faculty adequate for their needs. Many East European and Eurasian specialists were forced to leave academe for lack of job opportunities, thus serving as discouraging examples to others who initially may have been interested in pursuing studies in those fields. When the events of 1989-90 occurred, a loud lament was raised in the editorial pages of the *Chronicle of Higher Education,* the official organ of American academe, bewailing the lack of trained East European and Eurasian specialists. The fact was, higher education had only itself to blame for the situation.

Ethnic disturbances occurring between 1988 and 1991 in the Kosovo, Slovenian, and Croatian regions of the former Yugoslavia and in the Armenian, Azerbaijani, and Georgian republics of the former Soviet Union received a certain passing notice in the Western media. The independence movements of the Baltic republics also were highly publicized. Then, in 1991, with the advent of nationalistic and cultural warfare in the former Yugoslavia and with postcoup Soviet disintegration, media analysts and politicians were forced to add a consideration of ethnic animosities to their political-economic repertoire. Yet despite the broadening of analytical parameters that this addition entailed, we have remained handicapped by our inability to shake off simplistic perceptual approaches in our attempts to understand the events shaking Eastern Europe and the CIS.

Our latest analyses make increasing use of such adjectives as "historical," "religious," and "cultural" when attempting to explain the differences fueling nationalist unrest in the regions, but the terms are employed with an obviously limited perspective and understanding. In most of the analyses history rarely extends backward in time for more than sixty years. Thus, for example, the historical roots of the Croat-Serb conflict are considered to lie in Yugoslav events during World War II: The Croatian *Ustaše* was a creature organization of Hitler's Nazis, and Tito's mostly Serb partisans massacred thousands of Croats, whether *Ustaše* or not, at war's end. Likewise, both the confrontations between the Baltic states and the Soviets and that among the Romanians, Ukrainians, and Russians in Moldova are represented as stemming from the 1939 Ribbentrop-Molotov Pact. Religion as a component of analysis is essentially defined as "faith" and is primarily used regarding Islamic peoples, who constitute large population segments of Bosnia, Hercegovina, and the CIS states in Central Asia. They are usually portrayed in the context of conflict with their non-Muslim neighbors, such as the Bosnian Muslims with the Serbs, the Azerbaijanis with the Armenians, or the Ossetians with the Georgians, to name just three examples. The cultural factor is usually reduced to little more than mere descriptions of ethnic, usually religious and linguistic, differences.

Within the limited contexts imposed on their common usage in most Western analyses, none of these three terms—history, religion, and culture—in itself is satisfactory in providing the broader framework necessary for beneficially analyzing the situations evolving in Eastern Europe and the CIS, although they do point in the right direction.

One of the most critical keys to understanding events as they occur in Eastern Europe and the CIS lies in understanding the cultural forces that have historically operated in those regions. On the surface, this might appear a simple and straightforward undertaking. In reality, simplicity belies a complexity and sophistication not always readily apparent. Before the key can be used, therefore, the precise nature of the crucial tumblers in the lock—history and culture—must be clearly understood.

To quote from the book *1066 and All That,* history to the average person is "what you can remember." The average person appears to possess a historical awareness that spans her or his own lifetime, if that. People have little authentic understanding of the momentous issues involved in earlier events and how those events continue to shape their lives. True historical meaning is lost to most. The past, especially when it does not encompass personal memories, is the past. Period.

This seems particularly true of Americans. Perhaps this can be attributed to the fact that we Americans lack a historical consciousness because we possess such a short history of our own—two, three, or five hundred years at the very most. We have not been around long enough as a unique society to have developed strong, stable historical traditions. Given our lack of historical perspective, there is little wonder that we find it difficult to grasp the significance that history plays in the current affairs of other societies in the world. In Eastern Europe and Eurasia alone, peoples such as the Bulgarians, Serbs, Croats, Hungarians, Romanians, Albanians, Greeks, Czechs, Poles, Lithuanians, Georgians, Armenians, Turks, Tatars, and Russians possess strong, living traditions and a consciousness of their pasts that, for good or ill, often extend back in time for a thousand or more years. For them, history is alive today. It plays an important, continuing role in shaping their lives.

By considering history in terms of a people's long-held traditions and consciousness of their past, we are simultaneously raising the issue of their culture. Indeed, the two—history and culture—cannot be separated definitively. Both develop in parallel fashion in what is essentially a symbiotic relationship. Events of Eastern Europe and the CIS in large part are driven by powerfully authentic cultural forces, many involving concepts and emotions alien to Western thought.

Before one can gain an understanding of East European, Eurasian, and, indeed, world events, it is necessary to acquire a grasp of the traditional concept of culture. Simply stated, culture is the way a particular group of human beings (a society) adapts to its physical and human environment. The relationship between culture and environment is paramount, because a society's environment fashions the fundamental views of reality and the world shared by its members. These views, in turn, produce the group's various accepted means of environmental adaptation—its norms. Although cultural norms comprise such basic aspects of human existence as distinctive types of dress, cuisine, habits, tools, skills, and the various arts, the most fundamental expressions of culture are religious beliefs, languages, and philosophies. Culture provides groups of humans with their collective self-identity, thus shaping their every activity and institution, including churches, governments, and economies.

Culture, in the ideal sense, presupposes conformity among all the members of a given society. In the real sense, though, universal conformity within a culture does not exist. Since culture is a product of human design, it can be changed over time if enough people holding variant perceptions in common exert enough influence on the rest of their society to force the general acceptance of their views. Such a change usually occurs unconsciously over a long period of time. All cultures experience change, but not frequently. A change that forces a culture to divide into two or more uniquely different cultures is rare, indeed, and is extremely convulsive for the society involved. Most commonly, variant groups of people within the primary culture of a society constitute subcultures. While sharing in the fundamental core beliefs and institutions of the primary culture, subcultures possess enough variant traits to be readily distinguishable from the rest of their society. Distinguishing subcultural traits are particular variations in the norms expressed by the primary culture, often shaped by local or regional environments.

In the American context, most of the groups today commonly referred to as cultures are actually subcultures of the primary American culture—various ethnic groups, including Afro-Americans and Hispanics; regional groups, such as Southerners, Californians, New Englanders, and Midwesterners; and some authentic alternative lifestyle groups, such as gays and followers of the Hare Krishna cult. Although public emphasis tends to be placed on those unique traits that distinguish the individual subgroups from the others, all accept the fundamental moral, political, and economic values that constitute American society's perception of reality—that is, American culture. With the possible exception of certain Native American tribes living on reservations, one would be extremely hard-pressed to find an authentic primary culture in competition with the American anywhere in the country, certain groups' fears of Blacks, Hispanics, or gays notwithstanding. The term "subcultural pluralism" rather than "cultural pluralism" is the more accurate in describing American cultural reality.

Much the same might be said about all the major societies of Western Europe. Each exhibits a variety of ethnic, regional, and social subcultural diversity within its primary culture. In the United Kingdom, for instance, British culture encompasses such ethnic subcultures as the Welsh, Scottish, and Northern Irish; distinctive regional variations, such as can be found in Yorkshire and Cornwall, among others; and the commonly occurring social alternative lifestyle groups found in all Western cultures today. In France, French culture has its Breton, Norman, and Provençal linguistic variations, and a veritable smorgasbord of regional subcultural variety (as every wine and culinary connoisseur knows). Further examples can be made of every other Western European country and culture. While today all of them are facing rising internal cultural tensions resulting from a growing influx of immigrants from foreign societies with completely different cultures—Muslim Turks in Germany, Hindu Indians in England, Muslim North African Arabs and Afghan Turks in France, and various Orthodox East Europeans in all, to name only a few—in no case has the dominance of the primary cultures yet been seriously challenged within the borders of the individual Western states.

On the other hand, true cultural pluralism, meaning the existence of more than one unique culture within the borders of a single country, characterizes most of the East European and Eurasian states. For this reason, understanding the specific histories and cultures of the various peoples inhabiting Eastern Europe and Eurasia constitutes the logical framework for making sense of events in those regions.

Human culture operates within societies on two levels, the macro and the micro. Macroculture means civilization. Civilizations are nothing less than complex cultures shared by numerous people spread over large geographic areas, in which all important social activities (religion, leadership, livelihoods, defense, law, learning, and the like) are encompassed by highly developed, sophisticated institutions (churches, governments, economies, armed forces, courts, schools, and so forth). Moreover, every civilization is characterized by widespread urbanization, with the social differentiation and division of labor that it implies, and by a system of record keeping, usually in the form of a written language.

Nationality, which constitutes more than strict ethnicity, is now the primary expression of microculture. Within any given civilization there are a number of such cultures, each differentiated from the other by unique aspects of spoken language, customs, dress, cuisine, or any other particular trait that helps define culture. For example, within Western European civilization there are, among others, the American, French, English, and German microcultures. Because of the vast size and large population involved in any civilization, which are factors that guarantee pluralism at the macrocultural level, the cultural cement that binds the disparate microcultures together—the civilization's perception of reality—is most succinctly expressed through the fundamental form of religious belief that predominates among the human membership, although the expression of this core belief may vary among member cultures. For this reason, cultural historians often use religious and geographic names interchangeably in denoting individual civilizations—Hindu (Indic, Indian), Buddhist (Sinic, Far East Asian), Western Christian (Roman Catholic or Protestant, Western European), and Eastern Christian (Orthodox, Eastern European) civilizations. Uniquely, Islamic civilization is wholly denoted by religion. Ethnic or national names are most commonly used to identify microcultures. For example, such terms as French, German, English, Russian, Bulgarian, Polish, and Arabic are ethnic in nature; American, Canadian, Swiss, and Belgian are national.

Microculture does not necessarily require the presence of a macroculture. Numerous primitive, tribal cultures have existed outside the cultural frontiers of civilizations. Some, such as a few New Guinea and Amazonian groups, still do so today, although this situation grows rarer with each passing year. Most existing tribal societies, such as those found in Africa, Australia, and Latin America, have fallen under the strong cultural influence of civilizations. Whether civilization's interpenetration of these tribes' native cultures has proceeded to the point of successfully incorporating them into the macroculture still is a matter of some debate.

That primitive cultures, meaning microcultures independent of a macroculture, exist raises an important point about culture on its two levels. While every civilization undoubtedly is a culture, not every culture is, or will grow into, a civilization. History has shown that there have existed throughout the world less than seven hundred individual, documented cultures in the past six thousand years. During that same time there have arisen less than twenty-five civilizations, five of which exist today—the Western (Catholic/Protestant) and Eastern (Orthodox) European, the Islamic, the Indian (Hindu), and the Far East Asian (Buddhist/Shinto). To equate nationalities (microcultures), civilized though they may be through their membership in a civilization (macroculture), with civilizations themselves is a gross misrepresentation of reality. There are no such things as Polish, Serbian, English, French, German, American, and so on, civilizations. Although such equations have frequently appeared as book titles, they are merely expressions of nationalistic mythologies or pretensions.

The interactions among civilizations and nationalities over time have had the most profound effects on human development since the beginning of recorded history. On the macrocultural level, there can be no doubting the lasting impact made on Western European civilization by its centuries-old interactions with the Islamic world. These constant, often bloody, relations significantly helped shape the medieval development of the West and provided the fuel necessary for sparking the Renaissance. They motivated the Age of Discovery, contributed to the success of the Reformation, furnished a mathematical system (algebra) central to the Scientific Revolution, and serviced the energy needs of modern industrialization. Such phenomena as Western colonialism and imperialism in Africa, Asia, and the Americas were overt expressions of one macroculture's lasting impact on other, originally unrelated, microcultures. On the microcultural level, the French, German, English, American, and, in fact, all of the member microcultures of Western European civilization, are what they are today through centuries of interactions among themselves, both violent and benign. Although these examples have been drawn exclusively from one civilization—our own—similar cases can be cited from the others, whether located in Eastern Europe, Eurasia, or in any other region of the world.

Now that it has become apparent that the cold war holdovers of political and economic analyses are insufficient to fully explain the developments taking place in post-Communist Eastern Europe and Eurasia, we in the West find ourselves faced with problems regarding those regions. How are we going to act on the East European and Eurasian stages now that the only reality most of us have ever known as adults has disappeared? What will be our role in the new East European and Eurasian worlds? Is there some way we can effectively intervene to help stop the violence in these regions? Before we act or establish set policies addressing these issues, we had better gain a concrete understanding of the realities perceived by those regions' inhabitants. After all, we are dealing with human beings and not merely with terrain. If we are to gain a deeper, more balanced, and constructive understanding of events in Eastern Europe and the CIS, then we must be exposed to the complex maze of historical traditions and cultural interrelationships that are the underlying motivational forces acting, whether consciously or subconsciously, on those who are driving the events.

CULTURAL FAULTS

● ○ ●

November 1989 will stand symbolically as one of the most important dates in world history. It is hard to imagine a more stunning image than the fall of the Berlin Wall, signaling the collapse of Communist domination over Eastern Europe and the former Russian Empire. That the dismantling of the cold war icon was rooted in political developments at least three years in the making does little to diminish its awesome symbolism. The Wall came down and, like dominoes, so fell the Marxist regimes in East Germany, Hungary, Czechoslovakia, Poland, Bulgaria, Romania, Albania, and, finally, in the homeland of communism itself, the Soviet Union. The cold war was over; the West had triumphed. Most of the developed world rejoiced. Capitalism and liberal democracy had decisively demonstrated their intrinsic superiority over the scientific socialist dream of central planning and the dictatorship of the proletariat. Now the downtrodden people of the defunct East Bloc could finally, after one-half to three-quarters of a century, elect representative governments, install market economies, and rejoin their victorious European brethren. Peace, security, and expanding prosperity seemed assured. For some intellectuals in the United States, the victory of capitalist liberal democracy appeared so utterly decisive that the "end of history" was proclaimed, implying that the entire span of human existence merely represented a long developmental progression ultimately leading to the universal acceptance of capitalism and liberal democracy by all, after which there would be no further development since there would be no rational human need left to fill.

Despite the euphoria in the West, however, history did not end in 1989, nor did it end in 1991 with the failed coup in Moscow and the dissolution of the Soviet Communist party. Peace, security, and prosperity did not shower upon the land. Instead, in the wake of those momentous events, the European and Central Asian worlds witnessed some of the most deadly warfare, political disintegration, and economic disruption since the end of World War II. Dramatic, often devastating, eruptions followed one upon the other in rapid succession as the political, social, and economic constraints of communism were loosed. By Western standards and perceptions, many of the peoples inhabiting a freed Eastern Europe and Eurasia appeared deliberately determined to commit political and economic suicide. To Western eyes, the actions taken by peoples in the Balkans and in Eurasia following 1989 often seemed to verge on the incomprehensible. For many, they continue to seem so today.

The way human actions are perceived is a function of culture. In any society's observations and analyses of another's activities, the level of understanding attained will be a factor of the observer's own perception of reality—the observer's own culture. Actions taking place within and among other societies that do not fit, or cannot be made to fit neatly, into the observer's reality will, of necessity, be viewed as incomprehensible. To the Native North American tribal societies in the eighteenth and nineteenth centuries, the activities of the colonizing Western Europeans made no sense whatsoever, even though they realized that the intruders threatened their very existence. They failed to comprehend Western European realities and thus sealed their ultimate abject fate.

Western European civilization, which holds reason and causal relationships as fundamental premises of its reality, rejects the notion of incomprehensibility entirely. This causes difficulties for its members in making sense of activities taking place in non-Western societies. Either the foreigners' actions are measured perfunctorily by the unique moral standards of Western European civilization and subsequently labeled "barbaric," "ignorant," "tribal," or some other pejorative term, or an attempt is made to create a rational, analytical structure that places those actions within a context understandable to the Western mind. Since nothing truly constructive can be gained by the former approach (as the Native American societies discovered to their dismay), the effort must be made along the lines of the latter with regard to future Western relations with Eastern Europe and Eurasia.

Let us, then, construct a framework of cultural history that might prove both understandable and useful to Western Europeans when treating with Eastern Europe and Eurasia—and, by logical extension, with all non-Western cultures.

Since the beginning of recorded time, history has been shaped and driven by interactions among human societies and their cultures. In fact, these interactions are the very essence of history—the story of humankind's evolution from exclusively primitive local tribal societies and individual cultures into sophisticated civilizations spanning huge portions of the globe and encompassing the majority of all existing cultures. Not since the emergence of civilization as a cultural and social phenomenon some six thousand years ago in West Asia (Iraq) and North Africa (Egypt) has humankind escaped the determining factor of cultural interrelationships in human development. Every civilization, whether existing today or in the past, has been tempered and shaped by human contacts on the two levels of culture: interrelationships with other civilizations (macrocultural contacts) and interrelationships among its own member societies, which today are called nationalities (microcultural contacts). The interactions among civilizations ultimately determine the nature and state of the world in general. Those strictly among nationalities primarily affect the nature of their respective civilizations.

Of the human interplay that takes place on each of the two cultural levels, macro and micro, those involving civilizations possess the potential for the greatest degree of human convulsion. In Eastern Europe and Western Eurasia today we are witnessing the interactions of three civilizations—the Western European (Catholic/Protestant), the Eastern European (Orthodox) and the Islamic (Muslim). Discerning the interplay among them is crucial to our understanding of current developments in those regions.

To clarify the effort involved in our task, we might borrow from geology the concept of continental plate tectonics as a useful analogy. In the most simple expression of this analogy, every civilization can be seen as holding sway over a large, geographically defined core area where the fundamental worldview binding together its various constituent societies has undergone native, organic development. Each core area might then be viewed as a large plate superimposed on the map of the world. Focusing on the specific geographical regions of Europe and Western Eurasia, we find the Orthodox East European plate sandwiched between the Western European, to its west and northwest, and the Islamic, to its south and southeast. The locations where they are in contact with each other form cultural fault lines.

Since we are dealing with fluid human societies rather than with solid masses of earth and rock, the simple analogy must be modified accordingly. Human fault lines cannot be delineated neatly on a map by means of simple lines, as can their geological counterparts. Centuries of human interaction have occurred along the lines of contact among the three civilizations. As a result of the ebb and flow of historical events, microcultural societies of each have penetrated into geographic regions dominated by the others. Our plots of human cultural faults, therefore, are actually bands of gray on the map whose widths vary by location and history. Much like geological faults relative to seismographic and volcanic eruptions, these bands represent lines along which occur the most dramatic human disturbances, caused by friction among the differing macrocultural plates. Likewise, they are where future eruptions are likely. When the locations of the most explosive events that have occurred over the past few years in Eastern Europe and Eurasia are related to this sort of cultural geography, their general correlation with macrocultural fault lines is striking. It should come as no surprise that such has been the case for centuries.

The historical cultural fault line dividing the Western and Eastern European civilizations runs from the Baltic to the Adriatic seas, roughly encompassing the three Baltic republics; the regions of Belarus and Ukraine that border on Poland, Slovakia, and Hungary; Transylvania in Romania; the Vojvodina province of Serbia; the Slavonian border region separating Croatia and Serbia; all of Bosnia-Hercegovina; and the Dalmatian-Montenegrin border (see maps on pages xii-xvii). Even the most cursory glance at the history of those peoples living along this fault reveals the consistently disruptive nature of the East-West European macrocultural friction.

Violent human convulsions have consistently swept the fault separating the Eastern and Western European civilizations since the time of Western Europe's Middle Ages. Centuries of deadly Polish-Russian conflict pushed the cultural border in the northeast to and fro between Moscow and Warsaw until the second partition of Poland stabilized the frontier in 1793. The third partition of Poland in 1795 completely wiped the country from the map of Europe. Orthodox Russia received the largest share of Poland in that bit of international grand larceny, representing the first near-permanent inroad made by Eastern Europe into the West. Shortly thereafter, the tumult of the Napoleonic Wars renewed the European East-West macrocultural struggle in the massive French-Russian conflicts that eventually spanned the continent of Europe from Moscow to Paris, only to have the macrocultural border settle back into its pre-Napoleonic locale at their close in 1815. Two armed Polish uprisings against Russian rule erupted within the fault in 1830 and in 1864. During the first half of the twentieth century, the conflict between the two European civilizations along the German-Russian eastern fronts reached proportions unrivaled in violence, inhumanity, and devastation. Following the First World War, in a war with the newly created Soviet state (1920-21), a resurrected Poland drove the border with Eastern Europe eastward only to experience its return at the beginning of the Second World War (1939). In the aftermath of the latter war, the frontier of Eastern European civilization pushed farther west than ever before in history, reaching deep inside Germany to the doorstep of Vienna. Near the end of the twentieth century, with the collapse of Soviet-style communism between 1989 and 1991, the border separating the two European civilizations once again retreated eastward to its pre-1795 line of human demarcation. Simultaneously, new convulsions at the northern and southern extremities of the fault erupted.

The Baltic peoples, especially the Lithuanians, historically have viewed themselves as the guardians of Western European civilization's extreme northeastern frontier against Orthodox Eastern Europe. Pagan Lithuanians were in conflict with Orthodox Russians as early as the eleventh century, when they first became locked in what would evolve into a six hundred-year struggle for domination over the Belorussian and Ukrainian regions of Western Eurasia. The fourteenth-century union of Lithuania with Catholic Poland, which led to the conversion of the Lithuanians to Catholicism, transformed the Lithuanian-Russian conflict from the microcultural to the macrocultural level. Consequently, the Lithuanians were totally assimilated into Western European civilization through the cultural influence exerted on them by the highly Westernized Poles. Moreover, it was the Polish-Lithuanian union that drew the Poles permanently into the macrocultural struggle between Western and Eastern Europe, transforming the far-flung lands of Poland-Lithuania into the seismic epicenter of the cultural fault. The bloody three hundred-year history of this macrocultural conflict, which led to the disappearance of both Poland and Lithuania at the end of the eighteenth century and subsequently to two hundred years of Russian domination, bred among the Poles and Lithuanians an undying anti-Russian sentiment and concerns for stable national borders that exist to the present day.

The Baltic Latvians and Estonians, who never attained independent nationhood before the early twentieth century (and since then only for less than two decades), were originally brought into Western European civilization during medieval times primarily through their domination by foreign Westerners. First to arrive were the German Teutonic Knights. Later came the Lithuanians, the Poles, and the Swedes, as each successively sought political expansion in the Baltic region prior to the eighteenth century. By the time they were forcibly incorporated by Peter the Great into the Orthodox East European civilization of the Russian Empire in the early eighteenth century, these Baltic peoples already had been converted to Catholicism or Protestantism and were staunchly aware of their Western self-identities.

When the Baltic region is viewed from the perspective of macrocultural history, it can be seen as no accident that the recent struggle of the Western Lithuanians, Estonians, and Latvians for independence from East European Soviet (Russian) dominance was so adamant, and that the West, including the United States, was so supportive of their efforts. Once the control of the foreign civilization began to loosen because of internal stresses in the late 1980s, the deep-seated macrocultural animosity of the Baltic peoples toward the Russians precluded any successful compromise regarding their continued existence within the confines of an Eastern European civilization. Their demand for independence at any cost, even though independence meant existence as weak, small, and economically poor states in the community of strong, large, and wealthy Western nations, was as much an expression of macrocultural independence as it was of national liberation.

The rapid and potent Western support for Baltic independence, despite the potentially destabilizing effects on the international situation that their independence entailed, represented Western European civilization's gut reaction to reclaim and to protect its own. The macrocultural significance of the initial Western response to Baltic developments was underlined by the West's simultaneous refusal to support other non-Western independence movements within the Eurasian world, such as those of the Ukrainians, the Georgians, and the Azerbaijanis. On the other hand, Eastern European civilization's reticence to let go of a region that it historically claimed by conquest resulted first in Gorbachev's reluctance to submit to the rising tide of Baltic national movements and then in the violent clashes that erupted on the streets of Vilnius during 1988 and 1989.

Ultimately, internal troubles forced a grudging Eastern Europe to let go of the West's most northeasterly outposts. But the Baltic States' independence and reunion with the West did not stop the macrocultural friction between the two Europes in the region. The issues over the delay in Russian troop withdrawals and the Baltic republics' new, essentially anti-Russian citizenship laws have kept antagonisms simmering. So the fault has continued to tremor in the Baltics.

The Romanian province of Transylvania lies in the central region of the East-West European fault. Although relatively quiet throughout the dramatic events of 1989-90, it historically has been a hotbed of macrocultural turmoil between the two Europes. For nine hundred years, until its unification with the two other Romanian provinces of Wallachia and Moldavia in 1918, Transylvania was claimed and ruled by the westernized Hungarians. During that time, the Hungarian ruling establishment subjected the Orthodox Romanian majority to ever-increasing pressure from macrocultural discrimination. Hungarian pressure and mounting Romanian reactions caused such bitter mutual cultural animosities to develop between the two peoples that, once Hungary was beaten to its knees in World War I, the Transylvanian Romanians joyously tore themselves loose and flew into the open arms of their fellow East European conationals to the south and southeast, taking the entire territory of the province with them. Unfortunately, this development left numerous enclaves of West European Hungarians stranded inside Eastern Europe, where, in their turn, they were macroculturally discriminated against. In 1940 Hitler awarded a large slice of Transylvania to Hungary in return for a Hungarian alliance in his world war, but at war's end Hungary found itself once again on the losing side and its share of Transylvania reverted to Romania.

Since 1945 the situation of the Hungarian minority in Transylvania proved to be a continuous bone of contention between Hungary and Romania. The Hungarians, especially those expatriates in non-Communist Western countries, conducted a ceaseless public propaganda campaign against the barbarous treatment meted out to the Hungarian population in the province by their East European rulers. Though some of these claims were exaggerated, much was admittedly true. This was especially so under the regime of Nicolae Ceauşescu (1965-89) in the late 1970s and throughout the 1980s, when the proposed Romanian government policy of forced population transfers of Hungarians and the destruction of Hungarian villages in Transylvania gave overt expression to continuing anti-Hungarian macrocultural antagonisms. Ironically, the so-called Christmas Revolution in Romania of 1989, which toppled the Ceauşescu government and led to the summary execution of the megalomaniacal Communist boss and his sinister wife, was sparked by Transylvanian Hungarian street demonstrators in the city of Timişoara. Not as ironical but disquietingly foreseeable was the fact that, within three months of the successful overthrow of the Communist regime, Orthodox Romanians were beating Hungarians on those same streets of Timişoara. So the tremors along the East-West European fault in Transylvania have continued.

At the southern end of the East-West European fault, and far more explosive than the frictions in the Baltics and in Transylvania, lies the current warfare in the former Yugoslavia. At present, nowhere in Europe is the existence and immediacy of cultural faults more profoundly verified than in this conflict, which pits the highly Westernized Catholic Croats against the still somewhat Byzantine and Turkified Orthodox Serbs in a struggle having cultural roots traceable through a millennium. In fact, the fault separating Croats and Serbs has served as a decisive cultural divide since the late third century, when the Roman emperor Diocletian thought it necessary to administratively partition the empire he ruled into Latin western and Greek eastern halves. His division of the Greco-Roman world ensured that Europe ultimately would develop two related but separate civilizations.

Not surprising in our cultural context, when superimposed on a map of the Balkans today, the line dividing the Roman Empire decreed by Diocletian seventeen hundred years ago generally lies along the line separating Croats and Serbs in the region of Slavonia and bisecting Bosnia-Hercegovina. This line constitutes the southern extremity of the East-West European fault. The Catholic Croats and Slovenes, lying west of the fault, historically have been integral human components of Western European civilization by way of the Habsburg (later Austro-Hungarian) Empire. They experienced the same developmental stages in their history—the Renaissance, the Reformation, and the Scientific Revolution—as did the Germans, French, Italians, Hungarians, and other Western societies. The Serbs, however, lying east of the fault, have been part of Orthodox Eastern Europe since their emergence as a nation in the twelfth century, and have been almost wholly removed from the formative developments of the West. Their heritage resides in the Byzantine Empire and in their subsequent four hundred years of subjugation by the Ottoman Turkish Empire and its Islamic civilization. While Croats and Slovenes enjoyed the benefits of education at leading European universities and made important contributions to Western European culture, the Serbs existed in conditions of near illiteracy and social repression, submerged in an Islamic state that threatened to obliterate them as Europeans (that is to say, Christians) altogether. Warfare exploded in 1991 between Croats and Serbs over Slavonia and "Krajina"; it has since spilled over into Bosnia-Hercegovina with the addition of Muslim combatants. The intentionally destructive sieges of Dubrovnik, Sarajevo, and Vukovar (cities that lie squarely on the fault line and that serve as cultural symbols for Croats and Muslims), as well as the beastial conduct—ranging from mutilation of bodies, through torture of prisoners and mass, coordinated rapine, to "ethnic cleansing"—by all sides in the conflict, have been overt and ghastly expressions of deeply rooted macrocultural animosities given free reign.

Compounding the human turmoil in Eastern Europe and Eurasia caused by the cultural friction continuously occurring along the East-West European fault is the existence of a second fault line that separates the Eastern European and the Islamic civilizations. This line runs generally from west to east, beginning in the Balkan Peninsula and ending near the border of Mongolia, where it encounters the Far East Asian macrocultural plate.

At its western terminus—the Thracian border of Turkey-in-Europe bounded by the Aegean and Black seas—the East European–Islamic fault throws out an extension that resembles a long, somewhat scythe-shaped swath cutting northwestward into the Balkans through Bulgaria, Macedonia, Albania, and Kosovo, which eventually intersects with the East-West European fault in Bosnia-Hercegovina. From the Balkans the main fault circumvents the Black Sea into the Caucasus, continues along the borders of Turkey with Georgia and Armenia, and into Azerbaijan, where it turns northward along the western shores of the Caspian Sea and up the valley of the Volga River into the Russian Federated Republic. It then turns eastward once again, following, in a broad band, the border of the Russian Republic with Kazakhstan until ending at the frontier of Mongolia.

Formation of the Eurasian portion of the present East European–Islamic fault occurred over a period of ten centuries. Just as the northern and central sections of the East-West European fault originated in microcultural conflicts between Kievan Russians and Lithuanians, the roots of the Eurasian East European–Islamic fault lay in early microcultural struggles on the steppes between the Russians of Kiev and various nomadic Turkic and then Mongol peoples over the course of the ninth through thirteenth centuries. At the end of that period, the Russian East European world was effectively bottled in the cold, densely forested northwestern corner of Eurasia, confined by Western European civilization to its west, the forbidding forests and tundra of Siberia to its east, and the powerful state of the Mongol-Tatar Golden Horde to its south and southeast. Worse yet, because of military defeat and internal political collapse, the Russian Orthodox world was almost totally immersed in the Turko-Mongol cultural world of its dominant southern neighbor.

The Russian-Mongol conflict turned macrocultural when the Turkified Mongols of the Golden Horde converted to Islam in the early fourteenth century. By the end of that century the Russians were well on the way toward throwing off Mongol domination, and in the late fifteenth century they finally emerged completely independent of their Islamic masters. There then started a long, continuous process of Russian expansion into the southern and central Eurasian Islamic heartlands, beginning in earnest with Tsar Ivan IV Groznyi (the Terrible/ Dread) in the sixteenth century and continuing thereafter under Peter the Great (seventeenth-eighteenth centuries), Catherine II (eighteenth century), and especially under the nineteenth-century Russian rulers, Nicholas I and Alexander III. Great Britain and other Western powers viewed the nineteenth-century extension of the East European Russian Empire into Islamic Eurasia as far as Iran and Afghanistan as a threat to the interests of the British Empire (and, therefore, of Western European civilization). This expansion of the Russian Empire into southern and central Eurasia served to place the European limits of a broad-banded East European–Islamic fault deep within the confines of Eastern Europe's most imperialist state. When the Russian Empire was transformed into the Soviet Union in the early twentieth century, this broad Eurasian macrocultural fault within its borders remained.

While Russian Eastern Europe expanded against Islam in southern and central Eurasia, it also made similar and simultaneous advances to its southwest, toward the cradle of Eastern European civilization itself, the Islamic-controlled Balkan Peninsula.

Eastern European civilization had been created and shaped by the Byzantine (or Eastern Roman) Empire between the sixth and twelfth centuries. It was during that same period that the original East European–Islamic fault was formed, roughly conforming to the present southern and eastern borders of Turkey in West Asia. Byzantium was the first European state to face the explosion of Islam from out of the Arabian Peninsula in the mid-seventh century and was thus the first to be seriously mauled by the dynamic and militant force of that rising civilization. Before the fault settled into its earliest and long-standing West Asian boundaries in the eighth century, Constantinople, the capital of Byzantine Eastern Europe, just narrowly fended off two threatening Islamic sieges (in 673 and 717). Failure to do so in either case most likely would have had dire consequences for the futures of both European civilizations.

With the deposing of the increasingly complacent Arabs as the leading ethnic element in Islamic civilization by newly converted, more highly motivated Turks during the eleventh century, the situation along the East European–Islamic fault rapidly changed. By the end of that century the Turks had pushed Byzantine Eastern Europe almost completely out of West Asia, and the fault temporarily came to rest along the coastal regions of northern and western Anatolia. At the same time, the Eastern European regions of Armenia and Georgia in the Caucasus were swallowed by the expanding Islamic tide. This revival of militant Islamic activity in West Asia by the Turks ignited a reaction in the two European worlds known as the Crusades, which opened a brief West European–Islamic fault in the area of today's Syria, Lebanon, and Israel. Perhaps more important, the Crusades cemented the existence of a true East-West European cultural fault when Catholic Western warriors of the Fourth Crusade chose to attack, sack, and dismantle the East European Byzantine Empire in 1204 rather than to assail the Muslim Turks who ruled over the Christian Holy Lands. Although the Byzantine Empire was resurrected some sixty years later, the Western European Crusaders had dealt the East European Balkan world a blow that proved nearly fatal and created a deep-seated cultural animosity between the two Europes that has never disappeared. In the mid-fourteenth century the Islamic civilization, in the guise of a young, dynamic Ottoman Turkish state, pushed into the Balkans to stay. By the end of that century most of the non-Greek Orthodox Europeans in the region were defeated and incorporated directly into the rising Ottoman Empire. The conquest of Constantinople by the Turks in 1453 ended the Byzantine Empire for good. Soon thereafter, Orthodox Greece suffered the same fate as its Slavic neighbors. The Romanian Principalities of Wallachia and Moldavia fell to the Turks by the close of the fifteenth century, although they were retained as captive satellite states by the victors and not directly incorporated officially into their empire. The opening of the sixteenth century signaled the total submergence of Eastern European civilization in the Balkans into that of Islam.

Under Süleyman I the Magnificent, during the first half of the sixteenth century, the Ottoman Islamic world struck deep into the heart of Western Europe, incorporating most of Hungary (including, at the time, Transylvania as a dependency) and, in 1529, temporarily reaching the gates of Vienna. The western elements of the Islamic Mongol-Tatar world on the Russian steppes, the Crimean Tatars, were brought under Ottoman sway, so that by the close of the century the frontiers of Islam in Europe stretched continuously from the Adriatic Sea in Bosnia-Hercegovina, eastward along the northern borders of Hungary, Transylvania, Moldavia, and the Crimean Khanate, to the Volga River valley and beyond in central Eurasia. The fault thus formed faced both of the European civilizations. In the north of the Balkan Peninsula, Islam fronted the West European states of the Habsburg Empire and of Poland-Lithuania. In Eurasia, it abutted Russia, the only remaining independent Eastern European state.

Beginning in the late seventeenth century and continuing into the twentieth, the two European civilizations gradually drove the Islamic fault line in the Balkans southward. In the Western European theater, the conflict with the Turks became the central foreign policy issue of the Habsburg rulers of Central-Eastern Europe until their disappearance from the European political scene in 1918. On the East European front, in the late seventeenth century Russia commenced a series of twelve wars with the Ottoman Empire that ended only with World War I. These brought the borders of the powerful East European Russian Empire to the Danube River. Russia's expansion into the Balkans served to exacerbate East-West European macrocultural tensions, creating a long-standing international crisis known as the Eastern Question. By the mid-nineteenth century the Great Powers of both Eastern and Western Europe considered the Balkans strategically crucial to their own international interests. Their mutual macrocultural antagonisms over control of those regions in the Balkans liberated by the retreat of the European–Islamic fault played a major role in bringing about World War I.

While the Great Powers of the two Europes determinedly struggled against the Islamic Ottoman Empire, the native Eastern European peoples of the Balkans joined in the macrocultural conflict. National uprisings in the heart of the Balkans against continued Turkish Islamic rule won independence for Orthodox Serbs and Greeks in the early nineteenth century. Their lead was followed by the Orthodox Bulgarians in the third quarter of the century, by which time the near-prostrate Islamic Ottoman Empire had won the dubious distinction of "Sick Man of Europe." The piecemeal collapse of the Islamic frontier in the Balkans during the nineteenth and early twentieth centuries under strong pressures both from without and from within the Balkan world ensured that the rush for territorial spoils in the region by the newly resurrected, but small and weak, East European Balkan states of Greece, Serbia, Bulgaria, and Romania quickly became enmeshed in the larger tripartite macrocultural conflict that flared among Eastern Europeans, Western Europeans, and Muslims. By the close of the Balkan Wars in 1913, when the East European–Islamic fault in the Balkans took on its present form, the multicultural muddle was such that no neat band of gray straddling the modern Turkish-Bulgarian-Greek borders could be used to delineate the line clearly, and the English language had acquired a new word to denote a seemingly incomprehensible process of division within societies—"balkanization."

The tortuous history of the East European–Islamic macrocultural fault has been characterized throughout by lengthy and sweeping inroads made by each side against the other, always encompassing vast areas of land and millions of people. From the thirteenth through sixteenth centuries, the tide was in favor of Islam. Starting in the seventeenth century, it was reversed. Each time one side advanced, populations of the other's found themselves conquered subjects within the borders of the states representing the expanding civilization—the Mongol-Tatar Golden Horde and the Ottoman Empire in Islam; the Russian (later Soviet) Empire and the modern Balkan states of Bulgaria, Greece, Serbia, and Romania in Eastern Europe. The net result has been the creation of a wide human fault line spanning nearly a quarter of the globe, in which macrocultural conflict historically has been endemic.

In Eurasia, Eastern European civilization, under the mantle of the Russian Empire, reached its point of greatest penetration into the Islamic world by the late nineteenth century. Muslim groups such as the Tatar, Bashkir, and Chuvash peoples of the western steppes and the Volga River basin were among the earliest to be incorporated into the Russian state. Others in Central Asia, such as the Kazakhs, Uzbeks, Turkmenis, Tajiks, and Kirghizes, were finally conquered only in the later years of Russian expansion after long, bloody military campaigns, followed by Russian occupation and colonization. The relatively recent and living traditions of independence among these latter five Muslim societies helped ensure that each managed to preserve a certain measure of self-identity when the republics of the Soviet Union were formed in the early 1920s.

In the Caucasus, the Muslim Turkic Azerbaijanis, as well as a number of less populous Muslim Turkic groups, such as the Ossetians, were absorbed into the Russian Empire only in the middle of the nineteenth century after, again, hard-fought Russian military efforts against the Ottoman Empire and in the face of stubborn native guerilla resistance. Here, and in Central Asia, periodic local uprisings continuously rejected rule by a foreign civilization's imperial agents. During the Russian Civil War (1918-21), the Muslim-inhabited regions of Central Asia and the Caucasus were retained for the transformed Russian Empire only by violent, coercive Soviet military measures, which included confronting the Muslims' natural outside ally, post-Ottoman Turkey, along the Soviet-Turkish border in the southern Caucasus.

Events in the Eurasian regions of the former Soviet (Russian) Empire since the 1991 failed Moscow coup attempt have developed along lines that follow the history of the East European–Islamic fault. Anti-Russian unrest had already surfaced in Azerbaijan and Turkmenistan by late 1988. Following the 1991 abortive coup, the five Central Asian and the Azerbaijani Islamic republics, all relatively recent conquests of the Russian Empire, adamantly resisted any Russian attempt to maintain a political union that, given the historical linkage of the empire to Orthodox Russian control, the Muslims could only view as an effort to perpetuate an alien Eastern European civilization's dominance over them. They claimed their independence and, along with it, their readmission into the free Islamic world. All except the Tajiks, who are ethnically Iranian, turned to Turkey for political role models, guidance, and direct support in their efforts for independent existence. Turkey obliged them with open arms. The Islamic Tatar, Chuvash, and Bashkir peoples, incorporated into the Russian Empire centuries earlier and lacking deeply rooted traditions of independence, were forced to accept their positions within the new East European Russian and Ukrainian states. Yet even in these regions, the Muslim populations began voicing aspirations for increased political and cultural autonomy, and the Crimean Tatars, dispossessed of their patrimony by Stalin, started returning to their homelands.

Thus, the fault line in Ukraine and in Russia is far from completely dormant. Historic conflicts between Orthodox and Muslim populations along the Eurasian fault in the Caucasus have continued. Armenian Orthodox Christians have been in mortal conflict with Muslim Turks in Azerbaijan and in Turkey for centuries. The struggle began as early as the eighth century when the Armenians served as the easternmost bulwark of Byzantium's West Asian line of defense against a rapidly expanding Islamic world. Armenians were the first to suffer at the hands of the Turks in the eleventh century. During the Ottoman Empire's six hundred-years of leadership in West Asian Islamic life, the Armenians were generally unruly but tolerated subjects of that state, playing an important role in its economic and social life. When in the nineteenth century a large portion of the Armenian population in the Caucasus was reunited with Eastern European civilization in the Russian Empire, those left behind grew increasingly agitated over remaining within the Islamic world. The resulting macrocultural tensions between Armenians and Turks led to violent outbreaks that culminated in the Turks' perpetrating two massacres of Armenians, the first in the late 1800s and the second during World War I. Population transfers and Soviet rule over the Caucasus after 1921 capped Armenian-Turkish conflicts until, in 1989, Gorbachev's liberalizing policies loosened Moscow's tight grip on the Soviet Empire and the age-old macrocultural struggle between Armenians and Turks broke out with renewed violence over control of Nagorno Karabakh within Azerbaijan.

In the Balkans, the East European–Islamic fault has been particularly volatile. The Ottoman conquest of the region during the fourteenth and fifteenth centuries involved numerous and violent military operations before the Orthodox Christian states of the Bulgarians, Serbs, and Greeks were finally overcome. The vanquished Orthodox Christians were reduced to second-class status in the Muslim-led state that governed the Balkans for the ensuing four hundred years, creating a progressively more intolerant macrocultural animosity as time wore on. Christian uprisings and Turkish reprisals intensified, culminating in the various successful independence movements of the Balkan Orthodox Christians in the nineteenth century, all of which were mutually violent, with horrifying atrocities committed by all sides. By the time the tables had been turned and Eastern European civilization had again emerged dominant in the Balkans in the early decades of the twentieth century, the triumphant Balkan Orthodox world had developed a deep animosity toward its Islamic macrocultural foe.

All the newly established modern Orthodox East European states in the Balkans were faced, to a greater or lesser extent, with a common macrocultural problem—how to deal with their scattered but populous Muslim minorities.

Bulgaria and Yugoslavia postponed addressing this issue squarely to the second half of the twentieth century because of burning microcultural conflicts between themselves and with Greece, which were compounded by the chaos of World War II and the subsequent imposition of communism. Additionally, in Yugoslavia the dominant Serbs faced a running macrocultural diversion in their discord with the Western European Croats. Romania had microcultural problems with Russia regarding the region of Bessarabia, as well as major macrocultural antagonisms with the Western European Hungarians over Transylvania.

Until the outbreak of the recent war in Bosnia-Hercegovina, Greece proved to be the most active of the East European Balkan states in twentieth-century clashes along the East European–Islamic fault. Greece's forced participation in World War I on the side of the Entente against the Bulgarians and the Turks continued, in the case of the latter, after the close of the conflict in 1918. The liquidation of the moribund Ottoman Empire and the creation of a modern, nationalist Turkey led to the outbreak of Greek-Turkish warfare in the 1920s, with the Greeks unsuccessfully attempting to gain firm control of Turkey's Aegean coastal regions, regions that constituted ancient Ionia, the cradle of classical Greek civilization. The Greeks ultimately were pushed off the mainland of western Turkey to the Cyclades Islands lying just offshore. The exchanges of ethnic populations between Greece and Turkey that occurred shortly thereafter solidified the extension of the East European–Islamic fault from mainland Thrace in the Balkans southward through the Cyclades to Cyprus in the extreme southeast. There, in the mid-1970s, the Greek-Turkish macrocultural clash exploded once again, and it has continued to fester into the present.

In the 1950s the East European–Islamic macrocultural conflict in the Balkans bubbled to the surface in Bulgaria when Communist-inspired anti-Turkish policies led to mass emigrations of Muslims from the country to Turkey. Squalid refugee camps sprang up along the Bulgarian-Turkish border in Thrace, and thousands of refugees died from exposure. The affair caused an international incident of some portent. Although the crisis was papered over at the time, Bulgarian macrocultural animosity toward the Turks simmered on, only to boil anew in the mid-1980s in an official anti-Turkish cultural war conducted within the country by the government. This war ended only with the events following the overthrow of the Todor Zhivkov (1954-89) Communist regime in 1989. Since 1990 the Turks in Bulgaria have gone on to play an ever more significant role in Bulgarian political life, to the increasing unease of many Orthodox Bulgarians.

Similar macrocultural enmity bubbled below the surface in Yugoslav Bosnia-Hercegovina, Kosovo, and Macedonia throughout the 1950s. Major eruptions were repressed by the authority and power exerted by Tito, who attempted to defuse the generally embittered macro- and microcultural tensions in the artificially united country through the creation of federated, supposedly self-governing, republics and autonomous regions and through the promulgation of laws that protected ethnic and religious expression. The solutions imposed by Tito proved temporary. Cultural tensions, both micro and macro, intensified following his death in 1980, until the dissolution of Yugoslavia in 1991 freed them to recommence with renewed vigor. Armed combat then erupted in Croatia and Bosnia-Hercegovina among peoples representing all three of the civilizations that converge in the western Balkans.

While macrocultural frictions play a predominant historical role in shaping human relationships, the part played by microcultural discords cannot be ignored. We have already alluded to their importance a number of times in our overview of macrocultural interactions. With regard to microcultural frictions, our geological plate analogy continues to be useful. Every continental plate suffers internal stresses along geologically defined lines called fractures. Periodically, the pressures at the fractures build to sudden and violent seismic eruptions that shake and reshape regions of the plate itself. For example, the North American continental plate exhibits a major fracture that somewhat parallels the valley of the Mississippi River. In the early nineteenth century, convulsions swept this fracture with such intensity that shocks were felt as far afield as Canada and the eastern seaboard. The topography of the American Midwest was altered by a number of feet as a result of the eruption, and the course of the Mississippi River itself was changed at many points along its length. If civilizations (macrocultures) are considered analogous to continental plates, then the lines of contact among the various nationalities (microcultures) within them can be viewed as plate fractures. No civilization has ever been free of microcultural fractures and the constant frictions that occur along them. These frictions internally agitate and remold the cultural forms expressing both the microcultures of the nationalities and the civilization that they share in common.

Microcultural friction can be of two opposed sorts—benign or violent. By their very nature, the former kind constantly occur along the fractures but pass virtually unrecognized as frictions by the societies affected because they are so closely linked to the general macrocultural perceptions held by all. In Western European civilization, for instance, the spread of humanistic concepts from the northern Italian city-states to the rest of the Western microcultures north of the Alps in the fifteenth and sixteenth centuries did not require a convulsive process of human conflict. Nor was the seventeenth-century Scientific Revolution expanded from Poland into Bohemia, Austria, Italy, Belgium, and England through violent means. Likewise, over the course of the eighteenth century and into the nineteenth, the recipients viewed the spread of the Enlightenment and democratic ideals from France and of capitalistic industrialism and liberal ideals from England throughout all the Western microcultures as organic developments. In each of these cases, a cultural change originated in a particular microculture and was passed over a fracture to another microculture within the civilization, which then accepted it and, in turn, passed it on. Each change was accepted by all because it was perceived as a definitive expression of some aspect of the common Western European sense of reality.

More convulsive in the shaping of Western European civilization have been violent microcultural frictions. The English were forged into a unique society and microculture through centuries of conflict with Viking Scandinavians, Normans, Spaniards, the Irish, and the French. The developmental process for the French involved long, bloody struggles not only with the English, ending in the nineteenth century, but also with the Germans, which last erupted in the mid-twentieth century. As for the Germans, they largely became who and what they are today—divided among Germany, Austria, and Switzerland—through desperate conflicts with the French, various Scandinavian peoples, the Poles, the Italians, and the English.

Although the clashes of microcultures in these selected examples were all frictions drawn out over lengthy periods of time, violent, and costly in terms of human lives, they all solidified positive internal cultural developments for the societies involved. England's struggles resulted in the Magna Carta, the rise of parliamentary government, and its growth into a leading power in the Western world. The significant result of the Anglo-French Hundred Years War, which ended in the mid-fifteenth century, was the creation of a France that ever since has played an important role in the general cultural existence of Western Europe. The Franco- and Anglo-German conflicts of the nineteenth and twentieth centuries greatly contributed to the unification of over a hundred little local leftover medieval German duchies and principalities into today's large, potentially dynamic, powerhouse of Germany.

Violent microcultural frictions also have played their role in shaping the macroculture itself in Western civilization. One case in point was the Protestant Reformation of the sixteenth century and the resulting 150 years of religious warfare that began among the northern Germans. Though outwardly cloaked in religious forms, the Reformation was actually a successful struggle waged among Western microcultures to transform their macroculture from one dominated by a single religious institution (the Roman Catholic church) into one governed by the independent political institutions of the microcultures themselves. Similarly, the form of the newly anointed independent political institutions was determined through another case of microcultural convulsions in the late eighteenth and early nineteenth centuries espousing the concepts of nationalism. These first erupted in the rather localized American Revolution but thereafter were carried over the length and breadth of Western Europe by the French Revolution and the military campaigns of Napoleon. Prior to those two revolutions, the political institutions of Western microcultures were grounded in modified versions of pre-Reformation monarchies upheld by outdated socioeconomic systems stemming from medieval feudalism. By the time the frictions caused by the American and French eruptions subsided, the political macroculture of the West was firmly decided in favor of nationalistic liberal democracy, supported by an economy planted in industrial capitalism. In both of these cases—the end of medievalism and the rise of nationalism— inflamed microcultural frictions caused enormous human suffering and dislocation, and, in both, the Western European macroculture was violently pushed to a new developmental stage.

In Eastern Europe and Western Eurasia, microcultural fractures have played, and continue to play, a seminal role in molding the realities of the various societies inhabiting these regions on both the micro- and macrocultural levels. Let us now turn to a brief overview of the fractures within the Western and Eastern European civilizations that hold sway in the regions. We begin with the Western European.

While the great eastern macrocultural struggles with the Russians have predominated in the microcultural development of the Slavic Poles, the historical conflicts with fellow West European Germans across the Polish-German fracture to their west and north has always run a close second. Throughout their history, the Poles have been forced to adapt to existence in an area under constant threat from cultural enemies in the east and the west without the benefit of any geographically defensible borders. The repeated catastrophic results for the Poles in their macrocultural battles with the Russians from the mid-seventeenth century on owed much to the simultaneous microcultural conflict they were forced to wage with the Germans, which had begun as early as the fourteenth century in warfare against the Teutonic Knights and continued thereafter in intermittent disputes with the rising state of Prussia. Caught in a cultural pincers—macrocultural to their east, microcultural to their west—the Poles lost their statehood in the late eighteenth century partitions and, after a brief resurrection in 1918, lost it again in 1939 to the same enemies—the Germans and the Russians. Besides sparking the calamitous World War II, the Polish microcultural calamity of 1939 ultimately led to the broadening of the fracture with the Germans when, in 1945, both the eastern and western borders of the newly created Soviet satellite state of Poland were shifted westward, moving the country farther into the German-dominated regions of Central-Eastern Europe and giving it a sizable German population that potentially could stir up future German-Polish microcultural problems once Communist rule was eliminated. As might be expected, in early 1990 and intermittently thereafter, there occurred public demonstrations by Germans inhabiting regions in western and southwestern Poland voicing desires for unification with Germany. In an effort to head off such internal disturbances and to guarantee its frontiers as far as possible, the Polish government of Lech Wałęsa hastened to sign a treaty with Germany recognizing existing borders.

The Poles face further microcultural fractures to their northeast and south. Neither has been as disruptively active as that with the Germans, but both have been the source of distinct rumblings in the past. The Polish-Lithuanian fracture in the northeast first appeared in the fourteenth century when the two kingdoms were joined in a personal union by a marriage alliance between their ruling houses. By 1569, when this personal union finally was institutionalized legally, the non-Slavic Lithuanian microculture was being threatened by strong forces for cultural assimilation into that of the Poles. Russian conquest of the Lithuanians prior to the destruction of Poland in the eighteenth century arrested the process, freeing the Lithuanians from direct Polish influences for the next two centuries, as both were forced to consolidate their own cultures against the Russian macrocultural threat. When a state of Poland reemerged in 1918, the Lithuanians actively and successfully resisted efforts by ardent Polish nationalists to reconstruct the Greater Poland of old. Likewise, after both Poland and Lithuania won their independence from the Soviet Union in 1989, the Lithuanians made it clear that renewed Polish interference in their affairs was undesirable.

To the south, a fracture separates the Poles from the Slavic Czechs and Slovaks. In the thirteenth and early fourteenth centuries, strong Czech rulers of Bohemia confronted the Poles with determined assimilation efforts. The union with the Lithuanians was, in some measure, a Polish move to counter this cultural threat from the south. Over the next six centuries neither the Poles nor the Czechs relinquished their conflicting historical claims on the territory of

Silesia, which became the primary focus of seismic activity along the dividing fracture. The frictions along this cleft were compounded by the assimilation of the Czechs into a culturally German Habsburg Empire in the sixteenth
century, further complicating the deeper Polish-German microcultural rift. After
the two peoples gained independence in 1918, Polish-Czech animosities in the
area immediately surfaced in a heated border dispute over the province of
Teschen. In contrast, the Polish-Slovak fracture historically has been dormant,
because for the first thousand years of their history the Slovaks had been completely dominated by the Hungarians, with whom the Poles historically
enjoyed amicable relations, and because the Tatra Mountains posed a formi-
dable geographical separator.

Besides the fracture facing the Poles, the Czechs are bounded by other microcultural fractures to their west and east. The western Czech-German fracture
is of a long-standing and convulsive nature, originating in the ninth century.
At that time, the overtures toward independence from German microcultural
hegemony made by the fledgling Czech state of Greater Moravia proved
unsuccessful, and the Czechs were incorporated into the German-dominated
Holy Roman Empire in Central-Eastern Europe. The Czechs later reasserted
a certain measure of cultural independence with the rise of their Bohemian kingdom in the thirteenth century. Bohemia has since played an important role in
the affairs of Central-Eastern Europe. Its capital, Prague, emerged as a leading European cultural center in the fourteenth century. Unfortunately, throughout that early period of Bohemian efflorescence, the Czechs remained locked
in a microcultural struggle with their more numerous German neighbors that
ultimately led to their crushing defeat by the Habsburgs in 1620.

Not only did the Czech-Habsburg armed struggle of that time spark the Thirty
Years War in Europe, it also led to the direct incorporation of the Czechs into
the German Habsburg Empire and four centuries of attempted cultural
Germanization. In response to the German microcultural threat, Czechs
became leading exponents of the romantic nationalist-inspired Panslav movement that swept through Eastern Europe and Russia in the first half of the nineteenth century. Disappointed in their bid to gain independent recognition
similar to that won by the Hungarians in the creation of a Habsburg-led
Austro-Hungarian Empire in 1867, the Czechs actively sought the dissolution
of that state during World War I. By convincing the Slovaks to join with them,
they successfully won the independence of a Czecho-Slovak state in 1918 but
continued to face grave microcultural hostilities with the German minority
located in the new country's Sudet regions. These German-Czech microcultural clashes reached a boiling point in 1938, at which time Hitler, with the
tacit collaboration of Italy, England, and France, destroyed the young Czech

state in the Munich Agreements. Following 1945 the Czechs were forced to accept foreign macrocultural dominance by the Soviet Union, which ended with the Velvet Revolution of 1989. One of the first foreign policy efforts of the Vaclav Havel government after coming to power was to dampen potential outbreaks on the fracture with the Germans by negotiating border and trade agreements with Germany.

During most of the early existence of the Czech eastern fracture with the Slovaks, frictions were either nonexistent or benign. After all, until 1918 the agriculturally oriented Slovaks were dominated by the Hungarians, and, except for the brief semi-mythical state of Samo in the eighth century, they had never in their history enjoyed political independence. The two societies existed in separate worlds within heterogeneous Central-Eastern Europe: the Czechs in the German-dominated cultural sphere, the Slovaks in the Hungarian. This cultural dichotomy persisted into the period of the Austro-Hungarian state. In most respects, the two microcultures viewed each other as related, sharing similar unfortunate circumstances. Slovaks joined the Czechs in their Panslavic activities, and it took little persuasion by the Czechs to gain Slovak agreement in forming a united country at the end of World War I.

The creation of Czechoslovakia in 1918 proved the catalyst for sparking troublesome rumblings along the Czech-Slovak fracture. Czechs assumed a position of microcultural superiority in the country, justified, in their minds at least, by a long history of cultural leadership, political significance, and economic development in Central-Eastern Europe, as compared to the utter nonhistory and economic backwardness of their Slovak partners. The disgruntled Slovaks complained but had little recourse until, having crushed Czechoslovakia, Hitler bid to ensure its total disappearance by sanctioning an independent, neo-fascist, and nationalist Slovak government in 1939. Reunited after 1945, microcultural discordance continued between the two peoples until, when all restrictions were removed in 1989, the Slovaks once again pushed for independence from Czech domination in the state. The microcultural frictions resulted in the termination of the Havel government in 1992 and culminated in the definitive official dissolution of the unitary state on 1 January 1993 into two national ones, the Czech Republic and Slovakia, along the line of the microcultural fracture.

In turn, the Slovaks face a fracture with the Hungarians to their south. This microcultural cleft built up slowly over the course of a thousand years, during which time it remained outwardly dormant but inwardly compounded pressures that guaranteed, once a crack in the surface appeared during the course of World War I, that the eruption would be complete. Microcultural steam began to break the ground in the late nineteenth century when non-Slavic Hungarian cultural pressures on the Slovaks were intensified following the establishment of Austria-Hungary. Soon after the creation of Czechoslovakia, the Slovaks found themselves involved in a shooting war with the ill-fated, and short-lived, Hungarian Bolshevik regime of Béla Kun in 1919. The Hungarians never completely relinquished their historical claims on the region of Slovakia, so the Slovak-Hungarian fracture continued to emit low rumblings that have persisted into the present. Following 1989 new tensions emerged in disputes between the two microcultures over a proposed dam on the Danube River and growing restlessness among the Hungarian population of southern Slovakia, fanned by cultural agitation from Hungary.

Like that of the Poles, Hungarian microculture has been shaped by both micro- and macrocultural conflicts. The Hungarians lie on the West European side of the long macrocultural fault with Eastern Europe opposite Romanian Transylvania, to their east, and the Serb-dominated Vojvodina, to their south. In the north lies the already described fracture with the Slovaks, and to their southwest is another facing the Slavic Croats.

The Croats enjoyed a brief period of early independence in the eleventh century, but from 1102 until World War I they were joined to Hungary. Over that time, the Croats grew increasingly dependent on the Hungarians politically and experienced progressively more intense microcultural pressures from their dominant partners—especially to adopt the Hungarian language and mores. Their incorporation, together with the Hungarians, into the Habsburg Empire in the sixteenth century brought them into the German cultural sphere of Central-Eastern Europe, in which they were designated as the empire's Balkan border guardians against the advancing Ottoman Empire and Islamic civilization. The Croatian military border became a region exposed to Islamic macrocultural and Hungarian and German microcultural strains. Faced with the heavy duty of protecting their region of Western European civilization from that of Islam, the Croats began resisting their immediate microcultural antagonists, the Hungarians, in the early nineteenth century by attempting to play them off against the Slavs and the Germans of the empire. They readily joined in the Panslav movement of the Czechs and Slovaks and actively fought the Hungarian bid for independence from the Habsburg Empire in 1848-49, in vain hopes that the grateful German rulers would reward them with separation from Hungarian control.

Following the creation of Austria-Hungary, the Croats' frictions with the Hungarians intensified as Hungarian pretensions to cultural dominance in their half of the empire grew. When the attempt to gain recognition by the Habsburgs similar to that given the Hungarians failed, the Croats somewhat reluctantly decided to risk bridging the macrocultural fault to their south and threw their lot in with the Slavic East European Serbs during World War I. The resulting state of Yugoslavia formed after the war vindicated the Croats' misgivings. The Croats swiftly came to feel that they were being dominated by a people whose level of culture was greatly inferior to their own. Croat disgruntlement with their situation within Yugoslavia swiftly turned to active resistance in the guise of the *Ustaše* terrorist organization. When Hitler invaded the country in 1941, he found willing allies within fellow Western European Croat ultra-nationalist *Ustaše* circles, who proclaimed a neofascist independent Croatian state.

Croat-Serb macrocultural animosities reached fever pitch in World War II. Fascist Croatia was defeated by the Communist partisan movement led by Tito, and the Croats were once again brought into the Serb-dominated state of Yugoslavia in 1945. The violence and atrocities of the war served to intensify the macrocultural conflict, which was kept in check only by the power and prestige of Tito himself. When Tito died in 1980 the lid slowly came off the pot, and full-scale warfare erupted in 1991. Not surprisingly, the first countries approached by the Franjo Tudjman government of newly independent Croatia were Hungary and Austria, both of which quickly and publicly voiced their support and concern for their fellow Western Europeans. For the Croats, healing their fracture with the Hungarians proved to be more desirable than facing the fault with the Serbs. The Hungarians, worried about the possible fate of their conationals in the Vojvodina at the hands of the Serbs, reciprocated as much as possible, short of hostilities.

The Slavic Slovenes lie across a microcultural fracture to the north of the Croats. Prior to 1918 and their incorporation into the newly created Yugoslavia, the Slovenes had existed wholly within the German-dominated Central-Eastern European world of the Holy Roman and Habsburg empires since the eighth century. Their primary microcultural fracture faced the Germans of Austria to their north. Frictions along this line were benign, and the Slovene microculture became heavily Germanized. In fact, microcultural relations with the Austrian Germans were so close that, following the collapse of Austria-Hungary in 1918, over half of the Slovene population voted in a plebiscite to remain with their German neighbors in the new state of Austria. Their situation relative to the Croats resembled that of the Czechs and Slovaks—they were part of German-led Central-Eastern Europe, while the Croats were of the Hungarian-dominated world. The analogy continued to hold after those Slovenes who did not remain in Austria joined the Croats in Yugoslavia, but with a twist. Germanized Slovenia proved the most politically sophisticated and industrially dynamic republic in the country, which led to the Slovenes' growing resentment over political domination by the Serb

macrocultural foreigners and attempted cultural domination by the less developed, but Western, Croats. While the Czechs, whom they resembled so closely,
played the leading role in Czechoslovakia, the Slovenes were relegated to a
subordinate role in Yugoslavia.

By 1989, when Yugoslavia was beginning to show the strains of internal economic dissolution, the other peoples of the country looked to the Slovenes for
solutions. When their efforts failed to bring success by the end of 1990, they
were the first to realize that the artificially unified country could no longer sustain the internal economic and micro-macro cultural tensions. So in 1991 the
Slovenes led the process of dissolving Yugoslavia into its various microcultural components. The resulting warfare began in Slovenia but quickly retreated
to the south, where it settled into a blazing macrocultural struggle among members of all three civilizations present in the Balkans. After hostilities commenced,
the microcultural fracture with the Croats was soon emphasized when the
Slovenes closed their border with Croatia to supplies being sent the Croats for
their war effort against the Serbs. The Slovenes just as quickly moved to establish close political and economic ties to the Austrians, with whom they feel
more cultural affinity than with their fellow Slavs to the south.

Both the Croats and Slovenes share a microcultural fracture in the west with
the Italians. For the Slovenes, this fracture historically has been benign. As for
the Croats, since the eleventh century they have had numerous problems with
the Italians over the Croatian Adriatic coastline of Dalmatia. Venetian activity in the area caused frictions until the early nineteenth century, when the microcultural grating was transformed into a brief Franco-Croat one after the
occupation of Dalmatia by Napoleon in 1806, followed by Russian and
English interference after 1809. The northern course of the fracture formed the
Italian front for Austria-Hungary in World War I, after which, from 1920 until
1954, Croat/Slovene-Italian microcultural conflict flared over possession of
the Istrian Peninsula and its important ports of Trieste and Rijeka. The eventual international settlement of that problem gave Trieste and a small western
coastal strip of Istria to Italy, while the rest was granted to the Croat and Slovene
republics of Yugoslavia, with Croatia receiving the larger share.

Having observed the complexity of microcultural relationships among
Western European societies inhabiting Eastern Europe, let us now turn to sur-
veying the microcultural fractures in Eastern European civilization. We look
first to the Balkans.

The Serbs suffer from an unenviable cultural position. Their East European microculture lies at the point in the northwest Balkans where faults separating all three of the major macrocultures—Eastern and Western European, and Islamic—converge. To the Serbs' north and northwest lies Western European civilization in the shape of the Hungarians and the Croatians; to their west, the Islamic civilization of the Bosnian Muslims and the Albanians. This location historically has placed the Serbs at one of the most tumultuous epicenters of cultural fault convulsions in Eastern Europe.

Conflicts with the Islamic civilization began as early as the fourteenth century and continued throughout the subsequent four hundred years of Muslim domination in the Balkans. Following Serbian independence in the nineteenth century, and continuing thereafter, Serb-Muslim clashes were prevalent. The current war in Bosnia and the ongoing problems with the Muslim Albanian majority in the Serb-held Kosovo province are but the latest expressions of this half millennium of macrocultural combat. The Serbs' struggle against the Balkan Islamic world was complicated by macrocultural hostilities with the Western Europeans to their north, which actively began in 1878 and focused on Austria-Hungary's possession of Bosnia-Hercegovina and Croat efforts to gain political autonomy within that empire, taking those regions for themselves. Prior to that time, Serbs viewed the macrocultural fault with the West immediately to their north as offering a convenient source of support for their anti-Islamic activities, as numerous Orthodox Serbs had fled their Ottoman-controlled homeland for refuge just across the Danube in the Habsburg Empire. After 1878 the rapidly rising macrocultural tensions with the West over Bosnia-Hercegovina ultimately exploded into World War I and contributed to the internal instability of Yugoslavia that eventually led to the dissolution of that country in 1991.

As bad as the macrocultural condition of the Serbs may be, their microcultural situation is strained further by deep fractures to their south with both the Slavic Bulgarians and the Greeks.

Serbs and Bulgarians have clashed along their fracture since the ninth century. The Bulgarians were the first Slavic microculture in all of Eastern Europe to forge a state of their own, and the first to develop a sophisticated, elevated, and independent native culture through the creation of the Cyrillic alphabet. From Bulgaria, Cyrillic letters passed to the Serbs and to the Russians, providing them with the most essential vehicle for constructing their respective native Slavic microcultures. The Serbs were under Bulgarian sway until the eleventh-century destruction of the Bulgarian state by the Byzantine Empire. By the early thirteenth century the Serbs had firmly established their own state. Over the next century and a half Serbia contested control of the central Balkans with a resurrected Bulgaria, then briefly emerged in the mid-fourteenth century as the predominant Slavic power in the Balkans, only to be crushed, along with its traditional Bulgarian rival, by the advancing Ottoman Turks.

During the long period of Ottoman domination, the Serb-Bulgarian fracture remained dormant. The Serbs threw off direct Ottoman rule in 1829. When the Bulgarians finally managed to regain their independence in 1878, the fracture separating the two microcultures rapidly grew active over mutually exclusive claims on Macedonia that were advanced by each. The resulting struggle for the region spawned Europe's earliest forms of modern, organized political terrorism and opened a chasm along the Serb-Bulgarian fracture that never truly healed. Greece, seeking to expand northward and using ancient claims concerning Alexander the Great as justification, also entered the fray for Macedonia, breaking a new microcultural fracture with both the Serbs and the Bulgarians. Macedonia became the political prize for all three in the two Balkan Wars of the early twentieth century. In the first, while Bulgaria shouldered the main burden against the Turks in Thrace, Serbia and Greece occupied the contested region with relative ease and divided it between themselves, violating the terms of their alliance treaties with Bulgaria in the process. When they refused to give the Bulgarians their share of the Macedonian spoils, the Bulgarians attacked them in the second war, only to be trounced royally.

The Serb-Greek fracture created by their military successes in the Balkan Wars proved benign through World War I and into the closing years of World War II, at which time Tito actively intervened in behalf of the Greek Communists in the Greek Civil War (1946-49). The Greek distrust toward the Slavs in Macedonia engendered by that episode threw the Greeks into the arms of Western Europe and the North Atlantic Treaty Organization (NATO) and since 1991 has led them to oppose international recognition of Macedonia as an independent state. As for the Bulgarians, the microcultural conflict with the Serbs and the Greeks over Macedonia resulted in their joining the losing sides in both the world wars in vain hopes of permanently making good their claims on the region. The borders of Bulgaria with both Yugoslavia and Greece were heavily fortified after World War I, further emphasizing the microcultural fractures separating them. The Bulgarians, though signatories to international treaties recognizing existing borders, never completely relinquished their claims on the contested region, and in 1991 Bulgaria, quickly followed by Turkey, was the first nation to recognize the newly proclaimed Macedonian state.

Besides the microcultural fractures with the Serbs and the Greeks and the macrocultural fault with Turkey to their southeast, the Bulgarians face a microcultural fracture with the non-Slavic Romanians to their north.

The Romanians claim to be descendants of Romanized Dacians, who survived centuries of Slavic and Turkic invasions into the three Balkan regions of Wallachia, Moldavia, and Transylvania that they inhabited. Although the claim to Roman heritage has been challenged, there is no doubt that the Romanians, of whatever origin they may be, spent most of their early existence in the Balkans under strong cultural influences exerted by their Hungarian and Bulgarian neighbors. Between the ninth and early fourteenth centuries, the Romanians of Wallachia and Moldavia lived in the cultural orbit of the first and second Bulgarian empires, which were centered on lands across the Danube to the south. Romanians played an important role particularly in the development of the second medieval Bulgarian state but were not so culturally advanced as to be able to withstand completely the cultural pressures exerted by the more highly developed Bulgarians. They were converted to Orthodox Christianity during that time. Numerous Slavic Bulgarian words entered their language, and, until the end of the seventeenth century, they used the Cyrillic alphabet to write their essentially Latin-based tongue.

In Transylvania, the Orthodox Romanians were brought under the control of the expanding Catholic Hungarians in the eleventh and twelfth centuries. When the Romanians of Wallachia and Moldavia managed to create their own principalities in the early fourteenth century, they essentially existed as satellites of the Hungarian rulers of Transylvania. Those Romanians living south of the Danube in the region of Dobrudzha fell under the political and cultural authority of the Bulgarians. By the close of the fifteenth century, the Romanians of the Danubian Principalities had lost their independence, but fortunately not their very existence as states, to the advancing Muslim Ottoman Turks.

Bulgarian microcultural influence remained strong in Wallachia throughout the first three centuries of Islamic dominance in the Balkans. But in the eighteenth century Bulgarian was replaced by Greek cultural preeminence when the Romanians' Islamic masters began selling the thrones of the two principalities to wealthy Greek merchant families living in Istanbul. In reaction to this situation, the Romanians turned to their native microculture in efforts to resist all foreign cultural threats, whether Hungarian (macrocultural), Bulgarian (microcultural), or Russian (also microcultural). When Ottoman control collapsed in the principalities during the 1820s and their Greek puppet rulers were forced out, the Romanians were left facing all three.

The Romanian-Bulgarian fracture began trembling seriously in the late nineteenth century over claims to the Dobrudzha region south of the Danube River. Romania entered the Second Balkan War (1913) against Bulgaria for the express purpose of winning Dobrudzha, and succeeded. Between the world wars, the region was a bone of bitter contention between the two countries until a partition was finalized in 1940. Since that time the fracture between the two microcultures has remained relatively calm.

The Romanian-Russian fracture developed over the course of the eighteenth and nineteenth centuries as Russian southwestward expansion brought the two into direct contact in the region of Bessarabia, to which both laid claim. Most of the twelve Russo-Turkish wars involved the Romanian Principalities in some fashion, since they lay on the direct Russian invasion route into the Balkans. In the nineteenth century the repeated Russian presence north of the Danube virtually led to the establishment of a Russian protectorate in the principalities, essentially replacing Greek with Russian control. As a reward for their participation in the 1877-78 Russo-Turkish War, the Russians gave the Romanians complete independence from the Turks, though at the expense of ceding Bessarabia to Russia. Near the end of World War I, Romania annexed the region after the collapse of tsarist Russia and the outbreak of the Russian Civil War threw Bessarabia into political anarchy, only to lose it again to the Soviet Union in 1940 in a deal struck between Stalin and Hitler. The region, which contained a mixed ethnic population of Romanians, Turks, Bulgarians, Ukrainians, and Russians, was renamed Moldova. When it declared its independence following the 1991 failed Moscow coup, it immediately fell, once again, into bloody anarchy, with Romanians pushing for union with Romania and Russians forcibly resisting those efforts.

The major microcultural fracture of the Russians faces the Ukrainians, who inhabit the extreme western regions of Eurasia. Russia's historic roots lie in Ukraine—the name means borderland—with its capital, Kiev. There, in the ninth century, the earliest Russian state was formed and thrived. In the late tenth century the Russians of Kiev were converted to Orthodox Christianity and brought into the Eastern European civilization headed by Byzantium. The Mongol invasion from the east and continuous Lithuanian pressures from the west tore Russian Western Eurasia in half. In the north, the so-called Great Russians crystallized an Orthodox state around the city of Moscow over the course of the thirteenth to sixteenth centuries. During that same period the southern, Ukrainian, half, its population comprised mostly of Cossacks—essentially Orthodox Russians who had fled the growing centralizing authority of Moscow for the personal freedom offered by the uncertainties of life on the steppe—was gradually incorporated into Lithuania and, later, Poland-Lithuania. While the Russians of the Muscovite state were exposed to heavy Islamic macrocultural pressures from the Mongol-Tatar Golden Horde, the Ukrainians experienced an even heavier, more continuous, and longer-lasting macrocultural menace from their Roman Catholic Polish overlords. Though the majority of the Ukrainians managed to remain true to their Orthodox

Eastern European beliefs, a great many succumbed to westernizing pressures at the end of the sixteenth century, becoming Uniates—Orthodox Christians who, through compromising a few fundamental religious principles, placed themselves "in union" with the Roman Catholic church.

Throughout the seventeenth century Ukraine became the great battleground in the macrocultural struggle between Russia and Poland. Ukrainian society, split among three contesting religious faiths—Catholic, Uniate, and Orthodox —first weighed in on the side of the West. But mounting Polish macrocultural pressures and anti-Orthodox persecutions forced an Orthodox Cossack uprising in 1648 and the establishment of a Russian protectorate over the eastern Ukraine in 1654. By the end of the century Kiev was in Russian hands, and throughout the following century the rest of Ukraine was gradually incorporated into the Russian Empire as Poland progressively declined until it disappeared in 1795.

The Ukrainians, whose microculture was shaped by centuries of Western influences and Cossack traditions of freewheeling independence, were never happy about being directly incorporated into a Russian Empire controlled by the Great Russians of the north. Until the nineteenth century the major anti-government revolutions in the empire commonly originated in Ukraine among its Cossack populations, who resented the imposition of the inequitable Russian social system, grounded in Great Russian landownership and in serfdom. With the events of World War I, the Bolshevik Revolution, and the ensuing Russian Civil War, the Ukrainians made a major bid for independent existence but were ultimately defeated and forcibly incorporated into the Soviet Union in 1920. During Stalin's reign over the Soviet Union, Ukraine was particularly hard hit by the devastation and terror of forced collectivization and industrialization. Partially in an effort to mollify Ukrainian separatist sentiment in 1945, the Soviets permitted Ukraine to occupy a separate seat in the United Nations (UN). The failed 1991 Moscow coup resulted in the dissolution of the Soviet Union, with the Ukrainians playing a leading role in forcing the process. Since that time the Ukrainians and the Russians have been at loggerheads over control of the Black Sea fleet and of nuclear warheads located on Ukrainian territory.

Much the same can be said about the microcultural fracture separating the Belorussians (White Russians) from the Great Russians. Like the Ukrainians to their south, the Belorussians found themselves in the macrocultural battleground between the Polish-Lithuanians and the Russians, and, again like the Ukrainians, they experienced centuries of Polish-Lithuanian control before being incorporated into the Russian Empire at the close of the eighteenth century. In the chaos of postrevolution Bolshevik Russia, the Belorussians briefly enjoyed independence, but were swiftly incorporated into the new Soviet Union, receiving a separate seat in the UN, again like the Ukrainians, in 1945. Following 1991 the Belorussians proclaimed their independence, creating the state of Belarus, whose major city, Minsk, became the capital of the new CIS. Frictions with the Great Russians of the Russian Federated Republic over control of the numerous nuclear warheads located in Belarus have continued since.

Finally, in the Caucasus, a microcultural fracture exists between the Russians and the non-Slavic Orthodox Georgians. The Russian Empire succeeded in fully incorporating the Georgians only in the second half of the nineteenth century, after overcoming much armed resistance. Prior to that the Georgians had spent centuries as troublesome subjects of the Islamic Mongol-Tatar Horde and the Ottoman Empire. The collapse of the Russian Empire in World War I and the onset of the Russian Civil War led to a brief period of Georgian independence, which was forcibly ended by the Red Army in early 1921. Soon thereafter a Georgian Communist rose to become the single most powerful and influential leader in the Soviet Communist world—Josef Stalin. Yet, despite Stalin and his legacy, the Georgians, as a whole, were as discontented with their existence in the Soviet Union as were the peoples of the Baltic republics, Ukraine, Belarus, and Armenia. By the end of 1990, when the reforms of Gorbachev opened the door to possible liberation from direct Russian control, the Georgians, along with the Armenians and the Baltic peoples, declared their independence. The internal civil war that erupted soon thereafter precluded Georgia from joining the CIS in 1991.

This has been but the briefest, bare-bones outline of the macro- and microcultural tectonic picture of Eastern Europe and Western Eurasia. While it goes a long way toward helping us visualize the cultural complexities involved in the events that occur in these regions, it falls short in one important regard—it fails to account overtly for the inordinate impact that Western European civilization has made upon every other civilization, and nearly all microcultures, existing in the world today. Since the sixteenth century, the West's technological know-how, one of its dominant cultural developments, has placed it into contact and competition with virtually every human society, forcing them either to adapt or adopt, somehow and to some extent, Western macrocultural elements or face the possible destruction of their native cultural existence. Western military, economic, and communications technologies have compelled the rest of the world to take into serious account such Western cultural expressions as nationalism, capitalism, liberal democracy, socialism, and industrialism, all of which are dependent on the Western scientific-technological mentality. This situation has led Westerners to define the rest of the world in their own image, using such terms as "Third World" and "underdeveloped."

Yet, in keeping with our tectonic analogy, one might say that the gray area of the fault line separating Western European civilization's plate from all others encompasses the rest of the world in varying degrees of gradation. Therefore, since Western European macrocultural influence can be viewed as a universal given in our considerations of virtually all cultural interactions, the concept of core macrocultural plates and their respective human fault lines retains its validity. One simply must take the degree to which Western cultural elements have been adapted to the native macroculture into consideration in any detailed examination.

Bearing this last point in mind, the historical-cultural overview just outlined serves to provide a useful analytical framework within which we can begin to view events in Eastern Europe and Western Eurasia with a modicum of understanding and perspective. We can reasonably expect that future disruptions, should they occur, will continue to erupt in areas along the cultural faults, and that regions now dormant, such as Transylvania and Macedonia, are likely candidates for future disturbances. Moreover, using the cultural framework as outlined, it now makes sense that Hungary, Poland, the Czech Republic, Slovakia, Slovenia, and the Baltic republics appear to have the best chances of joining the modern European world with the least disruptive efforts. After all, that world is an original creation of Western European civilization and the peoples of those countries are, and have historically been, members of that macroculture. The East European countries, such as Bulgaria, Serbia, Romania, Albania, Bosnia, and the various Eurasian nations, including the Russian Federated Republic, are not members of Western European civilization, and so they are bound to experience more difficulties. For them, the process of "joining" Europe involves assimilating essentially foreign—Western—cultural elements. They may never succeed, but, then again, must they? But whether they do or do not, we Westerners should realize that no simple universal solutions, such as the mere institution of liberal democracy and market economics, have realistic chances of solving all the problems, especially in those societies where the organic cultural preconditions for them are lacking. Perhaps our Western cultural concepts will not work as we think they should in either an Eastern European or an Islamic context. We must recognize that our analyses are shaped by our own unique cultural perceptions. Any attempt at formulating a meaningful analysis of events in Eastern Europe and Eurasia must first take into account the complexity of long-standing, varied cultural interrelation-ships that exist among the societies located there on terms often much dif-ferent from our own. Once having achieved that, we might then proceed to deal with the regions in a mutually meaningful and useful manner.

Placing "Eastern Europe"

● ○ ●

An interesting human trait is the frequent use of certain words in common speech under the assumption that their definition is perfectly clear to users and listeners alike, when, in actuality, they are merely general expressions of indefinite, multifaceted ideas that possess varying meanings dependent on the individual perceptions of those who use and receive them. They are, in essence, generalities that are accepted and acted upon as specifics. They can range from mundane expressions that are encountered without a second thought, to terms that lie at the core of burning national debates. A good example of the latter is the term "middle class," which in the past few years increasingly has been heard in the media rolling off the tongues of a great many individuals from disparate backgrounds—ranging from the homeless to the wealthy; from the average wage-earner to the leaders of government—and imparting an interesting variety of innuendo. For all of the widespread and frequently heated debate over the middle class and its tax burdens, it should be obvious that the popular definition of "middle class" is so vague and so user- and receiver-dependent that the term has become all-encompassing, and thus practically meaningless. There are, of course, concrete definitions for "middle class" but these bear a decidedly Marxist connotation and so, for many Westerners, are taboo. Yet the use of the term persists and everyone continues to assume that she or he knows exactly what it means.

One of the more innocuous generalities that has grown common in popular usage, especially because of the course taken by international events in the past few years, is the term "Eastern Europe." Politicians, journalists, pundits, teachers, students, even average bread-winning workers, have been talking about or analyzing Eastern Europe since the dramatic collapse of the Berlin Wall in late 1989 ushered in a near-continuous stream of events with world-shaking portent. One would think that the object of all the discussion is well defined. The term has been in use for almost a century. Governments devised policies regarding "Eastern Europe" in the past and are continuing to do so today. Universities and colleges have taught, and their students have studied, "Eastern Europe" for a long time, and today academic interest in it is on the rise. The term itself appears self-explanatory. It simply means the eastern part of Europe. What can be simpler?

As one might expect, the answer to this question is that the premise for the question itself—that simplicity exists in defining Eastern Europe—is completely erroneous. At first glance, it would appear that geography defines Eastern Europe. This, however, presupposes that there exist geographically definable borders for Europe as a whole, beyond which lies all of non-Europe. But geographers, cartographers, and historians have been arguing for years over exactly what constitutes the eastern geographical limits of Europe without arriving at a definitive answer, let alone determining the dividing line between its eastern and western halves. So the premise requires a second glance. Perhaps it actually demands a political definition. After all, since the close of the 1940s the term "Eastern Europe" commonly has meant those countries in Europe that formed part of the Soviet-led East Bloc, and these certainly lay east of "Western Europe," or those European countries that did not. But this approach then raises additional questions as to whether Eastern Europe existed prior to 1948 and after 1989. If it did and does (and we know that this is true for the term itself), then what political form provides some sort of definitive continuity to Eastern Europe? Unlike Western Europe, the eastern half has not experienced a native, organic political progression from feudal societies, through centralized monarchies, to national states. Its political development has been disjointed and mostly subject to the whims of foreign political forces. Therefore, if a political premise is to be used, it for the most part must be focused outside of Eastern Europe itself.

Now that our first glance has proven somewhat unsatisfactory and our second has opened a real can of worms, we might consider a third glance at the premise from an ethnic point of view. Eastern Europe is often referred to as that part of Europe inhabited by Slavic peoples, as opposed to Western Europe, which is primarily the domain of Germanic and Latin inhabitants who lie to the west of the Slavs. Of course, this is true only in the most general sense. It ignores completely the important historical existence of such non-Slavic Europeans as the Hungarians, the Romanians, and the Greeks, let alone the Albanians and various Turkic peoples, who live in the region that must certainly be included in any definition of Eastern Europe. Our third glance thus proving not so very conclusive, we might attempt one last glance in this frustrating effort to pin down the term by taking a cultural perspective. Only from this point of view do we ultimately arrive at a truly precise definition of Eastern Europe. Unfortunately, the cultural approach is far less familiar to most Westerners than are the more commonly accepted geographical, political, and ethnic ones. Nevertheless, it is important, especially in light of continuing disturbing events in the Balkans and the CIS and increasing pressures for Western involvement in them, that we in the West gain a clearer understanding of Eastern Europe in all of its varied manifestations. So, let us proceed to examine each of the four possible approaches toward defining Eastern Europe—geographical, political, ethnic, and cultural—in greater detail.

By looking in a world atlas, one will notice that the region designated as "Europe" actually is a somewhat irregularly shaped, narrow, triangular peninsula of land jutting westward from the large landmass labeled "Asia." Two of the three sides of the European triangle are rather well defined by large bodies of water. Due north of Europe lie the Arctic Ocean and its component seas—the Barents, White, and the Norwegian—the North Sea, and the Baltic Sea. To its west yawns the Atlantic Ocean, and on its south are the Mediterranean Sea—with its component Tyrrhenian, Adriatic, Ionian, and Aegean seas—and the Black Sea. Large bodies of water create excellent, definitive borders for continents. It is the third, or eastern, frontier of the European triangle, fronting the Asian landmass, that presents a problem for geographical definition.

Older atlases might well show a line, generally running north and south, following the path of the Ural Mountains as the border between Europe and Asia. But it will be noticed that the Urals do not completely bisect the width of the landmass. They peter out into steppe country some four hundred miles north of the Aral Sea, so the continental border drawn from that point to the Caspian Sea, a distance of approximately eight hundred miles, abruptly turns westward in the shape of a large salient. This is so because, lacking any well-defined geographical land feature, it arbitrarily has been made to follow the northwestern border of the Kazakhstan Republic. One may quibble over this European-Asian boundary in the steppes, but surely, one might assume, the rest of its length along the Ural divide is beyond question.

Not so. The Urals are not the sort of geographical feature that can provide a definitive continental separation. With a maximum elevation of a bit over six thousand feet in a few places, the Urals are generally an old, low, weather-worn range of higher-than-average hills. They pose virtually no obstacle to the course of the Great Eurasian Plain that stretches east to west from eastern Siberia, near the Pacific Ocean, to the fields of Flanders, on the shores of the Atlantic. While the Urals may have stood as a mild buffer to Asiatic inroads into the heart of Europe throughout history, the gap of open steppe land to their south served as a veritable highway for Asian invaders, such as the Huns, Avars, Alans, Bulgars, Turks, and Mongols, who had an important, often devastating, impact on Europe and its historical development between the fifth and twelfth centuries. Later, beginning in the sixteenth century, the Urals failed to obstruct a reverse demographic movement—a steady stream of European inroads into the Siberian and steppe heartlands of Asia led by the Russians. At no time in historical memory did the Urals definitively separate Europe from Asia. In point of fact, no mountain range—not the Himalayas, the Alps, the Pyrenees, the Caucasus or the Rockies, all of which are higher and more forbidding than the Urals—has ever served as a definitive border for any continent.

One may then wonder just how the Ural Mountains commonly came to be accepted as the divide that supposedly provides Europe with its definitive eastern boundary. The answer, it seems, lies in politics. The Urals became the border of Europe because the great westernizing Russian tsar, Peter I the Great (1682-1725), willed it so. To Peter's mind, Russia could not become a great European power, accepted by other European powers, such as France, England, and the Habsburg Empire, if it were not physically located within the confines of the continent of Europe. So Peter ordered his court geographers to declare the Ural Mountains the eastern border of Europe on all of their officially issued maps. At the time, the Central Asian region that is today Kazakhstan remained outside the borders of the Russian Empire under Islamic, hence non-European, sway—thus the arbitrary drawing of the continental border in the southern steppes, based on Russia's actual frontier with Islamic Central Asia in that region. Since the Russian state came to play an important role in European affairs from the time of Peter on, the Russian definition of Europe's limits was accepted by all the member states of Europe as an expression of European realities.

In recent times geographers have attempted to overcome the problem of Europe's eastern border by labeling the entire landmass comprising both Europe and Asia "Eurasia." Although this term is technically more accurate, it tends to raise the neck hair of those who consider themselves Europeans, as opposed to Asians. They resent the idea that Europe, homeland of the world's most dominant civilization, is physically only a rather small outcrop of a huge, densely populated, un-European Asian continent. The Russians especially find the connotations of the term distasteful. Since historical Russia (that is, the area encompassed by the former Russian/Soviet Empire) geographically straddles territories in both Europe and Asia, the term "Eurasia," with its elimination of the Ural continental frontier, transforms the inhabitants of that state from Europeans into Eurasians. But in contemporary geographical terms, such indeed is the reality. Therefore, we are faced with a new arbitrary eastern border for Europe—the western boundaries of the former Russian/Soviet Empire. Today geographical Europe can be defined as the peninsula of land lying west of Belarus, Ukraine, and the Russian Federated Republic.

Having thus arrived at a modern eastern parameter for geographical Europe, we now must turn to the problem of geographically defining its eastern half.

Returning to our atlas, we will notice that the easternmost area of Europe (as we have just defined it) is characterized by two rather well delineated geographical regions lying on a south-north axis. The best defined of the two is the Balkan Peninsula in the extreme south. It is a rugged triangle of land bounded on the west by the Adriatic Sea, on the east by the Black Sea, on the southeast by the Aegean Sea, and with its southern tip jutting into the main body of the Mediterranean Sea. The broad northern land border of the Balkan triangle is generally formed by the Carpathian Mountains, although rivers, most notably the Danube, cut numerous gaps in this barrier.

Mountains characterize the terrain of the Balkan Peninsula. The very name "Balkan" is a Turkish term, meaning "mountain," and is now also the accepted name of a particular chain of mountains, known in classical times as the Hæmus, that bisects half the east-west width of the peninsula just south of the Danube River in today's Bulgaria. To the south of the Balkan Mountains stretch a series of mountain ranges—the Rilas (at 9,592 feet, the highest in the Balkan Peninsula), the Rhodopes, the Pirin, the Pindhos, and the Tagetus—to the tip of the peninsula in Greek Peloponnese. The western portion of the Balkan Peninsula is dominated by the Dinaric and Albanian Alps, which run parallel to the Adriatic coastline but spread extensively inland to the east. Close to 70 percent of the land in the Balkans is comprised of mountains.

Except for the narrow coastal plains, which vary in width from less than a mile in some areas, such as in parts of Dalmatia on the Adriatic Sea, to the extensive Thracian Plain in the peninsula's southeast, most of the lowlands in the interior of the Balkans are deep river valleys. The largest is that of the Danube, which cuts a swath into the heart of the peninsula between the Dinaric Alps and the Carpathian Mountains, narrowing at the so-called Iron Gates east of Belgrade, where the river literally carves a gorge separating the Carpathian and Balkan mountains, before widening once again into a broad, fertile plain extending to the Black Sea. Others, such as the Drava, Sava, Morava, and Iskŭr river valleys (which form important branches of the Danube watershed), the

Vardar, Struma, and Maritsa river valleys (which drain into the Aegean Sea), and the Krka, Neretva, and Drin river valleys (which flow to the Adriatic), provide the peninsula with both a modicum of shallow-layered arable land in the mountainous interior and the only lines of natural overland communications available.

Climatically, the Balkan Peninsula is not a unit. It enjoys a Mediterranean-type climate along its sea coasts and a continental one throughout most of its interior. The climatic line of division lies close to the coastline in most of the peninsula since the mountains, which form the climatic border, push close to the sea almost everywhere. This division between coast and mountains historically has been of political consequence as well. Often the coast, with its important seaports—Thessaloniki, Kavala, Piræus, Modon, Volos, Patras, and Nafplion (in Greece); Varna and Burgas (in Bulgaria); Vlorë and Durrës (in Albania); Rijeka, Zadar, Split, and Kotor (in Croatian Dalmatia); and, the greatest port of all, Istanbul, formerly Constantinople (in European Turkey)—was controlled by states foreign to those that existed in the mountainous interior, states such as Byzantium, Venice, France, and others—thus effectively barring the interior from friendly outlets to the seas.

The geography of the Balkans generally can be characterized as providing a harsh, divisive environment. The harshness of the land has played a decisive role in shaping the lives of those peoples who have inhabited the region since earliest recorded times. The mountainous terrain tended to separate human habitation in the peninsula among isolated river valleys and highland plateaus. This spawned the classical Greek city-state and, since medieval times, shaped the cultures and histories of the various groups of peoples inhabiting the interior, helping to create among them numerous unrelated microcultures and a plethora of submicrocultures. Moreover, in a region possessed of limited arable land, a harsh continental climate, and limited number of natural lines of communications for travel and commerce, life historically has been far from stable and prosperous. Centuries of fierce competition among the varied populations of the peninsula for control of the geographically restricted available natural resources have bred microcultures typified by extremes in their expression—communal generosity and stubborn territoriality; overt hospitality and brutal atrocity; bouts of fun-loving enjoyment and irrational violence. All exhibit one common characteristic: a sense of passionate, tenacious microcultural pride.

Immediately north of the Balkan Peninsula lies the other geographically definable region of Eastern Europe—the Danubian Basin. This region centers on the Danube River, one of the greatest of all European rivers. The Danube flows some 1,725 miles from its sources in the Black Mountains of southern Germany to its marshy mouth opening into the Black Sea. The basin defining the second region of Eastern Europe essentially consists of a broad, fertile plain, which stretches from the point the Danube enters the Balkan Peninsula northwestward to Vienna. It is surrounded by mountain chains and plateaus on its peripheries. Generally, the great arc of the Carpathian Mountains forms the basin's southeastern, eastern, and part of its northern borders. The Sudet and Ore mountains continue the northern frontier of the basin until they meet the Bohemian Forest-Šumava Mountains, which cut sharply south and southeastward. The Danube separates these Bohemian ranges from the chain of the Julian Alps in the west, which delineates the western extremity of the basin until it meets the Dinaric Alps in the southwest.

Two extensive mountain plateaus are nestled within the folds of the chains that serve as boundaries for the Danubian Basin. In the southeast is the Transylvanian (sometimes termed the Carpathian) Plateau. This triangular area is surrounded by the arc of the Carpathians on its south and northeast and by the less precipitous Bihor range on its west. Nearly all of the major river systems draining the Transylvanian Plateau, such as the Mureş, Criş, and Someş, flow through the Bihors into the great Tisza River system, one of the primary tributaries of the Danube in the heart of the basin itself. The Bihors thus pose no major geographical obstacle separating the Transylvanian Plateau from the basin proper. In the northwest lies the Bohemian Plateau, folded within the arc formed by the Sudet, Ore, and Bohemian Forest-Šumava mountains, and further bounded by the Bohemian-Moravian Highlands on its southeast. More an independent geographical entity than the Transylvanian Plateau, the Bohemian Plateau nevertheless is linked to the Danubian Basin by the Morava River system that carves its way southward through the Bohemian-Moravian Highlands to the Danube east of Vienna.

The heart of the Danubian Basin is composed of the wide Viennese Valley of the Danube and the great Pannonian Plain of Hungary. They both enjoy a continental climate and rich, fertile soil that have helped make the Danubian Basin a thriving agricultural region for centuries. The surrounding mountains and hills are rich in ores, minerals, and timber, all of which have contributed to the growth of industries in the basin. An extensive system of rivers draining into the Danube from every corner of the area has traditionally provided the Danubian Basin with an exceptional communications and transportation network, historically fostering political and economic unity in the area as a whole.

Geography has conspired to make the Danubian Basin one of the most important areas in Europe. In Roman times a good portion of the basin was organized into the province of Pannonia, a key element in the empire's border defenses against Germanic threats from the north and northeast and an important corridor for tying the empire's Gallic frontiers to its Balkan provinces. The great plain of Pannonia, which constitutes over half of the basin's flatlands, served as the core region for numerous transitory barbarian states that threatened the Roman Empire. Beginning with the Goths in the later fourth century, the Pannonian Plain successively attracted Huns, Avars, and finally, in the ninth century, Magyars (Hungarians), by its close resemblance to the steppe topography of their Eurasian homelands. Only the Magyars managed to plant permanent roots in the plain by forging ties with the Viennese Valley and by securing possession of the Dinaric and Carpathian mountain lines of defense.

Meanwhile, by the ninth century the Viennese Valley was firmly in the hands of Germans, who exploited the natural wealth of the area to such good political and economic effect that, by the early sixteenth century, the German Habsburg rulers of Vienna were able to begin consolidating all of the Danube Basin under their personal control. That process was completed by the end of the following century. At its close, the resources bestowed by a unified Danubian Basin guaranteed that the Habsburg Empire created by the process of consolidation held a recognized place among the Great Powers of Europe, along with France, England, Spain, and the Ottoman Empire. For as long as the Danubian Basin remained politically unified and its populations stayed loyal, the Habsburg Empire was able to retain its Great Power position in Europe. When that human unity in the basin began to collapse in the mid-nineteenth century under the blows of conflicting nationalisms, the Habsburg state fell into a decline from which it never recovered.

The dismemberment of the Habsburg state following World War I into small, independent national states recognized by the treaties of Versailles (1919-21) demonstrated the importance of the Danubian Basin as a geographical entity. Carving up its territory among the borders of four separate, highly competitive states (Austria, Hungary, Czechoslovakia, and Romania) completely disrupted the organic economic network of the basin that had thrived over the centuries because of Habsburg consolidation. None of the new countries created in the basin was blessed with sufficient natural resources for ensuring healthy economic, and thus political, existence. Austria, whose capital of Vienna had for centuries served as the basin's natural market and center for most commercial activity, was reduced to something akin to a huge head without a body. The other three states found themselves in the opposite situation. All were weak. They were given little time to forge new economic relationships that would have offset their weaknesses before being swept up by Hitler's Germany. Two—Austria and Czechoslovakia—disappeared completely by the end of 1938, while the other two were transformed into mere warehouses of human and natural resources for their fascist German masters after 1940.

Following World War II and the reemergence of the Versailles-created Danubian states, the disruption of the basin's natural unity continued. While Austria eventually made some progress in adjusting to its independent existence, the other states in the basin were incorporated into the artificially unified world of the Soviet-led East Bloc. Once that Bloc collapsed in 1989, those states once again were forced to face the serious problem of fashioning economic and political structures and relationships that might furnish the sort of regional stability that the unified Danubian Basin had provided in the past, or risk renewed weakness and disruption. The effort has already taken a toll with the 1993 division of the former Czechoslovak state into two smaller ones—the Czech Republic and Slovakia.

Immediately north of the Carpathian and Sudet mountains—the northern boundary of the Danubian Basin—the terrain falls off into a low, rolling plain extending some four hundred miles northward until ending at the southern shores of the Baltic Sea. This is a section of the Great Eurasian Plain. Although it is bounded on the south by mountains and on the north by sea, no notable land features serve to define either its eastern or western borders. Two extensive river systems, the Oder in the west and the Vistula in the east, drain the Great Plain in this area as they flow north to empty into the Baltic. Just as mountains do not serve as definitive geographical borders for continents, neither do rivers for regions. The geographical prominence of the open plain has given this third area of Eastern Europe its lasting name—Poland (from the Slavic word for field or plain, *pole*—thus, "Land of the Plain").

The topography of the southern third of the Polish Plain area is characterized by a gradual transition from the mountains in the south to the plain land proper in the north. The uplands that dissect this area create a number of definable subregions, consisting of highland plateaus and surrounding lowlands. These subregions, such as Silesia and Galicia, historically have been at the center of intense rivalries among Poles, Germans, Czechs, and Ukrainians, since they possess nearly all the available fertile agricultural and rich mineral resources in the area. The undulating Central Plain and the rather flat northern coastal plain offer little in the way of natural resources. Their soil is acidic, sandy, and often drowned by widespread marshland. The northern third of the plain is covered by thick pine forests that further conspire against soil fertility. Add a harsh northern continental climate to the natural topography and geology, and one can begin to understand why the microculture of the Prussian Germans, who hail from the most northern third of the Polish area, is renowned for exhibiting meticulous discipline, austerity, and tenacity. In their harsh, unfertile, boggy, darkly forested environment, the Prussian Germans needed to develop such traits to survive.

On the Central Plain, the Poles inhabiting the subregions of Greater Poland and Mazovia were faced with a number of environmental challenges. One was the dearth of natural resources offered by the plain itself. To compensate for this shortcoming, the Poles were forced to push southward into the more naturally rich uplands, establishing firm roots in the area now known as Little Poland, which lies between Silesia on its west and Galicia on its east. But this brought the Poles into competition with all of their immediate neighbors, who also were attempting to claim the same resources for themselves. A second challenge for the Poles was posed by the Central Plain's isolation from the major economic arteries of Europe, especially from the thriving Baltic Sea routes that linked northeastern Europe to the markets of England and Flanders. The only serviceable port on the Baltic in the Polish area was Gdańsk (Danzig), but it lay in Prussian German hands. The Poles' striving to gain and retain an outlet on the Baltic at Gdańsk lay at the heart of a centuries-long struggle between Poles and Germans.

Most crucial to the shaping of Polish microculture and history was a third environmental challenge posed by the Central Plain—the utter lack of natural frontiers to both east and west that could serve as defensive positions against the incursions of foreign enemies from either Eurasia or Western Europe. Since the time of their earliest establishment on the Central Plain some time in the ninth or tenth century, the Poles have struggled with the innate strategical disadvantage posed by the plain. Their conversion to Catholicism in the tenth century was a conscious effort to forestall Christian German attacks from the west by joining Western European civilization, thus eliminating the initial threat of genocidal warfare that the West felt justified in waging against pagan societies on its borders. The union with Lithuania in the fourteenth century not only assisted the Poles in their battles against the Prussian Germans (the Teutonic Knights) along the Baltic coast to their north, but also opened the opportunity for protecting their vulnerable eastern border against potential Mongol-Tatar invasion. When the Lithuanian Union drew the Poles into conflict with the Russian state centered in Moscow in the late fifteenth century, the Poles soon thereafter turned to an eastern border policy of offensive defense. They transformed the Lithuanian-held lands in Belarus and Ukraine from primarily buffer regions into springboards for eastern expansion against both Russia and the Mongol-Tatar Golden Horde. The strains of attempting to retain control of what amounted to almost unlimited open geographical space against Russian and Ukrainian enemies caused this policy to collapse in the seventeenth century.

By concentrating nearly all of their efforts and resources against the Russians on their vulnerable eastern frontier, the Poles had little left to counter increasing German pressure against their equally unprotected border in the west.

Caught in a pincer between two powerful, expansive enemies, the Poles were doomed to lose their independent state in the late eighteenth century, and this loss, which persisted for some 120 years, made a lasting impact on Polish microculture. Retreating into their Catholic faith to ward off the dominant cultural pressures of their Orthodox Russian and Lutheran German masters, the Poles developed a self-identity that rationalized the catastrophe that the plains environment had ultimately inflicted upon them. They equated themselves with the persecuted early Christians in an analogy both religious and national that assigned the perceived roles of Roman "persecutors" and Jewish "collaborators" to the Russians and Germans, respectively. To the Poles' collective mind, the land of Poland became Golgotha, with the Poles (Christ and the Christians) crucified for not accepting the rule of Orthodox Russia (pagan Rome) and its Lutheran German partners (the Jews, related in faith but considered flawed).

It is no accident that one of the most definitive expressions of modern Polish microculture is the novel written by the Polish Nobel laureate Henryk Sienkiewicz, published in 1896—*Quo Vadis: A Narrative of the Time of Nero*. To most non-Polish readers (and to those non-Poles who have seen the films based on the book), *Quo Vadis* is a stirring piece of historical fiction; to Poles, it is a glowing description of themselves, their past unfortunate fate, and the validity of their hopes for an ultimately glorious and victorious future in reward for maintaining true to their religious and national faith.

Although the Poles' hopes for a reconstituted independent state of their own were fulfilled at the end of World War I at the Versailles peace conference, paper agreements among powerful states could do little to solve the fundamental east-west border problem posed by the plains environment. From 1939 until 1989 the Poles were destined to suffer for a second time national crucifixion at the hands of the same two flanking neighbors. Once again a deal struck between Germans and Russians (Soviets) led to the swallowing of Poland by its macrocultural enemy to the east; only this time a fiction of independence was maintained and the country, reduced to the status of Soviet satellite, was not completely erased from the map. Following 1989, Poland was again freed of Russian control, but the environmental border problem remained, precariously restrained only by renewed treaties with traditional eastern and western enemies.

In discussing Eastern Europe, the three different geographical components are most readily identifiable as Southeastern Europe (the Balkan Peninsula area), Central-Eastern Europe (the Danubian Basin area), and Northeastern Europe (the Great Polish Plain area).

The intimate relationship between geography and political destiny in the case of Poland leads us into consideration of the second possible way of defining Eastern Europe—that is, politically. From 1948 until 1989 the West defined Eastern Europe as those European countries controlled by Communist governments. These lay to the east of the liberal-democratic states of Europe, forming a solid buffer zone between them and the Soviet Union. All of those states were considered (incorrectly, as it turned out) by the West as veritable carbon copies of the regime in the Soviet Union, which seemingly controlled their every activity. As a result, Eastern Europe was perceived as a monolithic whole—the so-called East Bloc—and was treated as such by the West throughout most of the cold war period. This politically defined Eastern Europe consisted of East Germany and Poland (located in Northeastern Europe), Czechoslovakia and Hungary (in Central-Eastern Europe), and Yugoslavia, Bulgaria, Romania, and Albania (situated in Southeastern Europe). All except Yugoslavia and Albania were members of the Soviet-led Warsaw Pact and Comecon (Council of Mutual Economic Assistance), a fact that emphasized their subordinate relationship to the Soviet Union.

Although the bloc concept provided a conveniently simplistic and generalized approach for the West's dealings with post-World War II Eastern Europe, the Yugoslav and Albanian exceptions negated its worth almost from the very beginning. Yugoslavia managed to escape the Soviet puppet status conferred on most of the other European Communist states through the independent leadership of its charismatic ruler, Josip (Broz) Tito. A successful commander of Communist antifascist partisans during World War II whose forces cleared Yugoslavia of the Nazis and their collaborators without the assistance of the Red Army, Tito emerged by 1945 as the popular, heroic political leader of the country. His military successes during the war, forceful personality, and iron control of a well-armed, numerous, and disciplined party organization ensured that Tito's grip on power became absolute. The Croatian neofascist *Ustaše* organization was crushed and the Serb royalist *četnik* war partisans discredited. He was able to impose on Yugoslavia a governing regime that, though dictatorial and often cruel, managed to knit the disparate peoples and cultures within the country's borders into a semblance of unity maintained by the sheer force of his personality and political will. Such a leader could not help but resent Soviet efforts to subordinate him and his government to the interests and whims of Stalin and his cretins in Moscow. The split between Tito and Stalin came in 1948, after which Yugoslavia pursued its own national-Communist interests. Under Tito's forceful control, Yugoslavia became a founding member of the Organization of Nonaligned States during the cold war, experimented with mixed socialist-capitalist economic endeavors, and served as a model for a form of communism that emphasized adaptation to specific national interests rather than blind adherence to the Soviet-style model.

Albania also parted with the Soviet-led East Bloc of Eastern Europe, but for different reasons from Yugoslavia. During World War II the Albanian Communist partisans represented an ideological wing of Tito's movement, accepting doctrinal, strategical, and tactical advice and, often, officer cadres from their more active and powerful comrades in Yugoslavia. Like Tito, Enver Hoxha, leader of the Albanian Communists, took undisputed control of Albania in 1944 without help from the Red Army. Until the Soviet-Yugoslav split in 1948, he used Tito as his mediator with Moscow, though he grew increasingly uneasy over Tito's deviations from the Soviet party line as voiced by Stalin. Following the split, Hoxha moved stoutly into the Stalinist camp to emphasize Albania's complete break with Yugoslav affiliation. When, after Stalin's death in 1953, Nikita Khrushchev repudiated the dictatorial and criminal regime of his predecessor at the Twentieth Congress of the Soviet Communist party (1956) and proceeded to give the Soviet Union a more flexible approach in both domestic and foreign policies, Hoxha saw this as a betrayal of true (Stalinist) communism. The split that openly erupted in 1960 between Khrushchev and Mao Tse-tung, the successful Chinese Communist leader, over this very issue provided Hoxha with the opportunity to guarantee Albania's independence from both Yugoslav and Soviet apostasy. He threw the country into the arms of the Red Chinese, where it remained until the 1970s and the repudiation of Maoism in China itself. Afterward, Albania attempted to go it alone in the Communist world, isolated and without much notable success.

Even if our hair-splitting over the Yugoslav and Albanian exceptions to the East Bloc concept is set aside and we accept European Communist governments as the premise for politically defining Eastern Europe, questions concerning the veracity of the definition itself remain. One of these has to do with Greece. Given our geographical definition just outlined, Greece obviously lies within the confines of Eastern Europe, being located at the extreme southern tip of the Balkan Peninsula in Southeastern Europe. But because the country successfully fended off an attempted Communist *putsch* after World War II and joined NATO, Greece is deemed a member of Western Europe in the political definition. (The fact that Greece also is seen as the ancient homeland of Western European civilization's Greco-Roman roots lends further credence to this idea.) The Greeks themselves revel in this Western identification, which has become an integral element in their sense of modern, nationalistic self-identity. Greece does not appear in a number of important publications dealing with Eastern Europe released over the past forty years, because the post-1948 definition is used. Works specifically dealing with the Balkans often have omitted consideration of Greece for the same reason, even though the country is undoubtedly situated on that peninsula and has played an important, near-continuous role in its historical developments. So in terms of Greece, especially within the Balkan context, the political definition of Eastern Europe becomes awkward and ahistorical—the claims of modern Greek nationalists notwithstanding.

A similar question about the Communist-based political definition of Eastern Europe can be raised regarding the former East Germany. In this case, it is a matter of inclusion rather than exclusion.

Until 1945 the regions constituting what came to be called East Germany (or, more accurately, the German Democratic Republic)—Saxony, Brandenburg, Thuringia, Lusatia, and Mecklenburg—were firmly ensconced in the world of Western Europe. Only the purely coincidental fact of Red Army operations in Europe at the end of World War II led to their political separation from the rest of Germany, which remained part of the West by the equally coincidental fact of American, British, and French military operations. No Germans, no matter which side of the East-West line they inhabited, ever truly accepted the Eastern European definition for those living in the German regions under Communist sway. The swiftness with which both East and West Germans embraced reunification after the fall of the Wall in 1989 (despite the trauma both knew the action would hold for them later) demonstrated the fallacy of the East European political definition as far as the Germans were concerned.

Now that communism has all but disappeared as a potent political force in all of the former Communist countries of Europe, a new trend in political and scholarly thinking calls for the elimination of the very term "Eastern Europe" from our vocabulary. The justification for this lies in attempts to crystallize Western-style, capitalistic, liberal-democratic societies in all of the ex-Communist states, thus transforming them into "Western" European countries. This approach epitomizes the flawed "end of history" philosophy that emerged among a few Western intellectuals following the events of 1989 in Berlin and elsewhere. Capitalistic liberal democracy undoubtedly is a sociopolitical cultural manifestation of Western European civilization, but there is a noticeable difference between its implementation among the former Communist states of Northeastern and Central-Eastern Europe, where the process appears rocky but is progressing, and among those in the area of Southeastern Europe, where the process is obstructed by intransigent internal political and ethnic divisiveness. Moreover, in no area of the formerly Communist Eastern Europe is it functioning anywhere near to accepted Western standards, let alone to the ideal.

While a half century of communism certainly is partly to blame for this situation, it cannot be considered the only cause, since the region of Eastern Europe has been a part of European political affairs for centuries. During those centuries the region was nearly always seen as being different somehow from its western counterpart.

Though at first it may seem surprising, an Eastern Europe comprised entirely of independent states has existed for little more than a quarter of a century. The countries of the region were created following the end of World War I and were truly independent states only until the end of World War II. Before and after (up until 1989, at least) that period, Eastern Europe primarily was dominated by foreign "superpowers," who bent and shaped the region to their various wills. We are all familiar with the post-World War II situation—the supremacy of the Soviet Union in the region. It, of course, gave us our working political definition of Eastern Europe for the second half of the twentieth century. Only a minority of us are familiar with the centuries-old political situation of Eastern Europe prior to the end of World War I, of which only the briefest of outlines can be given here.

During medieval times in the West, a number of independent monarchical states emerged in the region. The earliest of these arose in Southeastern Europe. First there was the East Roman Empire, which was the continuation of the old Roman Empire after the fall of its western half in the late fifth century. With its capital at Constantinople, in the extreme southeastern corner of the Balkan Peninsula, the East Roman Empire gradually was transformed over time into an essentially Greek state (the Byzantine Empire). Starting in the late seventh century with the rise of Bulgaria in the northeast, the Balkans witnessed the emergence of a series of smaller states—especially Serbia, Croatia, and Bosnia—between the ninth and twelfth centuries. All of those states were caught up in the general tug-of-war over dominance in Southeastern Europe between Orthodox Byzantium, on the one hand, and Catholic Rome and Venice, on the other. They all were heavily influenced, and often dependent on, one or the other of the contending sides. Eventually Bulgaria and Serbia gravitated permanently into the Byzantine orbit, while Croatia and Bosnia joined the Roman-Venetian sphere.

North of Southeastern Europe, in the Bohemian Plateau of Central-Eastern Europe, a Czech state of Great Moravia emerged in the ninth century but was swiftly brought under the political sway of the German-dominated Holy Roman Empire, within which the Czechs managed to consolidate a component state—the Kingdom of Bohemia—by the thirteenth century. Bohemia became one of the seven states within the empire that enjoyed the privilege of electing the Holy Roman Emperor and was the only state among them with the recognized status of kingdom. Also in the ninth century the Magyars entered Central-Eastern Europe and established a state of their own on the Pannonian Plain. Unlike their many nomadic Turkic predecessors, who had settled briefly in that area only to move on or disappear eventually, the Hungarians came to stay. By the end of the eleventh century they had brought the Transylvanian Plateau under their control and had gained European recognition as a kingdom. Soon thereafter, in 1102, Hungary acquired the Kingdom of Croatia, in the northwestern corner of Southeastern Europe, as a result of a personal political union—the Hungarian king becoming also the hereditary ruler of Croatia. When the two Romanian principalities of Wallachia and Moldavia arose in the fourteenth century south and east of the Carpathian Mountains, in the extreme northeast corner of Southeastern Europe, they swiftly became veritable satellites of the Hungarian state, though heavily influenced politically and culturally by the Byzantinized Bulgarian state to their south.

In Northeastern Europe a Polish state was consolidated in the late tenth century. Plagued by conflicts with the Prussian Teutonic Knights to its north and susceptible to attacks from the Mongol-Tatar hordes lying farther east on the open steppes, Poland was forced to unite in the fourteenth century with its eastern Lithuanian neighbors in an attempt to consolidate enough human and territorial resources to ensure its continued existence. This union, in which the Poles gained the upper hand by the mid-sixteenth century, permitted Poland to contain the Prussian Germans along the Baltic and made it, territorially, the single largest state in Europe by the early seventeenth century, stretching from the Baltic to the Black seas.

All of the medieval East European states lay in the mainstream of the general European political realities for their time. They all were monarchical states ruled, at first, by native royal dynasties. Their political and social organizations followed accepted European patterns, though cultural differences among them resulted in distinct variations as to how these were actually manifested. Power rested in the hands of landowning warrior classes that monopolized all important political, spiritual, and social positions. These elites guaranteed their dominance within the states by structuring their societies in such a way that the Christian church and the monarchy, with their respective hierarchies of subordinate clerics and warriors, governed in close partnership, with the spiritual justifying the temporal authority exerted by the ruling classes that dominated both. Because in warrior societies wealth and power lay in the ownership of land and in its resources, the economies of all medieval European states—with the possible exception of the northern Italian, commercially oriented city-states (such as Venice)—were agrarian, supplemented by craft industries. Agriculture and crafts supplied the ruling elites with the necessities that permitted them to devote their energies completely to their own interests. The majority of the populations in all of the European states—rural peasants and urban artisans and craftsmen—counted for little beyond their supporting role in the existence of the ruling elites and the institutions that those elites created for themselves. Interestingly, either for reasons of cultural differences or because of differing geographical factors, serfdom (the legal binding of peasants to the soil) did not attain the all-encompassing level of development among the medieval East European states as it did among those in the West. On the whole, other than in the social sphere of feudalism, the independent medieval East European states could not be differentiated politically from their Western European counterparts.

The political similarity between Eastern and Western Europe began to disappear in the late fourteenth century when the Southeast European states of Bulgaria and Serbia were crushed and then dismantled by the invading Ottoman Turks. In the following century the Byzantine Empire (medieval Greece), Bosnia, and the Romanian Principalities (Wallachia and Moldavia) suffered a similar fate. Except for the Romanian Principalities, which were preserved as puppet states in name only, all were directly incorporated into the rising Islamic empire of the Turks and, thus, were completely eliminated from the political map of Europe for close to five hundred years.

The political organization imposed on the populations of the former Southeast European states was utterly foreign to their old European traditions. Their native social elites were eliminated and replaced by Turkish functionaries of foreign ethnicity and religion. While the Turkish conquest spelled disaster for the former elites, it is doubtful that the change of both rulers and the system of governance had a profoundly negative impact on the general Christian populations of the former states. It, in fact, may have had quite the opposite effect. The Muslim Turks afforded their conquered non-Muslim subjects a large measure of local political autonomy, so long as they paid their taxes and did not impinge upon the religious precepts of their rulers. For all intents and purposes, the populations of the former Southeast European states merely exchanged one ruling elite for another, and the change, for as long as the Turkish system operated efficiently (for some two and a half centuries), may have had more of a positive than a negative effect—if any at all—on their political lives in general.

North of Southeastern Europe, the East European medieval states suffered a common political liability that led to the disappearance of their independence beginning in the fourteenth century. During that period all of the native ruling dynasties died out—the Árpáds in Hungary, the Přemysls in Bohemia, and the Piasts in Poland—and the elites of those states, exercising their traditional right to elect their rulers, turned to foreign ruling houses for new leadership. Thus, the following centuries found the royal houses of the Lithuanian Jagiełłos, the German Luxembergs, and the French Anjous ruling one, two, or sometimes all three of those states in various sorts of combinations. Within the medieval Western context of feudal government, such a situation may have made confusing sense, but, for the states themselves, it ultimately led to internal instability and political weakness. The crazy-quilt patterns of dynastic rule that emerged seriously undermined the central authority of the various rulers while reinforcing the anarchistic authority of those states' aristocratic elites, in whose hands were concentrated real political power that they used for their own personal benefit. These developments explain the rise of serfdom in those East European states north of the Balkans at the very time that that insidious institution was ending in the West, as well as their increasing political inability to fend off domination by more powerful centralized neighboring states to their west and east.

The almost inevitable loss of independence began for the Central-Eastern European states of Bohemia and Hungary in the first quarter of the sixteenth century when the Austrian ruling house of Habsburg gained the thrones of both and managed to cement its dynastic hold on them over the course of the following 150 years. By the close of the seventeenth century the dynastic problems of the Czechs and Hungarians were solved in favor of the Habsburgs at the cost of their respective states' independence. Until the end of World War I they more or less existed as formalities within the larger political framework of the Habsburg Empire. In the case of Poland in Northeastern Europe, dynastic problems continued long after the Habsburg takeover of the Central-East European states. Lithuanian Jagiełło, French Valois, Swedish Vasa, Hungarian Bathory, and other non-Polish ruling houses alternated with brief attempts at native rule until the end of the eighteenth century, during which time the political independence of the powerful Polish-Lithuanian nobility grew increasingly more independent from the central authority and the Polish rulers devolved into mere puppets of the powerful neighboring Russians and Germans. Polish independence was finally ended in 1795 when the Russians and the Germans tired of the anarchistic antics of the Polish-Lithuanian aristocracy and the accompanying charade of political independence. What had once been the state of Poland-Lithuania lay divided among the Russian, Habsburg, and Prussian empires until the close of World War I.

For a few decades following the destruction of Poland, there were no independent states to speak of in all of Eastern Europe. Every former state in the region had been assimilated, in one form or another over varying lengths of time, into the foreign Ottoman, Habsburg, Russian, or Prussian empires.

Interestingly, the Southeast European states that had been the earliest to disappear from Eastern Europe—Serbia, Greece, Montenegro, and Bulgaria—were the first to reemerge as independent countries. They managed gradually to throw off Ottoman rule over the course of the nineteenth century. To attain their renewed independence, the others north of the Balkans had to await the collapse of the remaining empires brought about by the results of World War I. But in most of the East European countries the varying legacies of long political domination by differing autocratic foreign powers retarded the development of deep-rooted political cultures. The various East Europeans subject to those empires essentially existed as minorities possessing varying degrees of limited governmental participation, ranging from virtually none at all, save at the local level (for example, the Slovaks under the Habsburgs or the Bulgarians under the Ottomans), to actual parliamentary representation (the Hungarians in the Habsburg Empire being the most developed case). They tended to continue longer in economic and social backwardness than their West European neighbors, and their societies remained predominantly peasant with highly developed folk customs. These factors, combined with the Western concepts of nationalism and the nation-state that were newly embraced by the various nationalities of Eastern Europe (which resulted in the creation of unevenly divided multiethnic, often artificial, states, such as Yugoslavia and Romania), ensured that between the two world wars the politically independent states of Eastern Europe were weak, both internally and externally, and, therefore, little more than pawns of their still-powerful western and eastern German and Russian (Soviet) neighbors. Only Greece managed to escape the essentially Soviet-dominated fate that befell the rest of Eastern Europe at the end of World War II through active British (and, later, American) intervention.

If a political definition of Eastern Europe is used, then that definition must be based on the dominant role played by powerful, autocratic foreign states lying outside the geographical limits of Eastern Europe and on the traditional political weakness of the East European states themselves. The foreign powers that dominated Eastern Europe for over half a millennium were those empires that disappeared as a result of World War I. For a brief period of four decades following World War II, the foreign power holding predominant sway in the region was the Soviet Union. Now, after 1989-90, the significant foreign political force in the region seems to be that exerted by the Western nations of the European Union and by the United States. But concerning this latest case, it is still too early to make any definitive judgment.

A third way of defining Eastern Europe is from an ethnic point of view. This approach leans heavily on language as the essential factor.

The most commonly used ethnic definition of Eastern Europe is based on the assumption that the predominant linguistic family of the region's inhabitants is Slavic, as opposed to the Germanic and Latin linguistic families that hold sway among the European peoples living to their west. Therefore, in this approach, Eastern Europe is considered synonymous with Slavic Europe, and Western Europe is equated with Latin/Germanic Europe. While such a definition may be acceptable in the broadest, most generalized of cases, it does little to serve the purposes of definitive accuracy. Despite Westerners' almost automatic equation of Slavs with Eastern Europe, the ethnic definition is far more accurate for Western Europe than it is for its eastern counterpart.

There is no doubting the fact that Slavic-speaking peoples form a majority in the total population of the East European geographical region. Bosniaks (Bosnian Muslims), Bulgarians, Croats, Czechs, Macedonians, Montenegrins, Moravians, Poles, Serbs, Slovaks, and Slovenes are all Slavic peoples living within the confines of Eastern Europe. One might even consider for this list Ukrainians, who, because of their inclusion for three centuries in Poland-Lithuania, and because of their presence in the region of Bukovina, which was held in turn by the Habsburg Empire and Romania for varying lengths of time, straddle the arbitrary border separating Eastern Europe from Eurasia. The same consideration might be made for the Belorussians, also because of their historic ties to Poland-Lithuania.

The ancestors of these Slavic peoples entered Eastern Europe during the fifth through seventh centuries from their original common homeland located somewhere north of the great Pripet Marshes, which separate today's Ukraine from Belarus. They came as part of the lengthy human migratory process that we Westerners call the Barbarian Invasions of Europe. Demographically pressed by westward-moving Turkic peoples from off the Great Eurasian Plain, some tribal groups of these early Slav migrants followed in the wake of German tribes that had moved into the territories of the Roman Empire farther to the west and southwest. They occupied and settled areas of Central-Eastern and Northeastern Europe vacated by those Germans. Over time the westward-moving Slavs developed distinct tribal cultures in their new habitats, leading to the emergence of separate Polish, Czech, Moravian, Slovak, Wend, and Sorb peoples. (The latter two today live within Germany and are almost extinct as Slavic cultures, despite recently renewed efforts to preserve their language and folk traditions.) These particular Slavic peoples collectively are known as the West Slavs.

Other Slavic tribal groups moved south and southwest from their Pripet homeland, eventually entering the Byzantine-controlled Balkan Peninsula as allies of the invading Turkic Avars during the sixth century. While the mounted Avars conducted themselves in Southeastern Europe in the tradition of Attila and his Huns—extorting hefty bribes from the Byzantine government through the threat of ceaseless raping, pillaging, and plundering—their Slavic infantry auxiliaries sought to settle a new, permanent homeland. These Slavic tribes roamed throughout Southeastern Europe, extending their migrations as far south as the Peloponnesian Peninsula of mainland Greece. The instability caused by the Avar presence, and the masses of tribal Slavs who followed in the invaders' train, forced many of the indigenous population in the Balkans to seek refuge along the narrow coastal peripheries of the peninsula. Others holed up in various walled cities or remained in the countryside, only to be ultimately assimilated into the cultures of the Slavic intruders.

When, by the seventh century, the Avars had moved farther west, their Slavic allies remained behind, settling much of the abandoned countryside in the peninsula's interior and causing serious political and financial problems for the shaken Byzantine Empire. That empire's plight grew so desperate that the emperor Heraclius (610-641) felt compelled to hire other Slavic tribes lying north of the Danube—the Croats and the Serbs—to defend the northwestern border of the Balkans against the still-menacing Avars, who had established themselves on the Pannonian Plain in Central-Eastern Europe, thus freeing available Byzantine forces for attempts to reestablish control over the Slav-populated interior. In exchange for their services, the two tribal groups were given settlement rights to territories that they defended. The Slavs who settled in Southeastern Europe—Bulgarians (eventually), Croats, Serbs, Slovenes, Montenegrins, and Macedonians—came to be called the South Slavs.

Finally, there was a third group of migratory Slavic tribes that tended to remain relatively close to the original Pripet homeland. Those members of this group who did migrate did so in an easterly or southeasterly direction, either into the forested regions of the northern Eurasian Plain or onto the vast, open steppes themselves. By the ninth century these tribes had been loosely united under the authority of the Kievan state. Kievan Russia is thought initially to have been formed and controlled by Swedish Viking raiders and merchants, who originally had been attracted by the wealth and grandeur of the Byzantine Empire farther south and who thereafter decided to settle on the steppes to take advantage of its commercial resources (both material and human) and close proximity to the markets of Byzantium. Over time the Viking rulers of Kiev were ethnically assimilated by their Slavic subjects. The Slavs of this third general group—Great Russians, White Russians, and Ukrainians—came to be known as the East Slavs.

Initially, all the Slavic tribes must have spoken dialects of a common Slavic language in the Pripet homeland. But the tribal migrations in three generally different directions and into three separate environments, coupled with the passage of time and the later intrusion and settlement of non-Slavic peoples into the central areas of Eastern Europe, resulted in the formation of three distinct subgroups of Slavic speakers, corresponding to the western, southern, and eastern tribes. This linguistic developmental process was not completed until the thirteenth or fourteenth century.

Many nineteenth-century nationalists among the various Slavic peoples refused to accept that the process of linguistic differentiation had occurred at all. By that time only the Russians of all the Slavic peoples possessed a state of their own. The rest were subject to foreign, mostly non-Slavic, empires. Infected by the wave of nationalistic sentiment that dominated the lives of Western Europeans at the time, and frustrated over their subordinate political, social, and cultural situations, the East European Slav nationalists, especially those within the Habsburg Empire, concocted an ideological movement known as Panslavism. Stressing what they claimed to be strong and continuous linguistic similarities among all Slavic-speaking peoples, these Panslavs dreamed of a united, independent Great Slavic state in Europe, in which the political and cultural potential of the Slavs would be demonstrated as equal to or better than their Germanic or Latin European neighbors. Russia was regarded as the primary example and the future core of Greater Slavdom, despite its somewhat sorry record in Poland over its treatment of fellow Slavs. But the facile linguistic parallels drawn by the Panslavs to support their beliefs proved superficial, at best, and the political realities existing among the European Great Powers, including Russia, precluded any possibility for creating a viable Greater Slavic state in Europe. The original Panslav euphoria met its tragic, and probably justifiable, end amid the turmoil of the 1848 revolutions, when the overly romanticized Russian Empire that the Panslavs idolized from afar showed itself to be just as reactionary as the non-Slavic European Great Powers. Russian troops assisted Prussian and Habsburg rulers in crushing their fellow Slavic nationalists' aspirations for independence. When the smoke cleared after the revolutions in 1849, romantic Panslavism lay smoldering in ruins.

The emotional strength of Panslav sentiment among the Slavs of Eastern Europe was not lost upon the Russians, who offered their own version to replace the original movement they had done much to discredit. Known as Slavophilism, this Russian variant on the theme of Slavic unity stressed nationalistic Russian leadership of and political domination over the Slavic world in general. The Slavophiles tied the myth of a Great Slavic state to the national interests of the Russian Empire, and they succeeded in winning over to their cause many in the Russian imperial government. Following 1848-49, they proceeded to assist fledgling nationalist movements among the various East European

Slavs, especially those who adhered to Orthodox Christianity in the strategically important Balkans, who lay under Ottoman and not Western European control, in efforts to further Russia's Great Power goals in Europe. Thus, as foreign policy moves in the complex power game played with England, France, Prussia, and the Habsburg Empire, the Russians supported the aspirations of the Serbs, the Montenegrins, and the Bulgarians at varying times and for quite specific purposes. The Slavophile legacy of Russia as the self-proclaimed leader of the Slavic world survived the debacle of the Russian Revolutions (1917), and echoes of it were used in Soviet attempts to smooth its domination over much of Eastern Europe during the period of the cold war.

The specter of Slavophilism has continued to haunt the minds of many Slavs in Eastern Europe, especially those who profess a Catholic/Protestant form of Christianity, who have once tasted Russian rule firsthand (as the Poles did), or who felt let down in their national aspirations by the Russians in the past (as did the Czechs, the Slovaks, and the Croatians, who had pinned their nationalist hopes on the Russians prior to 1848-49). In post-1992 Russia, the nationalist political elements once again voice programs and goals that harken back to the sentiments of the nineteenth-century Slavophile heyday. With its stress on Russian political and cultural supremacy among the Slavs, Slavic cultural superiority, and Russian imperialism, Slavophilism was dangerous to Europe in the past; it remains dangerous today.

Luckily, the idea of a Great Slavic Eastern Europe was a myth, even at the time of its inception. Although Slavs constituted a majority in the East European population since medieval times, the non-Slavic minority remained numerous, and they played a significant historical role in defining the ethnic character of Eastern Europe. The non-Slavs of the region have never felt themselves a part of some great Panslav world, and they consistently rejected the validity of Russian-led Slavophilism.

The ethnic picture of Eastern Europe has been affected by the continuous existence of indigenous peoples who predated the arrival of all others into the region. First there were the Southeast European Greeks, whose ancient and classical origins are so well known that they need not be described here. The Slavic invasion and settlement of the heart of their mainland Balkan possessions in the sixth and seventh centuries forced most of the Greek speakers to the coastal peripheries for ethnic survival. Only by a long, hard-fought process of military reconquest on the part of the Greek-speaking Byzantine Empire, lasting for the next two centuries, did the Greeks manage to regain control of the southern third of the Balkan Peninsula's interior. Even then pockets of Slavic-speaking populations managed to survive as far south as the Peloponneses and in the region of Macedonia to the north. During the five centuries of Ottoman supremacy in Southeastern Europe, the Greeks' Byzantine legacy assured their recognition as a privileged subject people by their Turkish masters, who stood in some awe of the empire they had ended. Through Ottoman sanction, Greeks eventually came to occupy the most important religious, political, and economic sectors of Ottoman society open to non-Muslims within the confines of Islamic sacred law. The Greek language was spread throughout the empire, leading to further assimilation of numerous non-Greek speakers in Southeastern Europe. Because of their role in Ottoman international commerce and a widespread interest in classical studies in Western Europe, the Greeks managed to maintain ties with the world outside the Ottoman Balkans through their language, a fact that furnished them with a pronounced advantage over the Southeast European Slavs once nationalistic concepts began to take root in the area during the eighteenth century.

Other surviving indigenous peoples in Southeast Europe include the Albanians inhabiting portions of the western Balkan coastline and their mountainous interiors, who speak a unique language that is thought to be descended from ancient Illyrian. If this is so, then they are among the oldest groups of peoples in all of Europe, whether east or west, akin in time, at least, to the Basques of northern Spain. Romanians claim a similar heritage. They speak a Latin-based language that, in Romanian national thinking, supposedly derives from over a century and a half of Roman occupation in the ancient region of Dacia during the second and third centuries.

Dacia once comprised the territories that today constitute Romania. According to the Romanian ethnic theory, when Roman Emperor Aurelian (270-275) withdrew his legions south of the Danube in 270, the Latinized Dacians remained behind, surviving successive waves of Germanic and Turkic invaders to ultimately reemerge in the thirteenth century ethnically unscathed. This contention is, of course, contested by many non-Romanians, who reject the possibility of Latin-Dacian survival under the adverse ethnic conditions that held in the area during the centuries of foreign invasions. They suggest that the Romanians originated south of the Danube as nomadic pastoral Latin speakers who migrated into present-day Romania some time after the arrival in the Danubian Basin of the Turkic Magyars. This contention uses the continued widespread existence of pastoralists, known as Vlahs, in every area of Southeastern Europe as part of its evidence. In fact, the name of the present Romanian province of Wallachia is derived from that of these goat-herding wanderers, meaning "Land of the Vlahs." The Romanians counter this argument by insisting that the Vlahs spread south into the Balkan interior from Romania. As of this moment, the question of Romanian ethnic origins is not settled definitively one way or another.

Riding into the heart of Central-Eastern Europe in the ninth century came a Turkic horde from off the Eurasian steppes. Led by tribal chiefs of the Árpád family, the Magyars established themselves on the Pannonian Plain, which they used as a home base for violent raids into civilized territories to their west and south, as had their invading Goth, Hun, and Avar predecessors. The destructiveness of their raids reawakened in the minds of the settled European peoples memories of the terrors inspired in the population of the Roman Empire by Attila and his Hun invaders, earning for the Magyars a new, and lasting, designation among their victims—Hungarians. Unlike their Turkic predecessors, however, the Magyars did not disintegrate or disappear from the European scene when they were decisively defeated by German forces in the mid-tenth century. Instead, they turned to consolidating their hold on the Pannonian Plain by securing control of the mountain defenses surrounding it, including the area of the Transylvanian Plateau and its Carpathian ramparts. By the opening of the eleventh century the Magyars had converted to Catholicism, established a strong, centralized Central-East European state and were recognized as members of the medieval European community by their contemporaries—the pope even conferred a kingly crown on their ruler, St. István I (1000-1038), in the year 1000.

The permanent settlement of the Turkic Magyars in the very heart of Eastern Europe had a decisive impact on the ethnic character of the region, especially with regard to the historical development of the Magyars' Slavic neighbors. In essence, the Magyars—a Turkic people, speaking a Finno-Ugric language related only to those spoken by Finns and Estonians in Europe—served as a dividing wedge isolating the three Slavic linguistic subgroups from each other. Although the original Turkic Magyars eventually mixed genetically with Slav and, perhaps, remnants of Avar peoples who had not been displaced by their incursion, the Hungarian people who emerged from that process tenaciously preserved the ancient Magyar language. The linguistic barrier that the Hungarians thus erected between the three components of the Slavic-speaking peoples ensured that the languages spoken within any one of the Slavic subgroups diverged greatly over time from those of the others, causing the emergence of definitive linguistic differences.

Other Turkic-speaking peoples besides the Magyars also found their way into Eastern Europe over the course of the centuries, where they played a minor though lasting role in the region's overall ethnic picture. Their impact was felt primarily in Southeastern Europe.

Two centuries prior to the coming of the Magyars into Central-Eastern Europe, Turkic Bulgars swept out of Eurasia and established a state south of the Danube in the old Roman province of Mœsia. By the ninth century they were challenging the Byzantine Empire for political hegemony in the Balkans, but by that time they also were well on the way toward ethnic assimilation into their numerous Slavic-speaking subject population. The conversion to Orthodox Christianity at mid-century of the Bulgar Turkic ruling aristocracy opened the gate to rapid and total Slavic assimilation, as well as to European recognition. Within a hundred years of the Bulgar conversion, most traces of their Turkic origins had disappeared, except for their name—the Bulgars had been transformed into Slavic Bulgarians.

Uz, Pecheneg, and Cuman Turkic tribes appeared in Southeastern Europe between the ninth and eleventh centuries. Most of them eventually suffered the ethnic fate of the Bulgars and left little lasting impression, though it is possible that some Turks living today in the eastern Balkans and the Gagauz Turks of Bessarabia (now known as Moldova) are direct ethnic descendants of those medieval Turkic interlopers. Furthermore, the Ottoman Turks' five-century rule over the Balkan Peninsula established numerous scattered enclaves of Turkish-speaking groups throughout much of the area, with a heavy concentration in the region of classical Thrace.

World War II had a devastating impact on the Jewish communities of Eastern Europe. Prior to the implementation of Hitler's "final solution" to the ethnic problem he perceived as stemming from the Jews of Europe, numerous Jews were found throughout Eastern Europe. Their situation varied according to the conditions prevailing in the three areas of the region. Those Jews who lived in the Northeastern and Central-Eastern areas hailed from the northern, Ashkenazi, branch of European Jewry. In the latter area, they maintained the primarily urban commercial and intellectual character they had developed in medieval Germany, while those in the former area additionally formed extensive rural peasant communities, which extended into the Ukrainian steppe country with the expansion into that region of Poland-Lithuania.

Medieval anti-Semitic pogroms in the German states forced many of the Ashkenazi Jews to seek livelihoods farther east, where the governing elites in the East European states originally were more tolerant of them because they were seen as beneficial for economic development. But the benevolent conditions changed with the initiation of the Jesuit-led Catholic Counter-Reformation in Eastern Europe during the seventeenth century. Poland, once a pillar of tolerance, was transformed into a bastion of anti-Semitism, especially after the end of the eighteenth century when Polish nationalism became synonymous with Roman Catholicism. Polish anti-Semitism greatly contributed to the more extreme form held by the Russians, who incorporated large numbers of formerly Polish-governed Jews in the Ukrainian and Belorussian lands acquired through the Polish Partitions. It was no coincidence that the infamous Jewish Pale established by the Russian government lay in those very territories. Similar reasons—the Catholic Counter-Reformation and rising nationalism—led to the deterioration of the position of the Jewish communities of Habsburg Central-Eastern Europe, especially in the more agrarian regions of the Hungarian-dominated eastern lands of the Habsburg Empire, where Jews came to be viewed as greedy partners of large landowners. The Jews of Northeastern and Central-Eastern Europe, caught in the historical mainstream of Germanic European anti-Semitism and more directly affected by Nazi Germany, suffered immensely in the Holocaust of World War II. After the war, large numbers of the surviving Ashkenazi Jews in the two areas of Eastern Europe migrated to the newly founded state of Israel.

The Jews of Southeastern Europe experienced a much different fate. There they were predominantly of southern, Sephardic, origin. While some were descendants of ancient Mediterranean Jewish merchant colonists, most were the offspring of Spanish Jews who had been expelled from Spain following the late fifteenth century *Reconquista* by the Catholic Spanish rulers and the Inquisition. Their long-standing association with the Islamic Spanish Moors, and their acknowledged commercial and intellectual skills, led the Turkish rulers of the Ottoman Empire to welcome them with open arms. Numerous Spanish Jews settled in the Ottoman eastern Mediterranean, where they were granted recognition of self-government (on an equal footing with the Christians of the empire) and additional privileges primarily within the Ottoman commercial class. Centered on the old Byzantine Greek port of Thessaloniki, which eventually acquired such a large Jewish population that it became known as a Jewish city, the Sephardic Jews came to dominate the international Levantine sea trade of the Ottoman Empire.

The lack of Ottoman anti-Semitism carried over into the post-Ottoman Balkan world. The independent states of twentieth-century Southeastern Europe continued to demonstrate a tolerance of Jews that was exceptional relative to conditions elsewhere in Europe. The rapid rise of anti-Semitism experienced in Romania during the period between the two world wars was caused by an inundation of Ashkenazi Jewish refugees fleeing the effects of the Bolshevik revolution and civil war in Russia and the rabid Polish nationalism of newly refounded Poland. The difference in Romanian perceptions between these northern Jews, who arrived as land managers for wealthy Romanian absentee landlords, and the native southern Jews, who were considered traditionally benevolent trading partners, sparked a radical reaction on the part of the Romanian peasantry, who were then suffering under the area's most inequitable land distribution system. Of all the peoples of Southeastern Europe, only the Romanians and the Croats, who historically were tied to

Central-Eastern Europe, spawned native neofascist, anti-Semitic movements before World War II and conducted Nazi-style anti-Semitic policies. After the German takeover of the Balkans in 1940, Serbs, Bulgarians, and Greeks, though Christian and not always gentle with their Jewish populations, did not follow Hitler's lead in carrying out systematic anti-Semitic pogroms. In fact, Bulgaria, officially Germany's ally, refused to send off to Germany and Poland its collected Jewish population for extermination. As happened in the north of Eastern Europe following the war, a great many of the Southeast European Jews also emigrated to Israel.

Finally, German speakers constitute a significant element in the ethnic picture of Eastern Europe. Heavy concentrations of Germans have existed in the western and northwestern corners of Central-Eastern Europe since early medieval times, representing the Austrian (or Southern) subgroup of the Germanic linguistic family. Other Germans have been native inhabitants of Silesia and the fluid western border of Northeastern Europe.

Starting with the twelfth century, various groups of Germans pushed eastward into Eastern Europe, usually at the behest of non-German East European rulers, who desired to use them as military forces or as commercial colonists to stimulate trade and ore mining. In this way the Piast rulers of Poland invited the Teutonic Knights into the Baltic region of Northeastern Europe to combat the threat posed to Poland's northern expansion by pagan Balt tribes collectively known as Prussians. The Knights succeeded in their task far beyond Piast expectations. Once the original Prussians were all but exterminated, those crusading mercenaries threw off Polish control and established a German state of their own on the Baltic, eventually adopting the ethnic name of their victims and inaugurating an intense German-Polish conflict that survived through the twentieth century.

At roughly the same time the Árpád rulers of Hungary brought into their Central-East European kingdom other Germanic crusading knights to help defend the Carpathian defense line against incursions by Eurasian Turks. They also invited in Saxon Germans to develop the economic resources of their Transylvanian holdings in the east of Hungary. These Germans settled into the area, founded towns, and persisted in maintaining their German ethnic self-identity into the present. The skills of the Saxons in developing mining and urbanization were so well known in the twelfth century that the Asen rulers of Bulgaria and the Nemanja rulers of Serbia in Southeastern Europe also brought them into their states as economic colonists. Thus, by the close of the European Middle Ages, numerous pockets of Germans could be found spread throughout all the areas of Eastern Europe, from the shores of the Baltic Sea to the heart of the Balkan Peninsula.

It was the Austrian Germans concentrated in Central-Eastern Europe who made the most lasting ethnic impact on the region. Beginning in the fifteenth century the European German world, both west and east, was centered on them as a consequence of their regional ruling house—the Habsburgs—acquiring hereditary control of the imperial throne of the German-dominated Holy Roman Empire. Even though the vast personal patrimony of the Habsburg family in Eastern Europe was ethnically varied—it ultimately encompassed most of the populations in Austria, Bohemia, Hungary, Transylvania, Slovakia, Croatia, Slovenia, Bosnia, Hercegovina, Silesia, Galicia, and Bukovina, at one time or another—and remained technically apart from the Habsburg-governed German Holy Roman Empire, which came to an official end in the early nineteenth century, it could not escape the ethnic import of its German ruling house. Today one only need travel through any of the disparate areas that once formed components of the Habsburg (as opposed to the Holy Roman) Empire to realize the lasting impact of the German language in Eastern Europe.

Through the Habsburgs, German became the lingua franca of Eastern Europe. After Bismarck expelled them from leadership of the German West European world in 1866, the modern Germany that he created took advantage of German linguistic prevalence in Eastern Europe to extend German imperial influence as far south as Ottoman Turkey. In the last quarter of the nineteenth century, the Germans created a nationalistic concept that demanded recognition of their uniqueness and strength by the rest of the world. They began collectively labeling Germany and its growing sphere in Eastern Europe, especially in the territories of the declining Habsburg Empire, *Mittel-Europa* (Middle or Central Europe). This term emphasized the perceived dominance of the German language as a common vehicle for expression in the region, while intimating German ethnic superiority over native non-German speakers. It also implied acceptance of the Ural Mountains as the eastern geographical border of Europe as a whole, thus relegating the areas inhabited by the East Slavs— Western Russia, Ukraine, and Belarus—and the Balts to "Eastern Europe." The dangerous and tragic implications of the term aptly were demonstrated by Hitler in his East European policy of *lebensraum* (living space) in World War II.

In the West the term "Central Europe" has become commonly used with regard to Eastern Europe without realizing its German ethnonational connotations. Many of the non-Slavic peoples of the region, especially the Hungarians, consciously retain its use because historically they have tended to associate themselves with the Germans to reinforce their ethnic differences with the Slavs. They dislike being regionally identified with Slavs, whom they often consider as either ethnically inferior to themselves or as insufficiently Westernized and, thus, open to Russian Slavophile imperialistic manipulation. Even Slavs in the region, such as the Poles, Czechs, Slovaks, Slovenes, and Croats, often choose to use the term as an expression of their "Europeanness," as opposed to affiliation with "Eurasian" Russians. A sense of historical reality has led to a descriptive modification of the term. It is now common to find the term expressed as "East-Central Europe" by both natives of the region and Westerners alike. (This term, meant to denote the entire region of Eastern Europe, should not be confused with our term, Central-Eastern Europe, which denotes only the central, Danubian Basin, area of the region.) While using "East-Central Europe" as a general term may imply a moderation of German ethnic chauvinism regarding the region, it does little to break with the original connotation.

In the final analysis, a definition based on ethnicity, whether Slavic or Germanic, proves more harmful than helpful in furthering our understanding of Eastern Europe as a whole.

A fourth and final approach toward defining Eastern Europe is one grounded in culture. This is a logical alternative implied by the previous three approaches, once their intrinsic shortcomings are recognized. In fact, these earlier definitions can be seen as progressively focusing our perceptions of Eastern Europe in a manner leading from a purely physical reality (after all, "European" implies much more than just the landscape) through two layers of increasingly more human social reality (institutional and linguistic) to the very core of European human reality—civilization itself. Only on the cultural level of civilization can Eastern Europe receive a definition that is truly comprehensive.

Before outlining this last approach, it should be understood that the very words "West" and "East," in themselves and by definition, are expressions of Western European civilization's culture. They are loaded terms that carry certain specific perceptual implications for all Westerners. To the Western mind, "East" is synonymous with such expressions as inferior, superstitious, dangerous, threatening, backward, corrupt, mysterious, weak, effeminate, and any number of other negative perceptions regarding humans and their societies. By corollary, "West" is associated with such opposite terms as superior, scientific, secure, benign, modern, virtuous, rational, strong, masculine, and various other positive individual or collective human attributes.

Such has been the case since the classical Greek ancestors of Western civilization attempted to make sense of their struggles for independent survival against incorporation into the Persian Empire. Herodotus, commonly recognized as the father of historical writing, was the first to characterize the Greeks' fifth-century B.C. wars with the Persians as a gigantic cultural struggle between superior Western (Greek) values and the morally degenerate East (Persia). From the time of Herodotus through the twentieth century, Westerners continuously have perceived a veritable litany of massive West-East struggles in similar terms—the campaigns waged by Alexander the Great against Persia and India; the centuries-long conflicts of the Roman and Byzantine empires with Seleucid and Sassanid Persia, as well as with assorted eastern barbarians; Byzantium's lengthy wars against various Arabic and Turkish empires; the Crusades; the conflicts between the medieval West and Byzantium; the thirteenth-century Mongol invasion of Europe; the five-century struggle with the Ottoman Turks in Southeastern Europe; Napoleon's bloody wars with the Russians; the "Eastern Question" in the nineteenth century that pitted the Western European Great Powers against Russia; the eastern fronts in both of the world wars; and the cold war, to highlight only the most notable of those conflicts.

The continual clashes viewed in such a manner over the course of some twenty-five centuries account for the sorry connotations made in the Western mind by the word "East" or its synonyms: "Orient" and "Asia." It should be borne in mind, however, that this perspective on human reality is utterly subjective—a cultural expression of Western European civilization alone—and has little to do with objectivity, which, ironically, is one of the very virtues that the West prides itself in possessing. Moreover, it should be recognized that, to people belonging to non-Western European civilizations, the realities are reversed. To their minds, Westerners are barbaric, threatening, incomprehensible, self-righteous, and all the rest of the usual negative human attributes. When attempting to deal objectively with more than one culture, this situation presents problems. In the West, such an approach lays itself open to attack as smacking of relativism—the sin of not blindly singing the praises of Western European civilization's greatness (that is, superiority). If Eastern Europe is to be understood in cultural terms, then it must be accepted that every civilization possesses its own measure of greatness, as well as its own fallacies and weaknesses, gauged by its own rules. Such is objective human cultural reality.

When we in the West speak of Europe in cultural terms, we commonly apply certain assumptions in doing so. For instance, we assume that Europe is that part of the world where human society experienced a certain organic historical continuum of stages—progressive development from ancient, through medieval and modern, to contemporary society. Driving this development can be discerned other human progressions that we assume also apply—progress from classical Hellenism, through the Dark Ages, the Renaissance, the

Reformation, the Counter-Reformation (the Baroque Age), the Scientific Revolution, and the Enlightenment, to the flowering of liberal democracy, nationalism, and the nation-state; and the economic progression from slave-holding, through feudalism and mercantilism, to the Industrial Revolution and capitalism. (Though the economic approach is primarily Marxist, we can exclude European communism as a stage to be considered, given the events of 1989 and later.)

If such are the factors that culturally define Europe as a whole, then Eastern Europe is merely the easternmost areas of geographical Europe where all the elements comprising the historical continuums involved in the definition have appeared among their populations. Areas whose inhabitants have not experienced them, therefore, are a priori not part of Europe. In examining the history of the Poles, Germans, Lithuanians, and Jews of Northeastern Europe, and that of the Czechs, Germans, Slovaks, Hungarians, Jews, and Ruthenians of Central-Eastern Europe, it is immediately evident that they all underwent the staged organic developments just outlined. In many cases they made seminal contributions to those developments—one need cite as illustration only a few individuals, such as the Poles Nicholas Copernicus (Mikołaj Kopernik) and Fryderyk Chopin, the Czechs Jan Hus and Franz Kafka, or the Hungarians Béla Bartók and Franz Liszt. In Southeastern Europe, the Slovenes and the Croats, through their long historical ties to the Habsburgs and the Hungarians of Central-Eastern Europe, also must be included under this cultural definition of Europe.

As for the Southeast European Albanians, Bulgarians, Greeks, Macedonians, Montenegrins, Romanians, Serbs, Turks, and Vlahs, their historical experiences do not coincide with the continuums assumed to represent European histori-cal reality. Their traditions do possess certain of the elements found in the rest of Europe, but such as they do possess do not constitute an unbroken organic development. For instance, these Balkan peoples all can lay valid claim to a common Greco-Roman European ancestry, but they did not experience a cul-tural Dark Ages, similar to the rest of the Europeans. Their Hellenic heritage is bound directly to the Byzantine Empire, which was nothing less than the east-ern half of the classical Roman Empire that survived for nearly a thousand years after the fall of the western half in 476. In Byzantium the living traditions of the classical world never disappeared, as they did in the West—therefore, there did not develop a Dark Age and the need for a Renaissance in the European sense. The Byzantine Empire represents classical culture, in its eastern, Greek form, given the freedom to develop organically for a millennium along lines defined in its own terms. These lines did not require a Reformation, and they may or may not have incorporated a Scientific Revolution or an Enlightenment.

(We can only speculate about these latter two matters, since the near-total conquest of Southeastern Europe by the Muslim Ottoman Turks during the fourteenth and fifteenth centuries and their subsequent five-hundred-year hold over the area froze non-Muslim cultural development.) When, beginning in the late eighteenth century, the subject peoples of the Ottoman Balkans fully embraced the European concepts of nationalism, the nation-state, and liberal democracy (with their industrial capitalist economic foundations), they did so like botanists attempting to produce new plant strains—by grafting them onto a different, but closely related, cultural trunk. They could attempt to do so because neither they nor the Europeans outside Southeastern Europe doubted that, despite the developmental differences in their cultures, the Balkan peoples were Europeans.

That being the case, what, then, makes them all European? With this question, we find ourselves once again facing the essential problem underlying all of the approaches toward defining Eastern Europe. That is: What exactly is Europe? Our geographical definition is arbitrary in delineating Europe's most critical eastern boundary. Both the political and ethnical explanations are dependent on the geographical, so that, if it is imprecise, then they are also. We are left with only a cultural approach on the level of civilization that can provide the definitive answer to the problem.

The historical continuums assumed by the cultural definition originally outlined earlier do not delineate a single, all-embracing European civilization. Quite specifically, they define the Western European civilization alone. This has interesting ramifications for approaching Eastern Europe from the cultural point of view. Poles, Austrians, Czechs, Slovaks, Hungarians, Slovenes, and Croats are all Western Europeans, and the current countries of Poland, Austria, the Czech Republic, Slovakia, Hungary, Slovenia, and Croatia are members of the Western European community of nations, even though they lie within the geographical confines of Eastern Europe. (The Baltic peoples—Lithuanians, Latvians, and Estonians, with their respective countries—also form part of cultural Western Europe, but they lie in geographical Eurasia.)

Albanians, Bulgarians, Greeks, Macedonians, Montenegrins, Romanians, Serbs, and Vlahs, inhabiting the current Southeast European countries of Albania, Bulgaria, Greece, Macedonia, Romania, and Yugoslavia (Serbia and Montenegro), are all members of the Eastern European civilization. It possesses its own, at times disrupted but nevertheless organic, historical continuum —from ancient, through lengthy classical-medieval and Islamic-dominated stages, to modern, without a fully developed contemporary stage as yet. Within this continuum can be discerned two predominant sociopolitical and economic human progressions—from classical Hellenism, through the Byzantine refinement of Hellenism and Ottoman immobilization, to the importation of nationalism, the nation-state, and liberal democracy; and from slave-holding, through pseudofeudalism and mercantilism, to capitalism, and, finally, the Industrial Revolution. As can be noted, these developments have enough in common with those in the Western European tradition to make them sister civilizations. On the other hand, they differ in enough important areas—in terms of factors totally lacking, one from the other, or in the order of their development—to ensure that they remain distinct civilizations.

Since peoples of both these civilizations consider themselves Europeans, there must exist between them a shared set of specific attributes that are uniquely European. We have already touched on one obvious trait—the Hellenic, Greco-Roman heritage. The hyphenation in the term is important. It emphasizes the cultural reality of the Hellenic legacy, in that it is composed of two related, but differing, traditions. At its base lies the sense of human reality created by the classical Greeks as a response to the harsh environment of their Balkan homeland. Forced to deal daily with the challenges of seas, mountains, and limited amounts of arable land, the Greeks came to view life as the constant interplay between individual humans and their physical surroundings. These could change from moment to moment, affecting the life of the individual accordingly. Knowing and understanding one's own body and the workings of the enveloping world beyond became supremely important.

The classical Greek reality, therefore, was one that saw time in one dimension—the present—but space in three. In other words, the individual human was seen as the supreme element in creation, whose life was lived constantly in the here and now, with virtually no past or future, because her or his physical surroundings constantly changed in some way. Each change created a new reality for the person. Reality perceived in such fashion shaped every outward manifestation of classical Greek culture. It explained the emphasis placed on realism and the sense of timelessness that characterize works of classical Greek art in all of its various forms—they were intended to express constant, ideal moments of human life frozen in time. It established the framework and context for Greek mythological and philosophical development—they attempted to help humans understand the arbitrary changes brought about in the physical world either by supernatural intervention on the part of humanlike gods (who also existed constantly in the present) or by some innate characteristics found in the various components of the environment itself. The Greeks' sense of reality spawned in them traits of humaneness and rationality in their approach to understanding the nature of all that existed around them. It also created in them deep-seated propensities toward mysticism, ritualism, and symbolism concerning man's relationship with the supernatural world that was believed ultimately to govern events occurring in the physical.

When, in the second century B.C., the Romans began their conquest of the eastern Mediterranean world by overpowering the Greeks, they swiftly recognized the superiority of Greek culture compared to their own. So, through slavish imitation, they co-opted most of the external components of Greek culture—artistic styles, philosophical studies, epic poetry, even the Greek mythological Olympian pantheon—while retaining certain fundamental elements of their own native cultural persona. The marshy, open, lowlands environment of the Romans' homeland in Latium helped form an agricultural society that understood the value of the small, independent, individual farmer as well as the need for strong individual commitment to a central authority, representing the will of all landowners and charged with ensuring the maintenance, expansion, and defense of all land held by the community. Individualism coupled with civic responsibilities nurtured in the Romans a practicality in dealing with the constantly changing present. Born of this practical reality were the Romans' highly developed predilections for legalism, efficiency, militarism, administration—in fact, all of the qualities needed for upholding the centrally governed, agricultural world of the Roman farmers-landowners.

The Greeks' realism and rationality sat well with the Romans' practicality, so the Roman conquerors flung open the door to the wholesale expropriation of Greek cultural forms. But the marriage of the two was not completely harmonious. One need only compare, for instance, any particular work of Greek sculpture with a Roman copy to see the subtle, but marked, differences—though the subject and pose may be the same, the Roman piece will have about it a roughness, a gaudiness, a noticeable sense of photographic realism that is completely lacking in the elegant, refined, and ideal Greek original. This dual quality permeated all aspects of what we call the Greco-Roman heritage. That duality was sustained through the use of both the Greek and the Latin languages in the Roman Mediterranean world, and the speakers of either one considered those of the other culturally inferior. Latin speakers predominantly inhabited the Roman provinces in the western portions of Europe and Africa. Greek speakers predominated in the European Balkan, eastern North African, and West Asian provinces.

When, in an attempt to stabilize the central government's control inside the state and to increase the efficiency of the military in defending the empire's borders against outside enemies, internal turmoil and increasing foreign pressures led Emperor Diocletian (284-305) to divide the sprawling Roman Empire into two administrative halves, he did so along the line marking the invisible human cultural divide in the northwestern corner of the Balkans that separated the Greek East and the Latin West. As a solution to the grave problems facing the empire at the end of the third century, Diocletian's splitting of the Roman state ultimately proved a failure, but it resoundingly succeeded in institutionalizing the demarcation—creating the hyphen, as it were—between the two distinct branches of Greco-Roman civilization. After Diocletian, these branches would develop historically along two increasingly divergent lines. Western European civilization has its roots planted in the western, Latin branch of Hellenism through the empire of Charlemagne, while Eastern European civilization is grounded in the eastern, Greek component by way of the Byzantine Empire.

A second European attribute is the vital role played by new peoples to the classical Hellenic world in forging the birth of both Western and Eastern European civilizations. Without the barbarian invasions of the fifth through ninth centuries, one can barely imagine Europe as anything other than a geographical term. Truly, the barbarians destroyed much of classical Hellenism, but that which they spared was injected with large doses of the barbarians' native cultures, creating a cultural mixture that became the alloy in which the European civilizations were cast.

Mostly Germanic peoples inundated the western, Latin-speaking regions of the Greco-Roman world. Slavs, and some Turks, settled in its eastern, Greek-speaking areas. This was no accident. The German tribes were the westernmost in a long chain of peoples that stretched across the Eurasian steppes to Mongolia in the east. When disturbances in China in the fourth and fifth centuries caused successive domino-effect waves of demographic pressures to sweep westward along that human chain, the Germans lying just outside the northern borders of Rome had nowhere else to move in response except into the empire itself. At first, they merely harried the eastern half, but eventually they were able to overwhelm the western. There they settled, decisively changing the demographic picture of the area. The key factors contributing to the German takeover were the chronic economic, military, and administrative weaknesses of the Western Roman Empire, relative to the eastern half. Diocletian had recognized this situation at the time he divided his state—he chose the eastern portion for himself. After the dust of the initial German invasions cleared, those interlopers established settled states of their own, loosely modeled after the empire that they had destroyed. The new states of the Germanic West retained a bastardized form of Latin Hellenism through the intermediacy of the papacy and the Roman Catholic church institution, which had survived the disruption of the invasions and which served as the cultural cement that lent cohesiveness to the new states.

The Slavs, who entered the Balkan possessions of the Eastern Roman Empire a century later than the German invasion of the West, never managed to destroy that portion of the classical Hellenic state. Their inroads may have cost the empire some territory, but its political, military, and economic strength ensured that it did not fall to the massive influx of outsiders. The coming of the Slavs helped crystallize the transformation of the East Roman into the Byzantine Empire, and Hellenic continuity was thus preserved. When Slavic states developed in the Balkans, they did so under a strong cultural influence exerted by their powerful Byzantine neighbor. Again, unlike developments in the West, where the Hellenic tradition was preserved among the newcomers by the slimmest of threads amid the dismantling of the old order, in the East a living Hellenic tradition was imposed on the newly settled Slavs by the sheer force of local Byzantine dominance in all fields of human endeavor. Over those Slavs whom the empire managed to incorporate directly within its borders, the Greek language gained sway. Those who remained outside the empire were brought into close cultural association with it through the invention of a uniquely Slavic written language—the Cyrillic—in the mid-ninth century, which was intentionally used to parallel Greek literary forms and which Byzantine Christian missionaries did much to create. An essential foundation for Eastern European civilization sprang from a living Hellenic tradition propagated among the Slavs in the orbit of Byzantium.

One last attribute—the most crucial—is needed for defining that which is culturally European. This essential factor is Christianity in its Hellenized form. Without it, the other two attributes are meaningless.

It was the early fourth century triumph of Christianity over the exhausted, fossilized traditional Hellenic mythology in the Roman Empire that decisively transformed Greco-Roman reality from a variable but constant present, existing in space (the three-dimensional realm), into one in which the present is but a single moment in a meaningful progression of directionally interlinked moments existing in both time and space—each moment possessing a past and a future. This innate sense of time (the fourth dimension) is central to the European mind. Rooted in the ancient Jewish and borrowing from the Hellenic cultures, Christianity gives universal meaning, outlined in its Old and New Testaments, to a reality that progressively links every event that has occurred since the creation of the physical universe and mankind to those arising in the present. Christian reality as directional progress is carried through into the future, culminating in the ultimate reason for all existence—human attainment of eternal spiritual life.

Of all the known ancient cultures, only the Judaic, out of which Christianity grew, shares with it such a profound sense of human historical development (hence the Judeo-Christian tradition in the European civilizations). The merger of Christian reality with Hellenic cultural forms was forged within the Greco-Roman world just prior to the coming of the barbarians, so that their Hellenization was accompanied more significantly by their Christianization. Thus Helleno-Christianity created the essential cultural mold that shaped both European civilizations, giving them their fundamental precepts concerning reality: an awareness of history (time) as the context for life; a belief in progress (directional cause and effect); an acceptance of motion (change) as a positive, universal constant; and a compulsion not only to understand change but to affect it actively in ways that ensure positive progress (free will and technology).

Though Greco-Roman tradition and the input of new peoples are important components in defining Europe culturally, without their combination with Christianity, they fail to delineate it completely. No one today would consider Syria, Jordan, Egypt, or Libya European states, yet they were once as Hellenized and overrun by outsiders as were, for instance, France, Italy, Greece, or Bulgaria. Christianity is the seminal factor in identifying Europe. Only those peoples who have completely assimilated the Judeo-Helleno-Christian worldview have ever been considered European, either by themselves or by outsiders. Since the early Middle Ages, those non-Christians who entered geographical Europe and found themselves in contact with the region's populous native Christian societies were faced with the choice of either joining them by converting or risking possible annihilation at their hands. This helps explain the importance of Christian conversion for relative latecomers—such as Bulgarians, Czechs, Hungarians, Poles, and Russians—into the European world. Their conversions, which occurred between the ninth and eleventh centuries, were their passkeys to membership in the European community that had arisen as a consequence of the earlier barbarian invasions. The borders of Europe became (and remain) synonymous with the limits of native Judeo-Helleno-Christian culture.

Because of the cultural division within the parent Greco-Roman civilization, its Helleno-Christian offspring can be considered analogous to twins. Just as is true in humans, the two siblings can remain different enough in character to ensure their separate individuality. This was indeed the case with regard to the birth of Europe. Instead of a single European civilization stemming from the demise of Hellenism, two European variants were born. Both expressed essentially the same bedrock Christian perception of reality framed in common Hellenic terms, but the forms of expression differed. The nature of the variant depended on the branch of Greco-Roman tradition out of which it developed.

That which grew out of the western, Roman part of the old Greco-Roman world couched Helleno-Christianity in terms of the legality, practicality, and militancy peculiar to the older hierarchical Latin Hellenic culture of the region. Thus, Latin-based Roman Catholicism, which institutionalized these basic traits in a Christian context, epitomized the cultural nature of Western European civilization at its most fundamental level. Every society that originally espoused the Catholic form of Christianity and adopted the Latin alphabet for its written language became a human component of Western Europe. Its twin emerged from the eastern, Greek half of the Hellenic world, where Christianity was expressed in the highly mystical, ritualized, and symbolical universality of the Greek Hellenic culture of the eastern Mediterranean. The Christian institutionalization of these traits occurred in the Greek-based Orthodoxy of the Byzantine Empire, which embodied the cultural essence of Eastern European civilization. Unlike the West, which brooked no deviation from its Latin-based culture, Orthodoxy demonstrated a true multicultural toleration—societies originally espousing the Orthodox form of Christianity were free to do so in their various languages, so long as they did not stray from Orthodox tenets. The various Orthodox societies constituted Eastern Europe.

With the cultural approach toward addressing the question of Europe, we at last find a definition that comes closest to being truly complete in itself. To be European is to be Christian, and vice versa. (Lest this statement be construed as a testimonial to the political agenda of the contemporary ultra-conservative religious right, it must be stressed that we are using the term "Christian" in this case as a general expression of culture—a perception of reality—and *not* as a specific faith. Even European atheists, whether they like to admit it or not, view the world through Christian-shaped cultural spectacles.) The two civilizations that constitute Europe in its totality are defined by the forms of Christianity that predominate within their respective component societies—Western Europe is Catholic (and its later-developed Protestant offshoots); Eastern Europe is Orthodox. In relating the two to a map, Western Europe geographically encompasses all of the regions normally accepted as forming the West, but also virtually all of Northeastern and Central-Eastern Europe, along with the northwest corner of Southeastern Europe as well. Eastern Europe, then, includes the rest of Southeastern Europe. It also should include all of western Eurasia (the Russians were converted to Orthodoxy in 988) and might be thought of as extending eastward to the Pacific Ocean, since Russian expansion through Siberia, beginning in the sixteenth century, carried with it its Orthodox culture.

The Russian case raises the one important question concerning cultural Eastern Europe: Can Vladivostok and the Kamchatka Peninsula realistically be considered part of Europe? The answer, of course, is that they cannot.

Geography rejects the notion. But more important, so does culture. Only in the western Eurasian heartlands of Russia does European Orthodoxy predominate as the native worldview. East of the Urals, cultural Europeanization is demographically weak. In many respects the spread of Eastern European civilization eastward through Siberia resembles the missionary propagation of Western European civilization throughout the world following the Age of Discovery—Christianity can be spread but it rarely comes to predominate in regions outside its homelands. (The Americas and Australia are the only notable exceptions.) Moreover, though the medieval ties of west Eurasian Russia with the East European fountainhead of Byzantium were strong, the thirteenth-century Mongol conquest of the Eurasian steppes severed them almost completely for close to two centuries. By the time Russia was able to reemerge as a potent Orthodox state in the fifteenth century, Byzantium was on the verge of final collapse, and the rest of the East European world in the Balkans was under virtual Islamic Ottoman control. Thus, history created a division within Eastern European civilization between the Balkan and the Russian branches, each experiencing a completely different development after the thirteenth century. This situation, and the predominantly non-European Asiatic character of Siberian Russia, raises the possibility that the Russian arm of Eastern European civilization actually may not be European at all, but a separate, Western Eurasian civilization in its own right. The point is a continuing focus for debate among cultural historians.

In any event, it is obvious that the term "Eastern Europe" is complex. It implies one, some, or all of the aspects that we have just investigated. Those who use the term should not do so lightly. They should be aware of exactly which approach (or combination of approaches) they are taking when using it, and make that clear to their audience. Otherwise, with regard to Eastern Europe, we Westerners stand to suffer continued confusion in our analyses and to retain only superficial understandings of the problems and events that shape life in the region.

ONE GOD, ONE EMPEROR, ONE EMPIRE

● ○ ●

In a private conversation, a noted professor of history at a reputable large university once lampooned his own opening lecture for an introductory course on world civilization in somewhat the following way: "In the beginning, there were rocks, and winds, and fires, and rains. And in the hot, slimy muck there arose little squiggly things that grew until, in 1789, the French Revolution broke out and history began."

While his exaggerated, loose parody of Scripture was amusing, he was making a serious inference to his personal perspective on history in general. As far as he was concerned, the 5,800 years of recorded human existence that preceded the events that sparked the modern age in Western European civilization's history were mere preamble to the truly significant developments of the nineteenth and twentieth centuries—they were interesting, perhaps, but of little consequence to today's world.

Our professor may have been stating his own view, but it is a view shared by a great many like-minded people hailing from all walks of life in the West today. Politicians, pundits, journalists, businesspeople, and most other Western professionals seem to have little use for a past that appears so utterly foreign to the world created by the Scientific Revolution and the Enlightenment, which together spawned the liberal–democratic capitalist nation-states that have come to epitomize the sociopolitical reality of the West.

Western reality worships rationalism. It reduces the "real" world to mathematically (or, at least, "logically") definable universal laws—of physical and human nature, of economics, of political systems—into which all existence is made to fit. There is no acceptable room in the Western mind for superstition or irrationality. By beginning the rationalistic process that ultimately would overthrow the absolute ruling monarchies of Europe (which justified their authority through their own religious convictions and those of their subjects, and which governed in personal, often socially and economically irrational, terms), the French Revolution indeed initiated a decisive watershed in the development of Western European civilization. In 1789 politically and economically modern, rational Western Europe was founded. Once established, it had little compunction in rejecting its prerevolutionary, superstitious past.

The West's scorn for its premodern past is, perhaps, understandable. It is even defensible if viewed as a development within the limits of its own cultural parameters. It simply is Western European civilization's perception of the West's present self as the optimum form of human reality. In the cynical expression of Voltaire, the capitalistic, technologically advanced, liberal–democratic nation-state is "the best of all possible worlds." And for Westerners, to whom such a world is the natural result of native organic cultural development, this very well may be the case—at least until some fresh cultural advances occur and open even newer possibilities.

The problem in all of this is that Westerners often fail to realize that their reality is merely a direct reflection of their own culture. This is not to denigrate Western European civilization—no intrinsic moral judgment between good or bad, right or wrong, is intended. It works for its members. The real rub comes when Westerners assume that the rest of the world's inhabitants, no matter their civilization or microculture, should be judged by Western standards of reality. Of course, this approach is not unique to Western Europeans. Every civilization or independent microculture sees itself as "the best of all possible worlds" and evaluates the nature of outsiders accordingly. Unfortunately, the worldwide political and economic position of dominance enjoyed by Western European civilization, won through the development and use of its undeniably effective technologies, renders Western cultural self-centeredness an obstacle to objectively understanding events that occur in cultures outside its own. Therefore, while it may be acceptable to argue that the modern Western world took shape only in the late eighteenth century, that does not mean that the pre-nineteenth century past of non-Western European societies is also dead today.

One of the important factors necessary for a Western understanding of current developments in Eastern European civilization is recognizing the continuing role played by certain cultural perceptions that first took shape over a millennium ago and that underwent close to nine hundred years of organic development among its member societies. Although often wrapped in a cloak of religious development, these perceptions primarily have to do with the nature and extent of political authority.

East European political culture is rooted in the reign of the Roman emperor Constantine I the Great (306-37). He emerged as sole ruler of the Roman state in 324 following the breakdown of the multiple-ruler system that Emperor Diocletian had instituted when he divided the empire into two administrative halves at the end of the third century. During twelve years of civil strife waged against imperial partners and pretenders to the throne, Constantine came to recognize the moral strength that the then illegal and persecuted Christian faith could lend to his efforts at reestablishing a powerful, centralized Roman state. Constantine viewed the internal instability that characterized the Roman Empire in the late third century, which brought Diocletian to divide it in the first place, as resulting from the decline of traditional Roman virtues and a lack of moral fiber that the old Hellenic religions could do little to correct. Rome was so full of gods and religions that they had lost any real meaning in the lives of the average Romans. Any one god was as good as any other, and all were equally trite.

Christianity, on the other hand, was different from the traditional Hellenic sects. It possessed a strong ethical-moral system and the necessary sanctions for enforcing its precepts. It also provided its adherents with a consistent meaning for human life, grounded in a historical perspective that viewed all existence as a progression from the creation of the universe to ultimate spiritual salvation in life everlasting. Everything, including the Roman Empire and its subjects, had its place in that continuum. Constantine recognized the utility of tying Christianity to the interests of a Roman state under his personal control. It could help to strengthen and perpetuate the empire, especially in the East where Christianity was prevalent, and bring unity to the Mediterranean world, which had begun to fall apart under the pressures exerted by Germanic tribes from outside the borders of the state. Already in Constantine's time, Christianity was spreading among those German enemies, so that it was wielding influence even beyond the empire's borders and might be used as a tool for expanding Roman authority. Most likely he also realized that a great many of the soldiers under his direct command were secretly Christian. For these reasons, Constantine took an active part in establishing Christianity as a state religion in the empire. (Christianity became *the* state religion only under a successor of Constantine, Emperor Theodosius I the Great [379-95].)

Like most religions, Christianity was associated with visions and miracles. According to Constantine's eulogists, his victory in the Battle of Milvian Bridge in 312, which brought him within a step of uncontested control of the imperial throne, was the result of both. The legend is famous. On the evening before the battle, Constantine looked into the sunset, saw a sign (a cross) with the device *in hoc signo vinces* ("In this sign, conquer"). He ordered that the sign be scratched on the shields of his soldiers for the battle, and, against strong odds, he emerged victorious. A year later (313), in recognition of this divine intervention, which he interpreted as coming from the Christian god, Constantine issued the Edict of Milan, giving legal status to the open practice of Christianity in the empire. From that time on he actively supported the spread of the Christian religion throughout the state.

If Christianity was to serve the political purposes that Constantine envisioned, it had to be correct—orthodox—in its beliefs. A religion divided in its own fundamental precepts had little to offer a ruler who sought to use it as a new, statewide vehicle for reinvigorating a declining empire with a shaken morale. Unfortunately, in the time of Constantine (and even up to the present day), Christianity suffered from internal differences of opinion. The dispute then raging centered on the structure and nature of the Divine Trinity—the most fundamental religious precept of the faith, since it defined the Christian deity. A unitary, single god who was composed simultaneously of three separate entities—Father, Son, and Spirit—was a bafflingly difficult concept to accept. Over the course of three centuries prior to Constantine's interest in Christianity, church leaders steeped in Hellenic philosophy arduously had applied their learning to the problem of making this totally illogical deity understandable to the religion's adherents.

Christians accepted the notion that their single god was composed of three individual "persons," even if to most that idea was incomprehensible from a rational point of view. Problems first arose over defining the exact nature of each person involved in the mix since, at least, the nature of an individual was a concept that could be readily understood. The three persons were each defined and redefined by a number of devout church intellectuals, many of whom acquired a certain mass following among the faithful. The early consensus that eventually developed was that the first and third persons in the Trinity—the Father and the Spirit—were divine by nature and substance, while the second person—the Son/Jesus Christ—possessed both divine and human natures but a divine substance.

While the Trinity concept became unquestioningly accepted by the Christians, the dual nature of Christ raised numerous questions. Was Christ really human, or was he a god who merely looked human? Was his flesh true human, living flesh, or was it some divine substance only? If Christ had a truly human body, did that mean he had two separate substances or a single one that was different from his partners in the Trinity? These might seem trivial hairsplitting questions to the modern Western mind, but they were utterly crucial to the Christian belief system—after all, the religion was called Christianity because the divinity of Christ lay at its very core.

By the early fourth century Christianity was divided over the issue of Christ's substance. Arius, a priest from Alexandria in Egypt, maintained that Christ possessed a substance that was different than that of the Father. Alexander, bishop of Alexandria, maintained that both Father and Son were of the same substance. Each of the two churchmen enjoyed widespread support among the Christian faithful, and neither could be reconciled in his belief with the other. Arianism eventually established roots in the western half of the Roman Empire and became the version of Christianity adopted by the German tribes lying beyond the northwestern frontiers prior to their entry into the empire itself. The philosophical conflict between Arius and Alexander escalated into fanaticism. Violent riots broke out in the streets of Alexandria and of other eastern Mediterranean cities as the zealot adherents of the two sides fought to win universal acceptance of their leaders' views. Each accused the other of heresy.

We have devoted some space to this essentially theological issue because it sets the stage for the earliest decisive steps in shaping the nature of Eastern European civilization's political culture.

Within a year after his victory over the last contender for the Roman imperial throne in 324, Constantine decided that a Christian church divided over an issue that lay at its very core would not do for his purpose: to give Christianity an official state position. Just as it was impermissible to tolerate civil strife in the political sphere, neither could religious disharmony within the Christian church be allowed. Taking advantage of a traditional Roman imperial title and office— that of Pontifex Maximus (Supreme Priest, or, more loosely, state umpire among gods and religions)—Constantine decided to bring order to the Christian church personally. In 325 he called a general meeting of all leading Christian church officials throughout the empire in the Anatolian city of Nicæa (today, İznik, Turkey). Constantine himself set the agenda and presided over the sessions. He ordered the church prelates to get down to business and settle the Arian problem, and he often entered directly into the theological discussions. By the close of what was to become known as the First Ecumenical Council of the

Christian church, the Arian concept of Christ's substance was branded as heresy, and the high bishops (patriarchs) of Rome, Alexandria, Jerusalem, and Antioch were given canonical privileges that elevated them equally to the highest level of authority within the church. The office of patriarch of Rome was afforded the honorary title of *pop* (pope), meaning "Father" in Greek, in recognition of its earliest holder, St. Simon/ Peter, Christ's disciple, and of its seat in the traditional ancient capital of the empire. The Christian church emerged from Nicæa as the accepted state religion of the emperor, with an administrative organization that mirrored that of the empire itself.

Perhaps just as important were the consequences of Nicæa on the emperor and his authority within an increasingly Christian Roman Empire. The prominent role played by Constantine in the affairs of the council left no doubt as to his intentions of linking the spiritual authority of Christianity closely to the civil authority of the state. Nicæa made Christianity an important element of the Roman Empire, and the active participation of the emperor in essentially church matters made it hard to distinguish between what was political and what was religious or dogmatic. By blatantly demonstrating his preference for Christianity, Constantine raised it above other religions within the state, a fact that, for all intents and purposes, sounded their death knell. The Christian leadership, of course, could only feel indebted to him for their church's meteoric rise from persecuted sect to favored faith. Constantine was hailed by the church as the "Thirteenth Apostle of Christ" and God's direct representative on earth. While, at first, these Christian accolades were personally bestowed upon Constantine, they swiftly were transferred to the imperial office, as Constantine's successors on the throne—with the brief exception of Julian the Apostate (361-63), who romantically and quite unsuccessfully attempted to revive official paganism—continued to solidify bonds with the Christian church as a matter of state interest.

The Christianization of the Roman Empire received further validation five years after the Council of Nicæa when Constantine dedicated a new capital city (on 11 May 330) erected on the site of the ancient Greek colonial port of Byzantium. Byzantium was located on an easily defensible triangular bit of land that lay on the European shore of the Bosphorus Strait at the point where it emptied into the Sea of Marmara. Directly on its north was the large, crescent-shaped mouth of a small river that emptied into the Bosphorus, which became known as the Golden Horn, forming the only natural, deep-water harbor in the region where the European Balkan Peninsula nearly abutted the Anatolian extension of West Asia. On its south stretched the Sea of Marmara, which found access to the Mediterranean Sea through the Dardanelles Strait. The Bosphorus-Marmara-Dardanelles seaway separated the European from the

West Asian landmasses and linked the interior of Eurasia beyond the Black Sea directly to the Mediterranean. Byzantium's Golden Horn was the only natural haven for all traffic on this crucial seaway. Moreover, the city was located at the most direct point along the continental divide for overland traffic to cross into the interiors of the two continents. Geography thus had bestowed upon the city a strategic importance as the economic and military crossroads of Europe and Asia. By fortifying the triangle of land on which the city sat, Byzantium could be transformed into an impregnable fortress-city controlling the intersection of all the important lines of communications then existing between the European and Asian worlds.

Constantine wished to give concrete expression to his state policy of reconstituting the Roman Empire on a Christian moral basis by founding a permanent, new imperial capital free of Hellenic pagan overtones. Ancient Rome was too heavily associated with the failed paganistic past (and, anyway, it had long ceased to be an effective location for the imperial capital in crucial military, economic, and administrative terms). Other cities, such as Milan in Italy and Lyon in France, which had served as imperial capitals at one time or another, had little to offer over Rome. They were situated in the western half of the empire, which was demographically and economically backward and poor in comparison with the eastern half, and which also was more seriously threatened by hostile forces from beyond its borders. Constantine realized that the new capital of a reinvigorated Christian Roman empire would have to be established in the East. And in the East, there was no better location for the new capital than Byzantium.

Legend has it that Constantine personally paced off the city limits of his new capital before work actually began. He intended to build a "New Rome" that would mirror, as far as possible, the original so that within the limits of his new city there would be seven hills, the Golden Horn would serve as the Tiber River; and all major civic buildings—Senate, Hippodrome, Forum, and such—would be near-carbon copies of those in the old capital. Orders were sent throughout the empire requisitioning building materials of the highest quality available. Old Rome and numerous other traditional urban centers were stripped of their finest works of sculpture, of precious metals, and of marbles for use in adorning Constantine's new Roman imperial capital on the Bosphorus. Yet despite all the intentional similarities between the new and the old capitals, Constantine ensured that a major, all-important difference was readily apparent—in his New Rome there was no place whatsoever given over to paganism. Instead, copies of old Roman Hellenistic temples were dedicated exclusively to Christian worship. New Rome—the City of Constantine (or Constantinople, in its Greek form [Konstantinopolis])—was to be the Christian capital of a Christian Roman Empire.

The founding of Constantinople gave symbolic but concrete reality to the new political ideology of Constantine. Christianity, the new state religion, represented the community of true believers on earth, whose borders were those of the Roman Empire. The church and the state were united in an indissoluble partnership, paralleling the nature of Christ Himself—two natures, one substance. Both partners were equally inspired and sustained by God, and their harmonious association was considered His ordained order of things for all human existence.

Among the Christian Romans there was no doubting the important role played by the emperor in forming this close, united partnership of church and state. It only was through the undisputed authority of the supreme temporal ruler of the empire that the Christian world-state was founded and could continue to survive. To guarantee the divine temporal order on earth, the Roman emperor served as God's supreme civil representative, charged with protecting the Christian empire against temporal and spiritual enemies both from within and from without its borders, and with expanding those borders whenever and as far as possible. He was assisted and strengthened in his tasks by an innate alliance with the Christian church leadership, the patriarchs, to whose number a fifth was added—that of Constantinople—shortly after the establishing of the new capital at Constantinople.

While there was only one accepted Christian emperor of the Christian empire, no single Christian prelate was recognized as the unqualified head of the church. The spiritual authority was shared equally among the patriarchs, who exerted it through the collective process of the ecumenical council. This collective spiritual authority was somewhat extended to the office of emperor, in recognition of the divine preference that he enjoyed as God's temporal representative, although decisions in matters of faith alone could be made only by the church leadership meeting in council, with or without the emperor's active participation. It was, however, the acknowledged duty of the emperor to see that the authority of the church and all governing decisions made by its leadership were effectively upheld throughout all the lands falling under his civil rule. Thus, the Roman emperor emerged from Constantine's efforts at revitalizing the empire through Christianity as the single dominant figure of authority in the Christian state. The seat of his authority rested in the Christian Roman imperial capital at Constantinople.

The ideology of the new Christian world-state eventually came to be expressed symbolically in the following catchphrase that epitomized the reality of the newly emerging European civilization of the fourth through sixth centuries: One God, one Emperor, one Empire. There was only one Christian God (the Trinity), whose direct temporal representative on earth was the one and only Christian (Roman) emperor residing in Constantinople, who, in turn, ruled over, protected, and nurtured the one Christian (Roman) empire, which constituted the God-ordained temporal body for the entire Christian community on earth. Thanks to Constantine, Christian Europe received a divinely sanctioned framework for strong, highly centralized, autocratic political authority.

It may be noticed that, in the preceding exposition of the political ideology espoused by Christian Rome, European civilization has been presented in the singular rather than in the plural. This is because, in describing Constantine's efforts at reshaping the political and moral structure of the Roman Empire, we actually have been addressing the crucial birth of Europe, in general, from out of the exhausted loins of the old Hellenic civilization.

In Constantine's time, the barbarian incursions into the empire were just beginning, and it was the inundation of the weak western half of the Roman Empire by Germanic invaders after Constantine and Nicæa that set the two cultural halves of the Hellenic world—Latin West and Greek East—off along rapidly diverging paths. Both halves originally held to the fundamental principles outlined in the universal God, Emperor, Empire mentality of the Christian state. It should be borne in mind that the Germans, who swept away much of the Hellenic world in the West, were Christian barbarians—Arian heretics, true, but Christians nonetheless. As they began to establish themselves in settled tribal states within the territories they had wrested from the empire, they were forced to turn to the only surviving source in the West capable of providing them with the administrative and literary expertise necessary for governing and operating sophisticated state apparatuses—the Christian church headed by the lone patriarch in the West, the Roman papacy.

The popular view of the situation in the West by the late fifth century is that of "the Fall of the Roman Empire." This is an interpretation of events based on hindsight and a decidedly Western viewpoint, first articulated by the English historian Edward Gibbon, in his extremely literate but culturally bigoted massive study, *The Decline and Fall of the Roman Empire,* the first volume of which appeared in 1776 (the same year in which the American Declaration of Independence first expressed the Enlightened principles of modern Western European civilization's new political philosophy of liberal democracy). Though Gibbon's contention that Greco-Roman civilization was corrupted by the rise of Christianity has been generally refuted, the powerful prose of his work has succeeded in leaving the general impression that the

Germanic invasions and occupation of the Western Roman Empire signified the willful total destruction of Hellenic civilization by the Germans and their Christian collaborators, resulting in the barbarization of Western society and, ultimately, in the Dark Ages. Moreover, his characterization of the East Roman Empire as dissolute, corrupt, ineffectual, and fossilized has never been completely overcome in Western perceptions.

We have good reason to believe that such was not the case.

On his deathbed in 337, the emperor Constantine I—who had raised Christianity to a position within the state equal to the civil authority, and who had molded a new definition for Roman imperial power based on that partnership—finally and officially joined the ranks of the Christian faithful by being baptized. Almost immediately, the empire was divided once again among his sons. With a few brief exceptions, the Roman Empire essentially remained divided into its two cultural-administrative halves, each with its own emperor (but that in the East consistently considered by all as the senior), until the end came for the western half in the later fifth century (traditionally, 476). Throughout that period and beyond, the legacy of Constantine served to preserve the concept of a universal Christian world-state ruled by the true Christian emperor from his Christian imperial capital at Constantinople.

All the evidence seems to indicate that the collapse of the Western Roman Empire at the disruptive hands of the German barbarians was an unintentional result of the political anarchy that accompanied their massive migration into and ultimate settlement of the region. Far from consciously attempting to destroy the Roman Empire, the Christian German invaders actively sought to become full-fledged, participating subjects in the Christian world-state. German tribal leaders, such as Stilicho the Vandal, Alaric the Visigoth, and Theodoric the Ostrogoth, actively sought and obtained imperial Roman titles and positions of authority. They married their children into the various Roman imperial families. They led their tribal forces in service to the Roman emperors, or to imperial pretenders of their choice, often fighting among themselves in the name of one or the other. It was they who furnished the military forces that turned back the incursions into the empire of Attila (445-53) and his Hunno-Turkish hordes. When in the late fifth century the partially Romanized German tribes settled into several tribal states in the territories of the western empire, their leaders at first made every effort to preserve the fiction that they governed as nominal provincial administrators of the Roman Empire, maintaining continuous communications with the emperor in Constantinople and long upholding puppet junior emperors in the West. Even Theodoric the Great (489-526), virtual independent ruler of an Ostrogothic state in Italy, maintained the fiction that he governed in the name of the one and only Christian Roman emperor in Constantinople, whose image Theodoric placed on the coins he issued instead of his own and in whose name all Ostrogothic laws were issued.

The pope, patriarch of Rome, and the western church organization he controlled served to ensure that the Christian German tribal leaders did not lose sight of true Christian political realities.

The pope and his subordinate church hierarchy subscribed completely to the political-religious imperial ideology that emerged from the Nicæan Council. That the Christian Germans, Arian heretics though most of them were, showed reverential deference to the church spared it the disruption suffered by other imperial institutions that were taken over in the West. The barbarians quickly sought to forge the political partnerships with the church that membership in the imperial Roman civilized world required according to the Christian worldview.

The German rulers of the newly emerging western states leaned heavily on the pope and his church organization for the expertise needed in building and maintaining sophisticated political structures. The church furnished them with the necessary education, personnel, and advice that their traditional tribal cultures could not supply. Along with the active political assistance furnished by the western church came a process of acculturation into the Christianized Nicæan version of Greco-Roman civilization in its western, Latinized Roman form. As the only direct representative of the Nicæan Roman Empire still effectively holding office in the West by the beginning of the sixth century, the pope acquired immense political and cultural prestige among the German rulers in the West, along with widespread practical authority within the Germanic sphere, by providing them with their lone source of ideological continuity to the collapsed imperial model of statehood. The lack of effective imperial authority in the West, coupled with this growing political role among the German states, resulted in the papal office assuming increased pretensions to leadership in both the spiritual and the temporal affairs of the Christian world far beyond the honorary position accorded it at Nicæa. As early as the reign of Pope Gelasius (492-96), contentions surfaced between the Latin papacy and both the Greek patriarch of Constantinople, an office recently elevated in status because of its close association with the imperial throne, and the emperor over the issue of primacy within the church. The resulting rivalry was the first indication of the universal Christian community's division along cultural lines.

The main stumbling block in the Western church-state relationship in the sixth century remained Arianism. The church and empire were Nicæan orthodox but most of the Germans remained heretics. This problem of heresy in the West set the stage for the last authentic effort to make the Constantinian Christian political ideology a working reality in all the former Greco-Roman world.

Emperor Justinian I the Great (527-65) came to the throne of Constantinople a somber man, sober and bookish. He seemed an easy target for manipulation by the circus factions of the Hippodrome in Constantinople that had developed into unofficial populist political parties wielding a great deal of influence on state affairs through threats of violence or street rioting. In 532 the factions attempted to force Justinian to make changes in his government bureaucracy that would serve to lessen the tax burden caused by near-continuous military confrontations with the traditional Persian enemy along the empire's eastern borders. They rioted in the streets of the capital, set fire to much of the city, and proclaimed Justinian's overthrow. He would have conceded to the popular uprising had it not been for his empress, Theodora—an ex-prostitute and actress, but also a woman of iron will and excellent political judgement. Admonished publicly by his wife to either live up to the ideal of an autocratic ruler or flee the throne and city like a coward, Justinian ruthlessly ordered his military to crush the uprising. This marked the last time the common people of the empire attempted to play a leading participatory role in the affairs of state. Over the bodies of 30,000 of his subjects, Justinian emerged as a ruler determined to solidify the autocratic power of his office and to realize the grandiose pretensions implied by the official imperial ideology of one God, one Emperor, one Empire.

For the rest of his reign following this affair, Justinian relentlessly pursued his imperial goals in both domestic and foreign policy to the point of driving his empire into near bankruptcy by the time of his death. Internally, Justinian concentrated on consolidating the basis of his supreme authority over the state by legal and religious means. He ordered the great collection and codification of Roman law that has since borne his name, which served as the fundamental legal basis of state government in much of both Eastern and Western Europe until the late eighteenth century. The Justinian Code not only furnished the state with a recognized body of traditional justice, it also entrenched as law the will of the absolute monarch. It made no bones about the fact that all civil law, whether traditional or by decree of the ruler, must necessarily be grounded in the scriptural law of the Christian Bible.

To further his policy of cementing autocratic power through Christianity, Justinian sponsored expensive building campaigns. While much effort and resources were spent on practical civic projects throughout the empire, such as on roads, bridges, and defensive fortresses, Justinian devoted particular attention to creating and propagating a new form of Christian church architecture that would express the power and glory of the partnership between Christianity and the Roman imperial office. The result was the domed cross-in-square architectural plan that became so characteristic of Orthodox Christian churches, epitomized in Justinian's great imperial cathedral in Constantinople—Hagia Sofia (The Holy Wisdom). The domed structure aimed at expressing the all-embracing, mystical Greek order of cultural reality. The church's broad, open, cubic internal space, with its large hovering dome seemingly suspended in the air above, emphasized the infinite universality that encompassed both heaven and earth, in which all men, including their overlords, were important members of a community united in faith. Stress was placed on dazzling internal decoration, at the expense of a somewhat bland external facade, to denote the mystical inner spirituality of this universal order.

The political symbolism involved in Justinian's religious architectural innovation was readily apparent to his Eastern Christian subjects. The divine order for human existence was the single community of all true believers living in daily close contact with the spiritual world. The natural temporal embodiment of the universal Christian community was the Roman Empire, ruled by its emperor—God's direct representative on earth—in accordance with the will of the church. It was the emperor who assured the continued beneficial relationship between the spiritual and temporal worlds for the good of the Christian community. In that liaison role, the outward character of the emperor was of little importance—he could be fat or thin, abusive or benign, miserly or profligate. Rather, it was the inner, hidden character of the office that mattered in the general order of things. The mystical nature of the Christian imperial ruler was further reinforced through borrowing numerous cultural elements from the neighboring Persian incarnation of the ancient Mesopotamian civilization that served to ritualize all aspects of autocratic political authority, which by the time of Justinian had become common in Constantinople. By removing consideration of the person of the ruler and concentrating on his mystical inner spiritual character, Justinian fashioned the final step necessary in shaping the ideological structure for Christian autocratic political power. The Hellenic tradition of deified Roman emperors was given its conclusive Christian facade.

Girded with this powerful, mystical Christian aura, Justinian commenced asserting his imperial claim to supreme earthly authority over the Christian world-state. His efforts to bring unity to the Roman world, which during his reign found its eastern provinces disrupted by a popular new heresy concerning the nature of Christ called Monophysitism, led him eventually to claim supreme spiritual authority, in the name of his role as God's direct representative, by attempting to legislate theological matters in the same manner as he had the empire's civil laws. Although he ultimately failed to make good on his assertion of imperial spiritual leadership, Justinian set a dangerous precedent in the area of imperial authority that never completely disappeared from the single God, Emperor, Empire political ideology. Justinian's pretension to supreme spiritual authority has come to be classified as Caesaropapism—control of the church by the state. It is a term that often has been used to describe Byzantine (eventually, East European) political realities by Western historians and theologians. Except for Justinian's failed efforts, and a few later isolated and brief cases, however, the term has been inappropriately applied. The traditional church-state relationship that characterized Byzantine (and, later, East European) political realities was one of union, harmony, and synthesis of the two, rather than the domination of one by the other.

When the western church, acting in the name of the Nicæan Christian community of Italy, appealed to Justinian for relief from Arian Ostrogothic rule, the emperor responded with a massive military effort to wrest North Africa (Italy's chief source of grain supply, and in Arian Vandal hands) and Italy from the control of the German heretics. Using the reestablishment of orthodox religious unity as a pretext, Justinian set out to re-create politically the undivided empire of the past, its capital to be centered on Christian Constantinople, with himself as the undisputed autocratic monarch. From 535 until 554 Justinian waged near-constant warfare in the West. At its successful conclusion, his empire had reincorporated the western lands of Italy, Sicily, most of North Africa, and the southern coastal regions of Spain. The Vandals and the Ostrogoths were utterly defeated and reduced to little political account. Administrative and religious unity of East and West was reestablished, and, over it all, Justinian briefly reigned supreme.

Justinian's reconquests in the West proved to be the swan song for a unified Christian Hellenic world-state. The costs of success for the empire in terms of financial and human resources had been prohibitive. Both the imperial treasury and the manpower of the military were exhausted. Two decades of conflict left Italy ravaged. Its non-German inhabitants, at first thankful for their liberation from heretical German rule, swiftly grew to resent the centralized, efficient taxation system imposed on them by the imperial government in Constantinople. Their economic woes were magnified by their growing awareness of the cultural differences that separated them from their East Roman liberators. While they both were Nicæan Christians, they rapidly sensed that Greek and Latin speakers, though outwardly adhering to the same beliefs, did not possess identical perceptions of their common faith. The practical, no-nonsense Latins soon came to resent the presence of the Greeks in Italy, whom they saw as being heartless, cunning, and altogether impractical. Fourteen years after

Justinian's victory, in 568, a new German tribal people, the Lombards, invaded Italy. The Latins offered the depleted and weak imperial defense forces little assistance in resisting the onslaught, and within four years the empire had lost most of the peninsula, except for Rome, Ravenna, and the southern regions centered on Naples.

Justinian died in 565, before the futility of his western policies was revealed fully, but signs of insuperable strain in maintaining them had arisen even prior to his death. Already in 559 Avar and Slavic forces had penetrated the Balkan possessions of the Eastern Empire, in a prelude to the inundations that followed for the next 150 years. These matters forced the empire to concentrate on defending and reclaiming its eastern European heartlands. In 540 warfare had been renewed with the traditional eastern enemy, Persia. Wars with the Persian Empire continued with periodic regularity under Justinian's successors until, in 630, during the reign of Heraclius, it ended in the empire's favor. But the victory proved sterile, since both protagonists were left utterly exhausted to face the new, dangerous threat from out of the Arabian Peninsula posed by the militantly religious Islamic Arabs, who first appeared as enemies on the imperial borders of Syria in 633. By the opening of the eighth century, Byzantium (as we may now call the Greek-speaking East Roman Empire) was faced with a life-and-death struggle both on its European Balkan front with the Bulgars and Slavs and on its West Asian front with the Arabs, who had swiftly stripped the empire of its Syrian, Egyptian, African, and Spanish territories.

Under such conditions, the emperor in Constantinople could spare few resources to maintain any sort of direct control over his few remaining holdings in Italy. Once again the pope in Rome was forced to play the leading role in representing imperial traditions in the West by default. It was by then obvious to all, in both East and West, that the one and only Roman emperor in Constantinople was unable to control the Christian western world effectively. There grew among western Christians an impression that, if the Roman emperor in the East was unable to rule in the West, then the situation had to be a demonstration of God's divine will—the eastern emperor surely no longer was the deity's direct representative on earth. To the Western mind, it followed that the Eastern Roman Empire had forfeited its claim to being the single Christian world-state.

By the beginning of the ninth century, this logic in the West was reinforced by the readily apparent growing cultural differences between Latin West and

Greek East. Lack of direct imperial control and geographical isolation from the four other eastern patriarchs had permitted the Latin papacy to fortify its claim to spiritual leadership within the Christian church vis-à-vis the Greek East as well as to function as an autonomous center of civil authority in the politically anarchistic Germanic West. To solidify its claim, the Roman church was not above forging documents that validated its pretensions, such as the infamous *Donation of Constantine,* which supposedly was issued to the pope by Constantine at the time he moved the imperial capital to Constantinople, delegating temporal authority in the West to that prelate as imperial vice-regent in the emperor's absence.

On Christmas Day 800, the papacy found an expedient, but decisive, solution to the imperial power vacuum that had emerged in the West. Standing on his claims to supreme spiritual and temporal authority, Pope Leo III decided to create a new Christian world-state—the Holy Roman Empire—by crowning Charlemagne (800-14), king of the Nicæan Christian Franks and leader of the most powerful Germanic state then existing in the West, as its emperor. Through the will and intercession of the pope, there came into existence two Christian Roman empires, each competing for possession of the single God, Emperor, Empire political reality of Europe. One—the West—was Latin in culture and conceived of the Christian world in terms of Roman Catholicism; the other—the East—was culturally Greek and adamantly tied to Orthodox Christianity. One was the calculated creation of a powerful church prelate, the other the organic creation of the original Constantinian-Nicæan partnership. From the ninth century on, neither would prove able to realize the theoretical ideal of universal Christian political unity. Both were doomed to remain regional in their authority and sectarian in their scope, while, at the same time, developing into increasingly irreconcilable competitors fighting for recognition of their unattainable claims to political hegemony within the general Christian world. With the pope's Christmas coronation of Charles, the division of Europe between two related but distinct civilizations was sealed.

In the West, the action of Pope Leo also sealed the fate of church-state relationships and the ultimate form that political authority would assume in Western Europe. Although outwardly adhering to the universal Nicæan political principle, by taking it upon himself to legitimize the new Christian emperor, Leo had actually modified the ideological formula. The symbolism of the coronation had inserted the office of Roman pope between God and the emperor: It essentially became one God, one Pope, one Emperor, one Christian Empire. The very act of the pope's anointing the emperor seemed to proclaim the ultimate supremacy of the church over the state. (It should be noted that the coronation of the Byzantine emperor *never* involved anointment by the Orthodox patriarch of

Constantinople but remained a secular affair of ritualized public acclamation by the senate, the military, and the population of the capital.)

In the politically anarchistic feudal structure that rapidly emerged in the West following the death of Charlemagne, the Roman popes managed to retain a certain measure of recognition of their commanding authority among the various German feudal rulers. The medieval Gothic architecture of the West gave physical expression to the strictly hierarchical, legalistic Latin-Roman cultural order of Western European political reality as fashioned by the popes, which emphasized the linear nature of authority from God, through the pope, to the temporal rulers, and, finally, to the common Christian subjects. The large-scale, towering narrowness of the structures, stressing the lowly position of common people on earth relative to their supreme overlords who resided, in stages, high above (the temporal below the spiritual), emphasized a total institutional devotion to the papal order of things.

When, by the fourteenth and fifteenth centuries, feudalism began to give way to the formation of centralized ethnic, regional monarchical states, the new rulers abjured such recognition of papal authority. No temporal ruler of an emerging centralized regional state worth his salt could afford to recognize the supremacy of a power whose center lay outside the borders of the territories under his control. The papal reaction to the rise of independent regional rulers—especially in its aggressive glorification of the church as an institution through expensive cultural programs, such as lavishly subsidizing the great Renaissance artists and architects and the erection of the extravagant St. Peter's Basilica in the Vatican—led to widespread corruption within the church and increasingly irrational pretensions of papal authority within the new states. This sparked the Protestant Reformation (begun by Martin Luther in 1515), which resulted in cementing the authority of the secular rulers in the West by the end of the sixteenth century, in the emergence of "Divine Right" (that is, rule by the "will of God") secular rulers in the seventeenth, and in the ultimate separation of church and state powers by the Enlightenment's liberal-democratic thinkers in the eighteenth.

In the East, no such lasting conflict between church and state over supremacy in the political sphere developed until the advent of communism in Russia during the early twentieth century. The traditional universal God, Emperor, Empire political ideology, which assumed a harmony of interests and power between church and state, continued in the Byzantine Empire until its demise in 1453 at the hands of the Ottoman Turks and thereafter among the various states that had existed within its cultural orbit.

Since the form of Christianity practiced was crucial in defining the political ideology in both the East and the West, conversions of tribal societies beyond the borders of the Roman imperial successor states to either Roman Catholicism or Eastern Orthodoxy spread their respective political spheres. By adopting Roman Catholicism the Slavs and Magyars of Northeastern and Central-Eastern Europe and the Croats of Southeastern Europe entered the political arena of the West—they adapted the Latin alphabet to fit the phonics of their various languages, recognized the spiritual supremacy of the pope, accepted royal crowns from the pope's hands, and entered into the tumultuous church-state relationships that characterized Western politics. In essence, their linguistic cultures were Latinized and their political cultures Germanized. On the other hand, the spread of the Byzantine political culture among peoples newly converted to Orthodox Christianity, such as the Bulgarians, Serbs, Romanians, and Russians, did not demand the Hellenization of their linguistic cultures. Still, it tied them just as tightly to the Greek cultural sphere of the East as the process among the others did to the Latin West.

The cultural orbit of the Byzantine Empire in the eastern European territories has been referred to as a commonwealth, reflecting the tolerance demonstrated by the Greek cultural leadership of the empire toward the microcultural autonomy afforded non-Greek societies within the Orthodox Christian world. Unlike the West, where microcultural assimilation into the Latin macroculture was viewed as a necessary prerequisite for entry into the Western Christian world, the Byzantines were content to permit ethnic diversity within their sphere so long as the fundamental religious and political tenets of the dominant Byzantine worldview were accepted. In Byzantine eyes, since the universal God, Emperor, Empire ideology was so intimately tied to the Orthodox form of Christianity, the very act of non-Greek peoples' acceptance of Orthodoxy assured the empire's undisputed leadership in the Orthodox world. In fact, the Byzantine government encouraged new Orthodox converts to further develop their native microcultures as a means of strengthening their resistance to foreign political-cultural threats (such as, from the West), thus tying them closely to the empire. By culturally linking the converts to the Byzantine orbit, the empire forged a lasting autocratic political culture for all of East European civilization.

The classic case of Byzantine concern for reinforcing non-Greek ethnic culture in service to the grand political ideology of the empire was the active role played by Greek emissaries in creating an alphabet for the Slavic languages in the ninth century. Cyril and Methodius, two Greek brothers from Thessaloniki, were directly associated with that important cultural development for the history of Eastern Europe.

Cyril was an accomplished linguist and philosopher, whose intellectual skills made him well known at court in Constantinople. Prior to his efforts in behalf of Slavic philology, he was sent at the head of a Byzantine delegation to the court of the Khazars, on the western Eurasian steppes, in an effort to win those powerful Turkic warriors to Orthodox Christianity and thus to implied Byzantine suzerainty. Although he failed in the goal of his mission (the Khazars eventually converted to Judaism!), he succeeded in greatly impressing Emperor Michael III (842-67) with his diplomatic and linguistic skills. When Prince Rostislav, ruler of a newly consolidated Czech Moravian state in Central-Eastern Europe, contacted the Byzantine court expressing his desire to convert himself and his people to Orthodox Christianity, and requested Byzantine assistance in resisting Catholic German political and cultural pressures in doing so, Cyril was asked to go as a missionary to the Czechs for the purpose of bringing them successfully into the Orthodox, hence Byzantine, fold.

Cyril realized the importance of reinforcing the Czechs' Slavic culture if he were to succeed in his mission. As a child, he was daily exposed to the Slavic language spoken in the immediate region of Thessaloniki. It is even conjectured that his wet-nurse may have been a Slav. In any event, he apparently was fluent in the local Slavic dialect. So he set out to construct a system of letters that could be used exclusively for writing Slavic. What emerged was the Glagolitic alphabet, a complicated, strange-looking series of signs rooted in a mixture of Greek, Phoenician, and assorted other eastern letters, into which Cyril translated the basic Orthodox liturgical texts. With his brother, Methodius, an able administrator and a devout cleric, in tow, he set out for Moravia in 863. There the two missionaries proved so successful in their religious and literary mission that the German Catholic church leadership vehemently denounced them to the pope. (At that time, the split between Catholic western and Orthodox eastern Christianity, though obviously growing, had not yet attained any sort of official institutional recognition—that would come with the so-called Great Schism of 1054.)

The row instigated by the Germans over the brothers' mission in Moravia became known as the "Three Language Heresy." The German church claimed that only Greek and Latin were acceptable "sacred" languages with divine authority to convey the Christian Scriptures. (Hebrew was acknowledged as the original language of the Old Testament but was not considered "Christian.") In Rome, Cyril eloquently defended his new Slavic alphabet at the papal court, stressing that, while Greek and Latin were both pagan in origin, the Glagolitic was Christian from its inception. The papacy, feeling threatened by increasing German efforts at church autonomy in the West, presaging the future political conflicts with German regional rulers, sided with Cyril, who died in Rome before having a chance to return to Moravia and build upon his victory. Methodius was raised to bishop of Moravia and did return, but proved unable to resist the mounting German pressure on his diocese. Upon his death in 885, Methodius' followers were expelled from Moravia by German church authorities. Later the brothers were canonized saints for their missionary efforts in behalf of the Slavs of Central-Eastern Europe, and today they are recognized as such by both the Orthodox and the Catholic churches. (In 1992 Pope John Paul II proclaimed them the *Catholic* patron saints of Eastern Europe!)

Circumstances transformed the failure of the Byzantine mission to the Moravians into a victory for Orthodoxy in the Slavic world. In 865 Prince Boris I (852-89), ruler of the Balkan state of Bulgaria, the principal competitor of the Byzantine Empire for political hegemony in the area, decided to join the Christian community of states by converting himself and his subjects, thus gaining recognition for his state as a brother member of the Christian European community and staving off possible extinction as an alien pagan threat by either of the neighboring Byzantine or Holy Roman empires. At first Boris turned to Rome and the German church, since Byzantium was his primary enemy. Emissaries were sent, but Pope Nicholas I refused both to grant Boris the title and crown of king and to authorize the founding of an autonomous Bulgarian state church organization. At the same time, the Byzantine Empire threatened the borders of Bulgaria with an army and a fleet, demanding that Boris convert to Orthodoxy. The harried ruler, attempting to gain as much for the Bulgarians as possible in the situation, chose Orthodoxy. Bulgaria became the first Slavic state to join the Byzantine Orthodox commonwealth.

Glagolitic had been the first Slavic literary alphabet, and it had gained some short-lived acceptance among many of the Slavs. Because it was created by a Byzantine monk, Glagolitic became associated with the Orthodox church, and its use was quickly eradicated among those Slavs who eventually joined the Roman Catholic world (such as the Czechs and the Poles), although Glagolitic letters managed to survive for centuries in isolated sectors of Croatia. While Glagolitic probably was already known in Bulgaria at the time of the conversion, Greek made the decisive initial literary impact immediately following the conversion. Greek prelates and Greek culture swiftly entered Bulgaria. For all intents and purposes, conversion immediately subordinated Bulgaria to Byzantine cultural dominance.

Things changed under Boris' son and successor, Simeon I (893-927). Simeon realized that, given the nature of the accepted Orthodox political ideology, religious-cultural subordination to the Byzantine Empire would eventually lead to political subservience as well. Bulgaria needed an independent state church organization of its own to assert the state's continued independent political existence in the Balkans. He was offered the opportunity to create just such a church when the Moravian disciples of Cyril and Methodius appeared on his borders after being expelled from their homeland by the Germans. Simeon lost little time capitalizing on this windfall. He offered them a royal welcome, brought them to court, and lavished rich patronage on them in support of their efforts to provide his state with Slavic liturgical works and with the training necessary for building a native Bulgarian church hierarchy.

From Simeon's farsighted policy, and from the work of the original disciples and their Bulgarian protégés, sprang a definitive Slavic literary culture based on a new, simplified alphabetical system—the Cyrillic. Mostly composed of modified Greek characters and named in honor of Cyril, creator of the original Slavic letters, Cyrillic was ingeniously precise in representing all of the phonics found in the Slavic languages. The original Greek liturgical texts in Bulgaria were quickly translated into Slavic using the new letters, and native Bulgarian clergy were trained in Cyrillic literacy. Soon the Greek hierarchy in Bulgaria was replaced by a native Bulgarian organization, providing Simeon with the necessary component for ensuring Bulgarian independence from Byzantium.

The creation of a viable Slavic literary language had portent far beyond merely the political independence of Bulgaria. All of Helleno-Christian culture lay open to the Slavic Bulgarians through translation. Quickly passing from translating originally Greek texts, the new Bulgarian literary workers commenced producing original works of their own, demonstrating that the Cyrillic alphabet was the most significant cultural tool created for the Slavs of Eastern Europe. Through it they were able to advance and expand their own native cultures in their own terms.

The Slavification of Byzantine Orthodox culture that occurred in Simeon's Bulgaria brought with it an assimilation of the traditional political ideology of the universal God, Emperor, and Empire. Simeon himself had been educated in Constantinople, where he had been sent as a hostage by his father, Boris, and where he had naturally imbibed Byzantine imperial ideology. Cyrillic Orthodoxy unified and strengthened the population under Simeon's rule and solidified his authority as ruler over the state. He was able to place into the field against Byzantium a cohesive military force that wrested control over most of the Balkans from the empire's hands. Bulgarian political expansion was accompanied by Cyrillic cultural expansion among the Slavic Serbs and Macedonians, and even among the Latin-speaking Romanians. Bulgarian military power forced Byzantium to recognize the autonomy of the Bulgarian church (a Bulgarian patriarchate was established in the Macedonian town of

Ohrid), though technically considered subordinate to the Greek patriarch of Constantinople by the Byzantines. The Bulgarian ruler was recognized as second in power and authority only to the emperor in Constantinople.

So complete was the assimilation by the Slavic Bulgarians of the Byzantine political ideology of the autocratic Christian ruler governing in partnership with the Orthodox church, no matter whether the culture was Greek or Slavic, and so powerful had the Bulgarian state become that, near the end of his life, Simeon was able to proclaim himself emperor—*tsar,* in Slavic—of the Romans and Bulgarians and have his claim taken seriously not only by Bulgarians but by some Byzantines themselves. Ultimate success appeared just within his grasp, and only the impregnable strength of Constantinople's defense walls prevented Simeon from being acknowledged as emperor in Byzantium. He died in 927 a frustrated but powerful ruler.

Byzantium's ninth-century policy of using an officially sanctioned Slavic form of Orthodoxy to bind the new peoples who had encroached upon the borders of the empire (Bulgarians) directly to the Nicæan imperial ideology, as well as to attempt expansion of its imperial authority into regions well beyond the former borders (Moravia), succeeded far beyond expectations. The culturally Greek Byzantine Empire managed to survive Simeon's Slavic imperial pretensions by the roll of history's dice. But survive it did. And having done so, Byzantium was unafraid to continue the policy among other emerging Slavic states in the Balkans and beyond.

In around 988 Russian Prince Vladimir I (ca. 980-1015) of Kiev turned to Constantinople and converted to Orthodox Christianity. His subjects were forced to follow his example. Vladimir lost little time in having the Cyrillic Slavic liturgy, which by his time had flourished in Bulgaria for over a century, imported into his lands. Unlike Bulgaria, which had had to work at developing the native Slavic Christian Cyrillic culture, Russia was able to enjoy instant Slavic Christianity, thanks to the Bulgarians. Along with the liturgical books came the secular political culture of Byzantium that had made the transition from Greek to Slavic culture in the Bulgarian Balkan heartland. Over time linguistic differences developed between the imported Bulgarian and the spoken Russian, causing the modification of the original Cyrillic literary language by Russianisms—the rise of Russian Church Slavonic—but the authoritarian political culture predicated on the universal God, Emperor, Empire ideology fit well with Vladimir and his successors on the Russian thrones of Kiev and, later, of Moscow. The Russian rulers were far enough removed from Constantinople to be able to afford formal recognition of the Byzantine emperor as supreme ruler on earth while, at the same time, exerting their authority unhindered by direct Byzantine intervention within their own lands.

In the ninth century an embryonic Serbian state emerged in the Raška region of the northwestern Balkans (roughly, today's Serbian province of Kosovo), but it was quickly subordinated to the expanding Bulgarian state and Christianized into Orthodoxy at the time of Bulgaria's conversion. Afterward, the Serbs threw off Bulgarian control by placing themselves under Byzantine suzerainty. Following Bulgaria's crushing military defeat by Byzantine Emperor Basil II *Boulgaroktonos* ["the Bulgar-killer"] (976-1025) and disappearance as a state in 1018, the Serbs of Zeta (today's Montenegro) gained independence from Byzantine control, beginning a lengthy state-building process that resulted in the emergence in the mid-twelfth century of a viable and expanding Serbian state in the Balkan northwest under the rule of a certain Nemanja, founder of the great medieval Serb ruling dynasty. Just as did the Bulgarians and Russians, the Orthodox Serbs had but one viable political model—the Byzantine Empire.

The Bulgarian state was resurrected from direct Byzantine domination by the Asen brothers, Peter IV (1185-97) and Ivan I (1190-96), in 1185—only to have a catastrophe strike Byzantium. French knights and Venetian mariners, constituting the military forces of the Fourth Crusade against the Muslim Turkish and Arab masters of the Holy Lands and Egypt, descended on Constantinople in 1203 under the pretext of installing a Greek pretender on the imperial throne in return for his financial and other material support of their crusading efforts. Although successful in their short term goal, their champion proved too much a creature of the Orthodox East to play the role of lackey for Catholic Westerners, whom the Byzantines looked upon as barbaric and less culturally developed (with some justification). In 1204 the Western Crusaders turned their greed and frustration on the Byzantines, whom they considered (just as justifiably) to have reneged on promises of support for their endeavor. The Crusaders eventually broke through the sea walls protecting Constantinople and, once inside, gave free rein to a venomous cultural animosity that has been rivaled in Southeastern Europe only by the carnage displayed in the latest warfare in Bosnia. The wholesale rapine, pillaging, and plundering inflicted by the Catholic warriors of Christ upon the stricken capital of the East, the largest and wealthiest city in the world at the time, was unprecedented. The Orthodox world never forgot or forgave the West for the sack of Constantinople, and the event created a gulf between the Eastern and Western European civilizations that has existed virtually unbridged into the present. The Latin Empire founded by the victorious Westerners was able to plant few roots in the midst of the hostile Orthodox East, and survived for less than sixty years. In 1261 the Greeks returned to Constantinople. Byzantium was revived, but only in a fatally weakened condition.

The autocratic political ideology of Byzantium survived the catastrophe in far more vigorous shape than did the empire itself. Slavic Orthodox Bulgaria had been one of the leading contenders for reestablishing the Orthodox empire following 1204. Only internal Bulgarian political anarchy permitted a Greek state centered on classical Nicæa ultimately to prevail. But the revived Greek empire itself fell into civil war in the early fourteenth century, leading to the successful rise of the Ottoman Turkish state in Anatolia and the emergence of Serbia, under its strong Orthodox ruler, Stefan Dušan (1331-55), as the dominant Christian state in the Balkans. Like the Bulgarian Simeon four centuries earlier, Dušan was completely committed to the universal God, Emperor, Empire Orthodox political ideology. He won Byzantine recognition of an autonomous Serbian Orthodox church organization (the Serbian patriarchate of Peć) on terms similar to the existing Bulgarian church, managed to acquire control over most of the Balkan interior and in 1346 proclaimed himself tsar of the Serbs, Greeks, Bulgarians, and Albanians. Unfortunately like Simeon, Dušan's assumption of the imperial throne in the Balkan Orthodox world was foiled. He suffered an untimely death in 1355, shortly before a planned attack on the weakened capital city of Constantinople could be launched.

Dušan's death spelled catastrophe for the Balkan Orthodox world. Just a year earlier, the Muslim Ottoman Turks had made their first permanent inroad into Europe by crossing the Dardanelles and occupying the fortress town of Gallipoli. From that European beachhead the Turks swiftly advanced against the then-disunited Orthodox Christian Balkan states. Byzantium, surrounded and cut off from the rest of Europe, was reduced to little more than the city of Constantinople itself. Its once-imperial emperor eventually was forced to travel to the West as a beggar seeking aid from the pope and the German Holy Roman Empire to stave off the inevitable Muslim conquest. At the Council of Florence in 1439, Emperor John VIII Palaiologos (1425-48) signed a document uniting the Orthodox and Catholic churches (technically healing the schism of 1054) on Catholic terms in hopes that it would bring Western military succor to the failing Eastern Roman Empire. But the pope and the Holy Roman Emperor had their own troubles with each other and the rising Western regional monarchies, so they could spare virtually nothing to help their desperate new ally.

In any event, most of the Orthodox clergy and nearly all of the Orthodox population in Eastern Europe refused to accept the union, which further weakened the dying empire of the East. Both Serbia and Bulgaria lapsed into internal anarchy following the death of Dušan, rendering the imperial titles of their nominal rulers meaningless and the military effectiveness of their armies nil. Within 150 years of the Turks securing their first foothold in Europe, almost all of the Balkan Peninsula—the entire Orthodox Christian world in Europe—lay in the hands of the Muslim Ottoman conquerors.

In one of history's great ironies, the conquest of the East European Orthodox world by the Muslim Turks served to perpetuate and strengthen the traditional imperial political ideal among the Christian subject peoples of the Ottoman Empire. By the time Sultan Mehmed II the Conqueror (1451-81) ended the Byzantine Empire by capturing Constantinople in 1453, the Turks had enjoyed over a century of close (if not altogether cordial) relations with their imperial enemy. Just as originally the Prophet Muhammad considered Islam the divinely inspired replacement for Christianity as the true faith, necessary because the Christians, wracked by internal heresies and corrupted by worldly concerns, had strayed from God's intended path, Mehmed saw himself as reestablishing the world-state of God on earth by substituting the Islamic empire for the Roman. Yet he wholeheartedly embraced the imperial One God, One Emperor, One Empire ideology of the Roman Empire, and he viewed his Islamic state as the logical continuation of that flawed predecessor. The lands he held in Europe were already known by the Turks as Rumeli (the Lands of the Romans), and he set up court in the former capital of Rum (the Roman Empire—the Byzantines, their Christian neighbors, and the Turks never conceived of the empire as anything other than Roman; Byzantine/Byzantium is a modern designation), now renamed Istanbul.

The Ottoman state as finalized by Mehmed leaned heavily on Byzantine bureaucratic, military, and ceremonial precedent. This was most evident, as far as the conquered Orthodox Christian subjects were concerned, in the establishment of the *millet* system for governing the non-Muslims within the empire.

Since the Ottoman Empire was an Islamic state, in which the religious and the political institutions were not just linked together but were indistinguishable from one another, state law was sacred law and could be applied only to Muslim believers. But the population of the Ottoman Empire at the time of Mehmed was predominantly Christian. (Expansion into the Islamic regions of West Asia and North Africa, which would tip the demographical scales in favor of Muslims, did not occur until half a century later.) Mehmed was forced to devise some way of governing his numerous non-Muslim subjects. Within a year of taking Constantinople, he hit on the solution: Non-Muslims could be held accountable to their own laws so long as they recognized the supreme authority of the Islamic sultan, did not intentionally besmirch Muslim beliefs, and agreed to pay not only the regular state taxes levied on all Ottoman subjects but certain special additional taxes as well. To ensure that his non-Muslim subjects adhered to this arrangement, Mehmed separated them into "nations"— *millets* —based on religious belief and not on ethnicity, and made the high church officials of each responsible for their administration and directly accountable to the sultan. Three non-Muslim *millets* were established after 1453—the Orthodox, the Armenian, and the Jewish. In mundane affairs, each was permitted wide latitude in autonomous self-government. For all practical purposes, they became official departments in the Ottoman central government.

Since Orthodox Christians comprised the single largest non-Muslim segment of the population in the European lands of the empire, the Orthodox *millet* ranked first in Ottoman imperial interests. It was headed by the Greek patriarch of Constantinople and administered by his subordinate church hierarchy. The office of patriarch was vacant immediately following the fall of Constantinople, so Mehmed's first order of business was to secure a prelate to serve in that post. In the past, the patriarch had been chosen by the Byzantine emperor in his roles as God's direct representative on earth and Thirteenth Apostle. With Byzantium destroyed, Mehmed, leader of the Islamic faithful and successor of the Prophet (*khalif*), tellingly appointed the new, postconquest patriarch— Bishop Gennadios Scholarios (1454-57, 1464), former leader of the anti-union Orthodox movement in Byzantium. Mehmed scrupulously followed Byzantine Orthodox tradition by ceremoniously investing the new leader of the Greek Orthodox church with his very symbols of office and issuing him an official diploma of investiture. From 1454 until the end of the Ottoman Empire, the Islamic sultan played the role of surrogate Christian emperor in determining who held the highest post in Orthodox Christendom.

Such an unlikely partnership between Muslim ruler and Orthodox Christianity was rationalized through the old imperial political ideology. Sultan and patriarch settled into a situation of mutual self-interest in which the actual religious differences between them grew blurred. The Orthodox Christians took to calling the sultan tsar. The high Orthodox hierarchy continued to enjoy the social and political prestige that it had during the pre-Ottoman past. If anything, the Greek church of Constantinople was strengthened in its authority, since it was given jurisdiction over the entire Orthodox population within the empire, including Bulgarians and Serbs, who had possessed autonomous churches of their own prior to the Ottoman conquest of the

Balkans. (These churches technically continued to exist until the third quarter of the eighteenth century but were subordinate to the Greek church centered in the capital.) The Ottoman-Orthodox partnership was one of the primary pillars of imperial stability for the Ottoman Empire.

That partnership began to break down in the late eighteenth century when Western nationalist ideas began to seep into the Ottoman Balkans by way of the empire's Greek international merchant communities abroad and through constant contacts of the Westerners of Central-Eastern Europe with the Serbs and Romanians along the military frontier in the northern Balkans. Interestingly, the Greek church organization of Istanbul consistently resisted the spread of anti-Ottoman national movements among its multiethnic membership in a futile effort to sustain the traditional autocratic political ideology in which it played such an important role. But even in its failure to stem the growing nationalistic tide in the Balkans, it unintentionally succeeded.

Throughout the nineteenth century, as newly independent Orthodox national states emerged in the Balkans, each resurrected the Nicæan autocratic political ideology along lines consistent with the newly adopted nationalist approach. Modern Serbia, Greece, Romania, and Bulgaria all found it inconceivable not to be ruled by a monarch closely associated with a national Orthodox church organization. In each case the form of government was technically that of a constitutional monarchy, whose laws expressed all the required liberal–democratic ideals. Yet in each case those ideals played second fiddle to the traditional ideology of the strong Christian ruler set on extending his authority to the maximum territory claimed by the nationalist program of his respective nation—even if the monarch himself was a foreigner because no acceptable native ruler could be found.

Serbia found its autocratic leadership in two native families—the Karadjordjević and the Obrenović houses—who alternated on the throne by means of bloody feuds and coups d'état from 1804 into 1941. No matter which house was in power at any given time, it usually dominated over the senate and national assembly in Belgrade thanks to the traditional partnership of the monarchy with the national Orthodox church and royal control of the military. The unifying ideological factor was the Serb monarchs' attempts to re-create "Greater Serbia"—imperial Serbia of the time of Tsar Dušan, when all of the northwestern and central Balkans lay under Serbian authority. This led Petr I Karadjordjević (1903-21) ultimately to defy Austria-Hungary for control of

Bosnia-Hercegovina in 1914. The results—World War I—were calamitous in the short term, but successful, at least for the Serbs, in the long.

Yugoslavia rose from the ashes of the war as a state dominated by the Serbs and their ruling monarchy, encompassing most of the territories claimed by the nationalists—and, unfortunately for the Serbs, more. When World War II swept the traditional royalty aside, it was replaced by the Communist monarch —Tito. Yugoslavia survived as a viable state only so long as did Tito, the living modern embodiment of the autocratic universal political ideology. At his death, the office was replaced by an ineffectual governing committee, in which leadership rotated among its members. The collapse of unitary rule caused by Tito's death ultimately led to the disintegration of the country. Slobodan Milošević has taken up the scepter of traditional authoritarian rule in Serbia, with the "Greater Serb" imperial connotations that it entails.

Few of the Greeks who fought for independence from the Ottoman Empire between 1821 and 1831 were aware of their great classical heritage. They only learned of it later from Western European classicists, who had sparked pro-Greek Western assistance for the rebels in the first place in the mistaken notion that the Ottoman Greeks were the living embodiment of their classical ancestors. Once Greece gained its independence (1831), the Greeks and their Western-imposed royal families (Bavarian Wittelsbachs [1831-62] and Danish Glücksburgs [1863-1967]) showed little respect for the outwardly liberal democratic constitutions that followed one upon the other. Far from espousing the Athenian democratic heritage, the modern Greeks most frequently looked to Byzantium for their national political models and ideals.

It was the reestablishment of the Greek-dominated Orthodox Byzantine Empire that served as the true national goal after 1831. The Greeks' national aspirations were summarized in the term *"Megale Idaia"* (The Great Idea), which envisioned the incorporation within the borders of the Greek nation-state of all territories that historically fell under the authority of the Orthodox Greek patriarchate of Constantinople, with that illustrious city—the Christian world-city—as capital. The Great Idea drove the expansionary process of the Greek state in the Balkans throughout the nineteenth and into the twentieth centuries. Because of it Greece became embroiled in conflicts with the Bulgarians over Macedonia and Western Thrace, including the Balkan Wars (1912-13) and the world wars, as well as a series of armed and diplomatic conflicts with Turkey, which saw the Greeks expelled from the Aegean coastal regions of Anatolia by the modern Turkish state of Mustafa Kemal (Atatürk—"Father of the Turks") in 1923, and which has continued into the present with the continuing crisis over Cyprus.

When the foreign monarchs of Greece were not abrogating their constitutions, proving ineffective as leaders, or being temporarily overthrown, the autocratic tradition of national imperialist government was upheld by strong Greek premiers or prime ministers who often acted as dictators. The model was set by Ioannes Capodistrias (1827-31), who at the very start of independence was the first to abrogate a constitution. His example was continued by Eleftherios Venizelos (1910-20, 1928-32), who maneuvered Greece into World War I on the side of the Entente and against Bulgaria over the objections of his king, and Ioannes Metaxas (1936-41), who established a dictatorship, among others who proved less prominent. These latter often included military takeovers led by such low lights as Theodore Pangalos (1925-26) and the Colonels, led by George Papadopoulos (1967-74). What all these men shared were the solving of internal political anarchy by imposing autocratic rule and the ultra-nationalist ideal of The Great Idea. Democracy has had a sorry record in the modern homeland of the ancient Athenians.

Although the Romanians never were under direct Byzantine control, their long medieval association with the Bulgarian Empire, and their relationship with the Ottoman Empire, instilled in them strong Byzantine-like Orthodox traditions. Throughout the eighteenth century the princely thrones of the Wallachian and Moldavian principalities were sold by the Ottoman sultans to members of wealthy Greek merchant families who lived in the Phanar (Lighthouse) district of Istanbul. Those Phanariote princes of the Romanian Principalities ruled their domains in true Byzantine autocratic fashion, surrounded by hollow ritual and dependent, sycophantic landowners and subject only to the whims or financial needs of the Turkish sultans. The continuous presence of Russian military forces on the borders of the two Romanian Principalities, beginning in the early nineteenth century, led to the displacement of their Phanariote Greek rulers by Orthodox Russians in 1829, who continued the autocratic political traditions of Eastern European civilization.

The Romanian revolution of 1848 resulted in successive periods of Russian and Austrian occupation of the Romanian Principalities until 1857. At a conference of all the European Great Powers in Paris in 1858, the two states of Wallachia and Moldavia were permitted to establish common institutions under separate princes. Alexander Cuza (1859-66) managed to win election as prince in both principalities, and, by 1862, the union of the two states was recognized as a single country, Romania. Cuza squelched all internal opposition to his rule by strengthening the legal powers of the princely office, but he was kidnapped and forced to abdicate in 1866. He was replaced by a foreign ruler, Prince Karl of Hohenzollern-Sigmaringen (1866-1914), who won complete independence for Romania in 1878 and raised himself to king in 1881. His reign was characterized by internal disturbances caused by the inequitable social divisions between the wealthy landowning minority and the poor peasant majority in the population, which resulted in long periods of martial law and the consequent entrenchment of royal power at the expense of the representative assembly of the country.

When royal power declined under King Ferdinand (1914-27), liberal democracy proved unable to exert stable government because of the continuing social unrest over land reform and anti-Semitism. Political assassination became the norm in Romanian politics. King Karl II (1930-45) was forced to deal harshly with the "Iron Guard" (officially named the "Legion of the Archangel Michael"), Europe's earliest fascist movement, by establishing a royal dictatorship and ordering the murder of the Guard's leadership in 1938. Royal dictatorship was replaced by the "dictatorship of the proletariat" after the close of World War II, when Red Army occupation of Romania led to complete Communist control of the government. The autocratic rule of party leader Gheorghe Gheorghiu-Dej (1952-65) was paled by that of Nicolae Ceauşescu, who seemed almost consciously attempting to reincarnate the Byzantine imperial traditions of Phanariote times. After Ceauşescu's fall in December 1989, the socialist Ion Iliescu regime secured and maintained its grip on power in supposedly democratic Romania by employing the familiar strong-arm tactics used by all previous Romanian governments since the mid-nineteenth century: In 1990 it brought hundreds of miners to the capital of Bucharest to beat the political opposition into submission.

Of all the Orthodox peoples of the Balkans, the Bulgarians had experienced both the imperial Byzantine autocratic tradition and the equally despotic Ottoman rule for the longest periods of time. When the Russians handed them their liberation from the Turks in 1878, they set out to write the most liberal of all European constitutions for their new country, based on American, Belgian, and Swedish models. Thought too politically immature to have a native ruling house by the European Great Powers, the Bulgarians invited Prince Alexander I of Battenberg (1878-86) to govern the country under Russian auspices. Alexander soon moved to increase princely power within the state, and, by 1881, he managed to change the constitution in his favor. In 1885 he increased the territory of Bulgaria by incorporating the Ottoman autonomous province of Eastern Rumelia over the violent protests of his Russian protectors. When the Russians withdrew their assistance and personnel from Bulgaria in hopes of weakening Alexander's government and army, he managed to successfully defend the expansion of the country against an invasion by the Serbs (1885-86), who were fearful of a rising Bulgarian threat to their own imperialist aspirations in the Balkans. But Alexander was kidnapped by Russian agents in 1886, and, although he succeeded in returning to Bulgaria, he soon abdicated.

The Bulgarian prime minister, Stefan Stambulov (1886-94), discovered a new candidate for the princely throne in Ferdinand I of Saxe-Coburg (1887-1918). Until his brutal murder by Macedonian revolutionaries in 1895, Stambulov dominated Ferdinand's reign. With his powerful prime minister dead and representative government in a shambles because of corrupt, self-serving policies perpetrated by an ever-increasing number of political parties, Ferdinand moved to reclaim the authority once held by his predecessor. In 1908, taking advantage of European public attention focused on Austria-Hungary's annexation of Bosnia-Hercegovina, Ferdinand proclaimed complete independence from Ottoman authority (until that date Bulgaria had been technically an autonomous state of the Turkish sultan) and had himself crowned tsar, in a conscious attempt to link himself and his state to the medieval Bulgarian imperial past—and to the overt expression of the traditional Byzantine universal political ideology. By his action, Ferdinand acquired supreme authority in the state, as well as a new nickname, "Foxy," and made public the official nationalist policy of re-creating the Bulgarian Empire in the Balkans.

Ferdinand's embracing of Bulgarian imperialism, especially with regard to acquiring Macedonia, led Bulgaria into the national catastrophes of the Balkan Wars (1912-13) and World War I on the side of the German Central Powers. Failure in both resulted in his abdication in 1918 and the enthronement of his son, Boris III (1918-43). The Bulgarians then attempted to make democracy work under their new ruler. In 1919 Aleksandŭr Stamboliiski, leader of the peasant Agrarian party, was elected prime minister (1919-23). While he espoused a policy of empowerment for the peasant masses, Stamboliiski proved ruthless in cementing near-autocratic power in his own hands. His attempts to quell pro-Macedonian expansionist nationalist activity led to his overthrow and assassination in 1923. With his death, effective central authority evaporated for a time in Bulgaria—nationalist agitation increased to anarchistic and dangerous levels, political parties proliferated until effective constitutional authority was unattainable, and winning parties in elections considered government a source of personal enrichment rather than a responsibility.

To cure the internal collapse of central authority, in 1935 Boris inaugurated a royal dictatorship. True to Bulgarian tradition, he attempted to reinforce his authority by tying his policy to the nationalist cause. Boris, a German by birth, allied his country with Hitler's Germany in hopes of winning Macedonia and Dobrudzha, although he was not by nature or inclination a fascist. He refused to exterminate Bulgaria's Jews and played no active role in Hitler's war against the Russians. Because of his refusal to declare war on the Soviet Union, Boris was summoned to Berlin by Hitler in 1943. Soon thereafter he died under mysterious circumstances. The Bulgarian government relapsed into ineffectiveness and was overthrown by the invading Red Army in late 1944. Two years later Bulgaria fell under Communist control, ruled by party leader Georgi Dimitrov (1946-49), a fervent admirer and associate of Stalin. Dimitrov's eventual successor emerged out of the ranks of the party leadership in 1954. Premier Todor Zhivkov became one of the longest-sitting heads of state in the post-World War II world (surpassed in longevity only by King Hussein of Jordan). He continued to govern in the autocratic traditions of the Byzantine and Stalinist veins until his downfall in November 1989, after which he became the first Communist ex-ruler to be placed on trial. Since his demise, the democratic government installed in 1990 has reverted to the sorry state that characterized Bulgarian political life following the deaths of Stambulov and Stamboliiski.

Although the modern Orthodox states of Southeastern Europe demonstrated little ability over the past century to move beyond the autocratic political heritage of the Byzantine Empire and its Ottoman successor, at least the geographical proximity of the region to Western European civilization helped mitigate somewhat the full impact of traditional centralized, absolutist rule. There were in Serbia, Greece, Romania, and Bulgaria borrowed semblances of Western-style constitutional governing institutions, such as national assemblies and senates, that monarchs or dictatorial prime ministers were forced to finesse or otherwise deal with in some manner. Such was not the case in the non-Balkan half of Orthodox Eastern Europe—Russia.

Kievan Russia joined the Eastern European civilization in the late tenth century through Byzantium, just as had Bulgaria before it and Serbia afterward. Like them, in Russia conversion to Orthodoxy entailed more than merely adopting a new religion. It meant embracing the Byzantine concept of political reality expressed in the universal God, Emperor, Empire ideology. Far from ending the political traditions of Byzantium on Russian soil, the demise of Kiev in the thirteenth century at the hands of the invading Mongols (often termed the Tatars by Westerners) ironically served only to intensify them within the resultant Russian successor state that was forged in the north of Western Eurasia by the grand princes of the city of Moscow over the course of the fourteenth and fifteenth centuries. The Mongol-Tatar state of the Golden Horde, centered on the steppes to the south, effectively cut off the Moscow-led Russians from direct contact with the heart of their Eastern European civilization in the Balkans. The Russians viewed their closest European neighbors, the

Lithuanians to the west, as enemies in struggles for control of the extreme western regions of Eurasia. Eventually the Lithuanians became members of Western European civilization, which Eastern Europeans viewed with general distrust and abhorrence following the Great Schism of the Christian religion in 1054 and, especially, after the horrifying example of the Fourth Crusade in 1204. Isolated in their forested northern Eurasian wilderness, the Russians centered on Moscow were left to consolidate their self-identity against non-Christian Asiatic dominance by reinforcing their Byzantine-style Orthodox culture.

Two cultural factors played leading roles in the rise of Moscow to Russian supremacy. One was the fact that, of all the Russian city princes in the lands politically subject to the autocratic Mongol *han* (ruler) of the Golden Horde, that of Moscow was the most grovelingly, but calculatedly, subservient. The *han* consistently tended to favor his most blatant Russian sycophant over less amenable princes in the Russian lands when it came to political and military support. Moscow managed to emerge as the official military bulwark of the Horde on its border with the Lithuanians in Western Eurasia. Despite periodic and disruptive raids by the Mongols, the princes of Moscow could depend on the support of the Horde as they progressively reduced their rival Russian princes to subordinates over the course of the fourteenth and fifteenth centuries. In consequence of the close Muscovite-Mongol relationship, numerous Asiatic cultural elements were slowly integrated into the native Orthodox cultural character, especially among the Russian upper classes. For example, by the fifteenth century the princely court in Moscow spoke Turkish as its official language (since by that time the Mongols of the Golden Horde had become ethnically assimilated into the Turkic population of the steppes that formed the demographic majority in the state); a large number of the Russian aristocracy, as well as the Cossacks, the common Russian border inhabitants of the steppes, affected Turkic dress and manners, and many adopted Turko-Mongol surnames (such as Godunov, famous for Boris, who rose to the office of tsar in 1598 and became the central hero of the noted Russian opera by Modest Musorgskii); and a pronounced predilection for premeditated cruelty—torture, flogging, mutilation, and the like—entered into Russian political and judicial life. (Similar trends were discernible in the Byzantine cultural traditions, though perhaps not in as frequent and as persistent a manner as was the case in the Mongol.)

The Asiatic elements that crept into the Russian microculture during the period of Mongol-Tatar dominance served to intensify the second cultural factor—the dominant Byzantine character of Russian political life. If anything, borrowings from the highly centralized, autocratic, and brutal political culture of the Mongols tended to accentuate the native culture—which stressed the universal God, Emperor, Empire ideology—among the Russians to a greater extreme than was the case for the Balkan peoples, who had experienced Byzantium directly. As the princes of Moscow eliminated political competition from their brother Russian princes during the period of Mongol-Tatar domination, they consistently elevated their official position within the Russian Orthodox world, first to Grand Prince in the mid-fourteenth century, and then to tsar, a title first used in the late fifteenth century at the end of Mongol domination and then continuously from the sixteenth century, as the Muscovite state expanded from its northern confines into a vast Eurasian empire. With the use of the imperial title, an extreme version of Byzantine autocracy was cemented as the fundamental Muscovite Russian political culture.

From its beginnings in the conquests of its Russian city-state neighbors, Muscovite Russia was an empire, and its rulers espoused the traditional Orthodox imperial ideals. By the time it emerged from beneath the sway of the Mongols, its imperial political model—the Byzantine Empire—had ceased to exist. Of all the Orthodox states in Eastern Europe, Russia alone survived by the late fifteenth century. This fact was not lost upon the Byzantinized Muscovite rulers and the Orthodox church of Russia. Vasili III (1505-33), who had begun using the title of tsar, as had his father Ivan III the Great (1462-1505), was convinced that his autocratic authority derived from the will of God, in the same fashion that the former Byzantine emperors were considered divinely chosen to be the "Thirteenth Apostles" and God's direct representatives on earth during their lifetimes. When in 1510 a reputable monk informed him by letter that he was the logical successor of the Byzantine emperors, Vasili needed little convincing.

In his letter to the ruler, Abbot Filotei formulated a Russian version of the traditional Byzantine political ideology known as the Third Rome Theory. According to Filotei, the first Rome (the Latin world) fell because of its pagan nature, so God established a second, Christian Rome centered on Constantinople (the Orthodox Byzantine Empire). But Constantinople had angered God by signing a religious union (Council of Florence, 1439) with the apostate Christians who had inherited the first Rome (the Catholics), so it was chastised by God, through his instrument, the Ottoman Turks, with conquest and disappearance in 1453. Only Moscow—the Third Rome—stood as capital for a living Orthodox imperial state, to which the mantle of Orthodox political leadership was rightly transfered from Constantinople by God. Although it would be wrong to misconstrue this political theory as a basis for urging Russia's world domination, as some scholars in the past have asserted, Filotei's theory provided Russian rulers with a strong claim to succeed to the Byzantine imperial tradition within the East European world.

The Third Rome Theory became the crowning element in the Russian translation of the traditional Orthodox political ideology of One God, One

Emperor, One Empire and served as the bedrock foundation for the Russian tsardom until its collapse in 1917, despite the overt Westernization of the ruling classes from the time of Peter the Great on. Though from the eighteenth through early twentieth centuries beards were cut à la the Western fashion, clothes were Westernized, political and social institutions within the country were given a Western veneer, and a small amount of industrial development occurred (relative to the size and population of the Russian Empire itself, but vast in proportion to any single European state), the centralized, autocratic authority of the tsar was never called into serious question. In fact, while Western Europe was undergoing a long, sometimes painful, transition to constitutionally ordered liberal democracy in the nineteenth century, the Russian Empire entrenched the absolute authority of its ruler even further. The modern "Europeanized" political ideology of Russia emerged in a new official slogan created during the reign of Tsar Alexander III (1881-94), to which all subjects of the Russian Empire were expected to subscribe—Autocracy (absolute political authority vested in the tsar and his governing bureaucracy), Orthodoxy (the official state church, which validated the tsar's supreme authority), and Nationalism (loyalty to the Russian Empire, ruled by the tsar). Little separates this ideological trinity from its medieval Byzantine and Third Rome counterparts.

By its very definition, the Russian Orthodox political ideology, whether medieval or modern, left no room for democratic participation in governing. Rising and widespread social and political discontent among the subservient and politically meaningless masses of the empire's population, coupled with the military debacle suffered by the Russians in the Russo-Japanese War of 1904-5, forced Tsar Nicholas II (1894-1917) to grant a form of representative assembly—the Duma—in 1906. Although it remained in existence through the First Russian Revolution in 1917, the assembly was never permitted to function as a truly democratic institution. The ruler dissolved and reconstituted it almost at will, so that, during the crucial period of February-October 1917, when the revolution had placed Russia's future in the balance, no one within or from outside the assembly possessed the political experience to make representative government work. It, like the tsar and his government, became an easy prey to Vladimir Ilyich Lenin and the Bolsheviks, who realized the force of continued autocratic political traditions in a country that knew no other form of workable governance.

Communism was a Western (German), thus foreign, ideology imposed by force on Eastern European Russian society. But Lenin and Josef Stalin, who succeeded him and shaped Soviet communism into its lasting order, made it acceptable to most of the subjects of the former Russian Empire for over half a century by expropriating many of the forms and most of the political ideology of the overthrown imperial state. The old empire, which the Russians viewed as their rightful and historic state, was retained as the Soviet Union. The party replaced the Orthodox church as the supreme institution that lent validation to divinely inspired political authority, with Karl Marx (and later a trinity of Marx, Lenin, and Stalin) as the deity. Authority rested in the hands of the party leader, who was Marx's (Marx-Lenin-Stalin's) leading disciple and direct representative on earth. The Soviet political ideology was thus: One God (Marx-Lenin-Stalin), One Emperor (the secretary-general of the Soviet Communist party), One Empire (the Soviet Union). The party secretary-general ruled the new socialist empire in much the same autocratic and absolutist manner as did the former tsars. Many of the organizational elements of the Soviet governing body were directly modeled after old imperial counterparts, including the NKVD (later, the KGB), which paralleled the imperial *Okhrana* secret police of the nineteenth century, which, in turn, had its roots in the *Oprichnina* of Ivan IV, founded in 1564.

Autocracy, absolutism, centralization, divine sanction—such are the terms that historically and consistently describe the political culture of Eastern European civilization for well over a thousand years. The degree to which they are manifested among the member microcultures of that civilization varies, depending on their geographical proximity to Western European civilization and its powerful cultural influences, as well as on the circumstances of their individual historical development.

The Orthodox peoples of Southeastern Europe experienced close to two centuries of strong Western cultural contact, the effects of which were assisted by the circumstance of five hundred years of previous Islamic domination, thus providing fertile soil for imported Western nationalistic concepts and the outward forms of liberal democracy that appeared to be part and parcel of the nation-state idea. While traditional Byzantine-like autocratic tendencies have dominated the governments in all of the post-Ottoman Southeast European states, Greece has shown the greatest amount of Westernization, probably because the Greeks have been exposed to the Western world through their centuries-old commercial activities, have enjoyed the active and direct interests of Westerners aware of their own Hellenic cultural roots, and have not experienced the post-World War II era of Communist control that reinforced the traditional autocratic political culture of Eastern Europe among their non-Greek

Balkan neighbors. One may argue over the pecking order among the remaining Balkan states as to which is more Westernized and less Byzantine in its political culture, but the fact that such is the case demonstrates that none truly share the liberal-democratic political tradition.

Among the new states that have emerged in Western Eurasia following the breakup of the Russian/Soviet Empire, the more extreme Russian form of the autocratic Byzantine political tradition has left a deeper cultural mark. Least autocratic, in relative terms at least, are Ukraine and Belarus, which once enjoyed the benefit of direct Western political influences into the eighteenth century by way of Poland-Lithuania. But one must not place too much emphasis on this fact, since the imposition of Russian imperial rule for over two centuries had a lasting impact on both. And as for the Russians, the easternmost of the East Europeans, their eleven-year experience of Western-style democratic government in the early days of the twentieth century was limited in the extreme and mostly fictitious. For all intents and purposes, the Russians have known only the Byzantine imperial ideology of autocracy.

Westerners are naive if they believe that the autocratic political culture of Eastern European civilization can be overcome swiftly by Western European liberal democracy. The presidency of the Russian Federated Republic will most likely resemble more a personal monarchy than the presidency of the United States for years to come, whether the holder of that office is Boris Yeltsin or some other political strongman. The West will be forced to deal with men the likes of Slobodan Milošević and Radovan Karadžić in Serbia and Serbian Bosnia (if that state manages to retain any real independence from its ethnically related neighbor for long), who personify the traditional Balkan autocratic tradition outwardly cloaked in non-Byzantine forms for Western consumption. They may speak the political language of the West, but the meaning of their words is a far cry from Western understanding. The post-1989 Romanian government, whether the Iliescu regime or that of some successor, will most likely proceed along Phanariote lines, exerting subtle, but forceful when necessary, intimidation on the population to maintain power and to suppress its Westernized Hungarian minority. In Bulgaria, the one Orthodox country in the Balkans in which no strong political personality has yet emerged since the demise of communism, the government appears doomed to flounder in ineffectual political limbo until such an individual is found.

If change to true and effective Western-style liberal democracy is to occur throughout Eastern European civilization, it will require not months or years but decades, perhaps even a century or more, of unbroken, persistent, and determined cultivation on the part of the East Europeans themselves, aided by continuous and effective Western support. Such a change is traumatic and exceedingly difficult to accomplish, and usually disruptive for all concerned. This is so because the process involves a fundamental alteration in the very macroculture of Eastern Europe demanding the total assimilation of a foreign cultural perception. History has shown that such changes, if they take place at all, do not happen overnight: "Rome wasn't built in a day," and neither were the two European civilizations.

The very idea that Eastern European civilization *must* make the dramatic and upsetting change to Western political institutions is a cultural projection on the part of the West. A growing number of East Europeans and a few Westerners have questioned whether liberal democracy is really a necessary prerequisite for the future stability and well-being of the East European states. Every country in Eastern Europe has some would-be claimant to the pre-Communist royal throne living in exile in the West and waiting in the wings for an opportunity to return. Each monarch-in-exile has a small amount of internal popular support, whether real in political terms or merely sentimental in nature. Although the idea of a return to monarchy in Eastern Europe rubs most Westerners the wrong way (despite the existing Western constitutional, hereditary monarchies of such countries as England, Belgium, the Netherlands, and the Scandinavian states) and is repugnant to those who currently hold political power in the region, it is not beyond the realm of possibility that, should the initial attempts to establish working liberal–democratic governments fail or merely prove too politically painful, monarchies or dictatorships disguised as democracies might become less disruptive and more viable options in the eyes of peoples whose political culture is fundamentally autocratic.

A thousand years of cultural tradition cannot be swept away in one stroke merely because the West wishes it so. This is a lesson of history that events taking place today in areas around the world—not merely in Eastern Europe and in Western Eurasia—are beginning to teach us.

NATION OR *MILLET*?

● ○ ●

The clash of civilizations lies at the very core of the horrendous violence and the uncompromising animosity manifested by all sides in the most recent warfare in the Balkans. In Bosnia-Hercegovina, a territory less than half the size of the state of Pennsylvania, the cultural fault lines of three historically and mutually antagonistic civilizations—the Western European, the Eastern European, and the Islamic—converge. Localized genocide, "ethnic cleansing," organized rapine, and assorted other dehumanizing actions have been inflicted by all sides in the Bosnian war on each other with an indifference that can be explained only as stemming from authentic cultural hatred. Such venomous enmity is utterly irrational but, by being so, is close to boundless. Though it can be expressed most fundamentally only in terms of religious or ethnic animosity, it is rooted in each side's unquestioned "feeling" or "belief" that the others pose a mortal threat to some, or all, of their human sense of reality and to their own unique place within it. When warfare taps such deeply embedded reservoirs of cultural antipathy, its fury tends to transcend purely political, economic, or social constraints.

While the extreme violence of the Bosnian war has been fed by cultural antagonisms among member societies of three different civilizations, it would be a mistake to blame those animosities for starting or for pursuing the fighting. The war was begun and fought for political reasons. Yet even in these, there were underlying cultural factors that must be considered. These had to do with the nature of the political institutions that the warring sides espoused as their objective. Since the institutions created by every society are shaped in the image of their culture, the various sides' fight for political victory in Bosnia-Hercegovina represented a cultural struggle on a more philosophical, less personal level than the killing, raping, and "cleansing." But a cultural struggle it was nonetheless.

At issue in the political battles in Bosnia-Hercegovina—and potentially in all of the former Communist states of Eastern European civilization, whether the struggle is violent or otherwise—was the imposition of either a Western-style or a native, non-Western political structure. In fact, this remains the political issue that faces not only the newly independent states of Eastern Europe but also the entire non-Western world as the twentieth century draws to its close. But specifically for the Balkan regions of Bosnia-Hercegovina, Albania, Kosovo, Macedonia, and perhaps Bulgaria, the essential political cultural issue pits Western against Islamic forms.

Liberal democracy, industrial capitalism, and nationalism comprise the ideological trinity of Western European civilization's modern political culture. They have come to be institutionally expressed in the West's unique political creation—the nation-state. Because all four are products of Western European culture—the West's perception of political reality—few of us in the West recognize just how distinctive they truly are. Throughout the entire six thousand years of recorded history, at no time and in no place other than in the core area of Western European civilization has any human society spawned a native political culture in exactly these terms. The Athenians of ancient Greece, whom we like to hold up as classical political ancestors of the West, never developed a comprehensive capitalistic economic philosophy; they essentially were farmers and traders. Athenian democracy was extremely limited in its franchise to the point that it more closely resembled an oligarchy than anything else. Since only the relatively few in Athens' population with voting privileges were considered citizens of the state, while all the rest of the city's inhabitants were political, and often social, nonentities, there was no trace of nationalism present, at least as we know it. Without nationalism, there was no sense of nation; the state was the city of Athens and its environs. Athens may have been a Greek city-state, but it was not Greece.

A similar analysis leading to similar conclusions can be made of Rome, the West's other cultural ancestor. Granted, Rome developed from a city-state into a large world-state, but for that very reason it did not represent a nation-state as we know it. Rome was an empire ruled first by an oligarchy (under restricted republican forms) and then by an emperor-autocrat. Its inhabitants were subjects (despite their official designation as citizens) and multicultural in the extreme (with no true sense of common nationality). Rome's economy was agricultural and mercantile, not consciously capitalistic. Athens and Rome may have been the cultural parents of Western European civilization, but they definitely did not evolve the political culture of their offspring. When the most closely related civilization to the Western European—Hellenic civilization— failed to create political institutions resembling it, one cannot expect such development in civilizations even farther removed in culture, such as the Islamic, Indic, Mesopotamian, or Far East Asian. The West's political culture is its own unique creation.

The roots of that culture lie in the West's medieval struggle between the temporal (secular monarchies) and the spiritual (the papacy) leaderships in society for supreme worldly authority, begun when Pope Leo III crowned the Frank king Charlemagne emperor of a West-centered Holy Roman Empire in 800. Through investiture conflicts and outright military combat, Western society was dominated for the next five hundred years by the spiritual authority of Rome. Papal grasp on political supremacy was loosened in the early fourteenth century when the French king Philip IV the Fair (1294-1314) imposed on the papacy the so-called Avignon Captivity, which first overtly exerted the strength of the temporal power, in the guise of regional (some scholars like to use the word "national") secular rulers, over the spiritual. Despite its ability to break free from direct temporal control after some seventy years, and thereafter to continue asserting its claim to political supremacy in the West, the papacy never recovered completely from the political blow inflicted on it by the French monarchy.

The Protestant Reformation initiated by the German monk Martin Luther in 1515 further undermined the claims to temporal authority made by the papacy. While the Reformers may originally have been sincere in their religious beliefs, the success of their cause was the result of the political ambitions held by regional rulers who allied themselves with the Reformation to entrench their temporal authority against the claims of the weakened papacy. The real importance of the Reformation for Western European civilization was not the reform of Christianity but the decisive victory of the temporal over the spiritual authority in its political culture. One need only consider the "reform" of the church in England by King Henry VIII (1509-47)—who, through royal decree, successfully transformed the former Roman Catholic church organization in his realm into an English state church ruled by the secular monarch simply because of a dispute with the papacy over his right to marry and divorce in the interests of his kingdom and dynasty—to understand the true significance of the Reformation for the West.

A century and a half of religious-political warfare in Western Europe, initiated by the Reformation, was needed to finalize the secular authority's victory in its struggle for political supremacy. By the mid-seventeenth century a new Western cultural development was under way that further undermined any possible future claims to supreme temporal leadership by the spiritual author-ities. The Scientific Revolution, spawned by such men as the Pole Nicholas Copernicus (1473-1543), the Englishman Francis Bacon (1561-1626), the Italian Galileo Galilei (1564-1642), and the German Johannes Kepler (1571-1630), and brought to full philosophical fruition by the Frenchman René Descartes (1596-1650) and the Englishman Isaac Newton (1642-1727), destroyed the Western perception of the physical universe (hence, physical real-ity) as a divinely ordained, unchanging, mystical, human-centered structure. The West had inherited that view from the classical Hellenistic models devel-oped by Aristotle and Ptolemy, the nature of which ultimately could be explained only by superstition (religious belief). The scientists substituted rational thought (mathematics) for superstition and were able to construct a phys-ical reality that conformed to the operations of universal laws, which were defined by mathematical systems that the scientists themselves designed. Despite resistance from the Christian churches and from some of the secular rulers in the West, the scientists were able to win general acceptance of their new perception of physical reality that effectively removed the divine com-ponent from the workings of the universe.

Success for the scientific point of view in Western European civilization was cemented in the eighteenth century by another cultural development given birth by the Scientific Revolution—the Enlightenment. It grew out of the intellec-tual rationalism that took root in the political thinking of the Englishman John Locke (1632-1704), as viewed in combination with the concepts of the Newtonian universe by a French intellectual, François Voltaire (1694-1778). Centered in France, the new intellectual movement begun by Voltaire was spread throughout the West by the undeniably skilled and effective writings of him-self and of such other like-minded figures as Baron de Montesquieu (1689-1755) and Denis Diderot (1713-84).

The aims of the Enlighteners were to discover and to implement universal "natural" (in conformity with nature) laws through the use of "reason" (con-structive questioning based more on experience and observation than on math-ematics) that could be applied to all aspects of human social existence, including the economic and the political. Just as Western science had elimi-nated the necessity of direct and continuous divine intervention in the opera-tion of physical reality, the natural laws sought by the Enlighteners were thought also to function independently of God's constant intercession. According to Enlightenment ideas, once these natural laws were discovered and implemented, the results would bring humankind progress (not of the spir-itual sort in the hereafter that Christianity promised, but of a material kind on earth—the first purely secular expression of this concept) that ultimately led to the "natural rights" of happiness and freedom for the individual, as well as for society in general. A human society governed by natural laws thus had no need of the traditional linkage of religion with politics, since each would be relegated to its respective and separate "natural" sphere of human endeavor, spiritual and secular. The Enlightenment gave the West its intellectual rationale for the separation of church and state.

While such ideas, especially that concerning freedom, were potentially revolutionary in a period in which the political culture was dominated by secular monarchs who justified their rule through the concept of Divine Right ("God wills it"), their explosive impact was somewhat dampened when the monarchs themselves bought into the Enlightenment by claiming to reorder the nature of their rule in conformity with certain of the natural laws espoused by the intellectuals under the guise of a public relations image characterized as Enlightened Despotism.

A new secular political culture developed in symbiotic parallel with the Enlightenment—liberal democracy. Its founder was John Locke, whose political arguments in 1690 justifying the Glorious Revolution of 1688 in England, which cemented parliamentary control over monarchical government, helped inspire Voltaire to launch the Enlightenment in the first place. Locke was the intellectual father of such concepts as government by the consent of the governed, the separation of powers within the government to ensure against despotic rule, and the right of the governed to rise up in revolution against a government that was despotic. All of these concepts were defined in a legal instrument—a contract between government and governed—called a constitution. He characterized a despotic government as one that either broke the contract or did not guarantee its governed certain "inalienable ('natural') rights" with which he declared all individuals were born: life, liberty, and property ownership. This latter right was particularly important to Locke, who defined happiness as a function of owning property, and liberty as its unfettered acquisition and defense. He considered all actions of individuals to be motivated by self-interest, which was expressed through owning property, and all social structures to be determined by its protection. Because, in Locke's view, property ownership was crucial to human political organization, it followed that his concept of government by the consent of the governed actually meant by the consent of the property owners in the state. The political ideals of Locke came to be crystallized into the Western ideology known as liberalism.

The idea that a constitution—a governing contract—was a rational and "natural" basis for government joined that of Enlightened Despotism in the political thinking of the Western European Enlighteners. But Locke's constitutional approach also made a deep impact on the political thought of a French intellectual who reacted against the pseudoscientific bent of the Enlightenment. Though influenced by it, Jean-Jacques Rousseau (1712-78) rejected its notion of reason as the dominant human characteristic in favor of emotion. He trusted in nature, but a nature that was unspoiled by the corrupting forces of civilization. His political thought encompassed a structure in which all persons were active citizens who participated in shaping the laws that governed their society. All citizens helped make the laws, and all agreed to obey them because they had helped form them. In Rousseau's eyes, this active agreement constituted human liberty. No one in such a society had the right to dominate another—there were no hereditary monarchs, no overweening church hierarchies, and no privileged nobility. There was only a society of loyal and active equals who willingly suppressed many of their personal self-interests in favor of those of the group as a whole. Rousseau held the "general will" of society paramount in his political model. That will was legally expressed in the constitution of the state founded on his premises—a social contract (the title that he gave the book in which his ideas were expressed in 1762)—that both guaranteed the individual freedoms of its citizens and delineated their collective responsibilities to the state. What Rousseau offered the West politically was a form of simple, pure, and ideal democracy.

Locke's liberalism and Rousseau's democracy were wedded together by the two late eighteenth century events that reshaped the Western European political culture into its modern form—the American and the French revolutions. The American Revolution (1775-83), with the Declaration of Independence (1776) that it issued and with the Constitution (1787) that it ultimately created, first demonstrated to the rest of the Western world that a society was capable of successfully instituting a form of government philosophically grounded in the precepts of the Enlightenment, liberalism, and democracy. But the newly established United States of America was too isolated geographically from the core area of Western European civilization's remaining societies to have a direct impact on them beyond setting an example. The decisive political upheaval in the West came only with the French Revolution (1789-99) and the French imperial wars of Napoleon Bonaparte (1799-1815).

France lay in the heart of the core region of Western Europe, so its revolution against the traditional political order in the West (the Divine Right despotism of regional monarchies) could not help but ignite violent storms of reaction among the monarchs ruling its surrounding societies. The declaration of human rights issued by the French revolutionary leadership (1789), which originally was conceived of as only a preamble to a constitution (but, as it turned out, to three successive and not very satisfactory ones), expressed all the ideals of liberalism and democracy in a more radical tone than in the American example. It sounded the tocsin for general political revolution throughout all of Western Europe. In 1792 war was declared by the French on the old political order in the West, and war continued until Napoleon found his Waterloo in 1815.

The Revolutionary and Napoleonic wars spread the ideals of liberal democracy over the length and breadth of Western Europe, even reaching into regions of Eastern European civilization (in the Balkans with the "Illyrian Provinces" [1806-13] and Russia [1812]) for short periods of time. By an ironic twist of fate, though the French were defeated on the battlefield, their political concepts ultimately emerged victorious in the West. This victory can be greatly attributed to two other cultural developments that were accelerated by the enormity of the conflict in terms of the number of people and states involved in the wars: the rise of industrialized capitalist economics and their linkage to the interests of nationalism and the nation-state.

The Industrial Revolution in Western European civilization began in England in the early years of the eighteenth century. It was sparked by rising rural productivity and the availability of ready cash for investment and consumption that resulted from improved agricultural techniques and growing British colonial enterprises. Money and markets for consumer products developed that needed only to be tapped. The opportunity was not lost on a segment of the English population that was ready-made to play the role of dedicated mass producers—the various communities of Anabaptist-type religious dissenters against the official Anglican state religion (like the Puritans and Quakers), who, by law, were excluded from all of the traditional philosophically "respectable" careers in English society (such as landholding and the government), so had been forced into the more "ignoble" monetary professions (for example, banking). It was they who refined the so-called Protestant work ethic, tying persistent and productive labor to divine order and any resulting material prosperity to divine favor. They found no better way of demonstrating God's approval of themselves and their religious beliefs than by working to satisfy the rising demands for goods that English agricultural and commercial prosperity had created.

Manufacturing operations blossomed in the English countryside, feeding on the technological developments that grew out of the Scientific Revolution. Increased goods production led to increased demand, resulting in larger production plants and expanding technologies, which, in turn, created new industries to serve the older ones. The Industrial Revolution brought about one of the most rapid social and economic transformations in human history. In less than a hundred years from its inception around 1720, every aspect of society was affected—employment, housing, transportation, urbanization, and social classes, among others—as industrialism exploded into one of the most all-encompassing forces in English society. From England, it quickly spread to the European continent, where, by the end of the eighteenth century in France and Germany, it was fast on the road toward catching up with its English parent.

Industrial capitalism found its philosophical roots in the idea of "universal natural laws" propagated by the Enlightenment and in the propertied self-interest of liberalism. In 1758 François Quesnay first publicly broached the idea that natural economic laws existed and that they should be discovered and permitted to operate without hindrance. He was followed by Adam Smith, who in 1776 "discovered" the first, and most fundamental, of such laws—that of supply and demand—and its "necessary" political corollary—laissez-faire (government noninterference). According to Smith, a society's economic well-being depended on the free and unfettered, self-interested pursuit of prosperity (profits) by each of its individual members in a competitive marketplace. Claiming to have unearthed another natural law related to supply and demand, which made population growth always more rapid than increases in food supplies, in 1798 Thomas Malthus asserted that poverty was inevitable in every society, but especially in one that was industrialized, because industrialists would always grow wealthier while their workers' wages would sink ever lower. He advocated laissez-faire with regard to governmental social assistance for the poor so that fewer poverty-stricken children would be born, thus lessening population demands on available food supplies. Finally, in 1817 David Ricardo uncovered the "iron law of wages," which viewed labor as a commodity that was bought and sold just like any other. This law, too, sprang from the fundamental precept of supply and demand: When labor (the potential work force) was abundant, it was inexpensive (low wages); when it was scarce, it was expensive (high wages). A society with a plentiful supply of labor would always experience lower levels of wages than one with fewer available workers. Once again, Ricardo advocated laissez-faire regarding wages, leaving them to Smith's law as the only "natural" thing to do.

The classical economists of industrial capitalism planted that economic system squarely within the intellectual political culture of liberal democracy, with their emphasis on individual self-interest (property and profits) and on freely operating economic laws guaranteed by a government whose primary purpose it was to protect them at all costs. Liberalism and industrial capitalism went hand in hand in an optimum partnership between politics and economics. That partnership was cemented by the wars of the French Revolution and Napoleon. The ideological nature of those wars brought about the earliest appearance of massed armies, fielded by governments on all sides. For the first time in history, every state involved in the fighting was forced to mobilize all of its available resources, on a scale previously unheard of, in its effort to gain victory. With the advent of mass military formations came the need to equip, clothe, and feed the millions of men under arms. Governments turned to the industrial sector of their societies for the necessary mass production of the materials of war. The relationships sparked by military need brought benefits to all parties involved—the wherewithal to field the required military forces for the government, profits for the industrialists, and employment for the work force. When the wars ended, far from disconnecting the relationships that had been forged, the political-economic partnership remained in place. This was primarily due to the last Western cultural development that grew out of the wars—modern nationalism and its political expression through the nation-state.

The Western European concept of nationalism—the self-identification of a group of people with a state and government distinct from all others—did not originate with the liberal democratic revolutions of the late eighteenth and early nineteenth centuries. Its roots were sunk with the emergence of regional monarchies, such as the French, English, and Spanish, in the twelfth century. The concept matured with the progressive success of the regional monarchs in throwing off papal temporal authority over the centuries that followed. But we should not confuse the nationalism of the pre-French revolutionary era with the form that is familiar to us today. None of the Western European states prior to the American and French revolutions was a nation-state—a state that supposedly delineated the territory inhabited and governed by a particular ethnic group. All were, instead, states that encompassed all the lands held subject by a particular monarchy, which governed them by means of a privileged, restrictive elite, whose justification for its existence lay in its feudal landholding past and whose numbers were small relative to the general population of the state. Only the Western European regional aristocracies, from whose ranks the monarchs sprang, had any real attachment to their states. The majority of the population in every state counted for little in the political scheme of things beyond serving as the primary source of royal and aristocratic revenues. Until the end of the eighteenth century, the word "nation" simply meant the aristocracy of a particular state, and not its general population. Thus, the English Magna Carta (1215), some modern interpretations to the contrary, was far more a reassertion on the part of the English aristocratic elite of age-old Germanic traditions of government through an assembly of notables than it was an expression of political concern for the interests of the English population as a whole. Prior to the liberal democratic American and French revolutions in Western European civilization, the nation was synonymous strictly with the nobility.

The French revolutionary and Napoleonic wars changed the nature of nationalism. The overthrow of the French monarchy, the revocation of aristocratic privileges, and the installation of liberal democratic governing forms gave the general French population a political voice and a personal stake in the state. The state thus represented the French in their totality—culturally, ethnically, politically, socially, and economically. Its borders were considered sacrosanct boundaries, within which the French people reigned supreme, free to live and govern as they chose. When the English, Austrian, and Prussian monarchies threatened to intervene militarily inside France to restore the old aristocratic regime, the French reacted with a mass rising in support of their new political order—the first time in history that the majority of the population in a Western European state had done so. French victories and their resulting territorial expansion pressured the Western monarchies into fielding ever larger armies in efforts to outman their militantly nationalistic opponents. But their efforts to defeat the new form of mass nationalism that motivated the men in the ranks of their enemy ultimately proved successful only because they too were forced to instigate that very same sort of nationalism among their own populations to increase the numbers of their military recruits. Immediately after the wars were ended, in 1815, the victorious monarchies bent all of their repressive efforts toward suppressing the nationalistic genie that they had unbottled, but to no avail. The revolutions of 1830 and 1848 pushed the Western monarchies into eventually compromising with the new nationalism and the liberal-democratic forms that were its fundamental political expression.

The aftermath of the wars, which saw in Western Europe the last attempts on the part of the traditional prerevolutionary monarchies to retain undisputed political power under a regime of state repression characterized by the Habsburg chancellor, Prince Klemens von Metternich (1809-48), spawned a new form of nationalism tied closely to the rise of Romanticism. Reacting against the devastation of the wars and the social-political regimentation imposed by the victorious monarchies, the Romantics represented a young generation of intellectuals and artists who came to blame the rationalism of the Enlightenment, which dominated the thought of the European political establishments, and the rampant materialism created by the Industrial Revolution for the situation. They rejected them and their classical Hellenic roots in favor of emotionalism and escapism—primarily into a fictionalized medieval past, a past that was dominated by human emotion (that is, religion) and that had permitted the peoples of Western Europe to express their native cultures without corruption by foreign (classical) elements.

In the Romantic view of reality, which had its intellectual roots in Rousseau, each ethnic group of people carried within itself a consciousness of its special cultural uniqueness that was fundamentally expressed through the group's common religious beliefs and, most important, its common language. For the Romantics, religion (Catholicism on the Continent, Protestantism in England) was the emotional expression of civilization and language was the key to human group self-identity—language defined "the people." To discover the true character of any people's culture, one had to know and understand the group's historical past, which could be reconstructed only by analyzing historical and linguistic evidence. In their quest to uncover the medieval origins of the various Western European peoples, the nineteenth-century Romantics gave birth to modern historical study, which required the collection and interpretation of primary source materials. They used historical documentation to validate the pasts of peoples rather than merely those of states.

The Romantics also created a completely new field of intellectual inquiry—ethnography—by their emphasis on the importance of peasant folk songs and legends as the primary vehicles for expressing any given people's native culture in its purest, most emotional form, undistorted by literary conventions or by languages spoken by neighboring, but different, ethnic groups. The tales collected and published in Germany by the Grimm brothers, Wilhelm and Jacob, or by Hans Christian Andersen in Denmark, were intended to be read as more than just interesting children's stories; they were presented to demonstrate the very soul of German or Danish culture.

It did not take long for the Romantic sense of national consciousness—the people's awareness of their common origins, language, and history—to be integrated with the military sort of nationalism created by the French revolutionary and Napoleonic wars in Western Europe. Every ethnic group of people now possessed a history and a culture of its own, with a unique past, character, territory, interests, and aspirations. The group as a whole constituted the "nation," and the role of the state created by the group was to represent and defend that uniqueness politically, socially, economically, and territorially.

Thus evolved the Western concept of the nation-state as the ultimate, most "natural" form of political organization. All aspects of human reality ideally were encompassed by its structure. The borders of the state were those that delineated the sovereign territory inhabited by a particular ethnic group (the nation), which was distinguishable from all others by its specific language, religion, dress, customs, and mores. Its liberal-democratic government, in which all members of the group had a patriotic stake but no privileged interest groups predominated, ruled in the interests of the nation and in conformity with the Enlightened natural laws that governed human reality, free of any constraints imposed by direct religious interference. Industrial capitalism, predicated on the gainful implementation of technologies rooted in science, supported and expanded the economic well-being of the nation, providing goods, profits, employment, and property for the nation, and furnished the material wherewithal to defend militarily its sovereignty against threats from foreign nations. Given the cultural evolution in the West that led to the development of the nation-state concept, by the end of the nineteenth century the societies of Western European civilization believed it truly represented the "best of all possible worlds."

Perhaps. But if it was the finest political expression of Western European cultural evolution, it most certainly also was extremely divisive and inherently violent. This became openly apparent after the middle of the nineteenth century, when the intellectual stimulus of Charles Darwin's theory of natural selection ("the survival of the fittest": *On the Origin of Species* [1859] and *The Descent of Man* [1871]), as first applied to nation-state politics by Napoleon III

(1852-70) of France and Otto von Bismarck (1862-90) of Germany, fed a series of inter-European national wars that in the twentieth century erupted into two global cataclysms and numerous local conflicts within the worldwide context of the cold war.

The Romantic notion of a nation's special cultural uniqueness implied a sense of group self-superiority, which variously could be expressed as xenophobia (the "we're-number-one" syndrome, which virtually all Western nation-states have demonstrated in some degree, in one form, or at one time or another), racism (Nazi Germany, for example), or messianism (the American claim to "Manifest Destiny," or the Soviet claim to leadership in international communism). Operating hand in hand with national self-superiority was an innate suspicion of all other national groups, which, depending on circumstances, posed potential threats to any given nation's national interests, whether they be political, economic, or territorial. From its inception, modern nationalism spawned an "Us Against Them" group mentality that ensured relations among nations would be highly competitive and often antagonistic. The highest expression of national self-superiority was possession of a sovereign nation-state, whose borders definitively delineated the territory over which the nation held dominant sway. Borders meant lines drawn on maps that reflected inviolable lines on the surface of the earth ideally separating distinct nationalities. But at no time in modern history have lines on a map neatly and definitively been able to separate any two neighboring nationalities on the actual ground. The utter inability of borders to represent an ideal, all-inclusive expression of the nation-state could not help but create bitter territorial disputes among neighboring nations, which laid claim to the persons and lands of conationals who inevitably were left living on the "wrong side" of virtually every nation-state border. This fact, the so-called national minorities problem, combined with modern nationalism's innate senses of self-superiority and suspicion of others, led to national conflict as an endemic element in the modern Western European nation-state political culture.

Romantic nationalism and the concept of the nation-state had a powerful impact on the numerous European ethnic groups of geographical Eastern Europe. At the opening of the nineteenth century, all of them were submerged within multinational (or, more accurately, anational) empires—Habsburg Austria, Russia, Prussia, and Ottoman—whose political structures were grounded in the aristocratic privileges of foreign ruling houses—the Austrian Habsburgs, the Russian Romanovs, the Prussian Hohenzollerns, and the Turkish Osmanlis. For those not German, Russian, or Turkish, political life in the empires offered no advantages, in many cases not even recognizing their existence beyond listings in tax registers. Given their political circumstances, the various European ethnic groups of Northeastern, Central-Eastern, and

Southeastern Europe formed a ready and willing audience for the emotional appeal of Western European Romantic nationalism—with its emphasis on the unique value of every ethnic group, based on its shared history and language, and on every group's "natural right" to possess a political organization—a nation-state—of its own.

Nationalism and the nation-state were the primary attributes of Western European political culture that attracted the attention and fired the blood of the subject peoples of geographical Eastern Europe. The emotional appeal of a people's value being determined by its own history and culture, and not by the past of the dominant aristocracy who controlled the states in which the people lived, proved to be an explosively revolutionary force that ultimately, by the end of 1918, would sweep away the empires of the region. The ideas of liberal democracy and industrial capitalism, while noticed, were relegated to varying subordinate levels in their priorities, depending on the recipients' own civilization and their place within it.

For example, the Western European peoples, such as the Hungarians, Czechs, Croats, and Poles, possessed a strong sense of their past history (developed to a high level—sometimes to the point of fictionalization—under Romantic influences) and long-standing political cultures rooted in premodern aristocratic nationalism and powerful noble assemblies that had not been obliterated totally by their incorporation into the multinational empires. It took little effort to adapt their past traditions to the new liberal-democratic culture of the West. Other Western peoples, such as the Slovaks, were without a history of their own because they had never developed a strong, independent premodern aristocracy to represent their national interests. To have any chance whatsoever for shaping a nation-state of their own, they were forced to resort to outright forgery in re-creating the sort of historical past that modern nationalism required. In the end, the Slovaks succeeded in achieving this only in 1993. The same can be said of the Slovenes and of the Carpatho-Ruthenians.

Only the Czechs, the Poles, and the Slovenes, of all these East European nationalities, experienced industrial development on a significant scale prior to the twentieth century, and that only because the Habsburg and Prussian monarchies thought it in their own interests. When industrialization for the rest came during the period of communism, it was rooted in ideological (the party needed "workers" to represent) rather than economic necessities. (This goes a long way toward explaining the dilapidated and environmentally destructive nature of industry in the former Communist world—the states were more concerned with politics than with workable economics or the needs of the population.)

The East European peoples of Southeastern Europe were even more attracted by the emotional linguistic and historical components of modern Western nationalism and the nation-state concept than were the Western peoples to their north. While the others at least lay under political subjection to foreign but culturally related European empires, the Balkan Europeans were subject to a state ruled by a monarchy and governed by principles rooted in a completely non-European civilization. Though the endemic national animosities that accompanied the growth of nationalism and of nation-states was hot and contentious among nations of similar civilization (among Western Hungarians and Slovaks or Croats, or Czechs and Slovaks, or Poles and Germans; or among Eastern Bulgarians and Serbs or Greeks or Romanians), and violent, often bloody between nations of Western and Eastern European civilizations (Poles and Russians; Hungarians and Romanians; or Serbs and Croats), it proved downright vicious when East European nations were pitted against Islamic peoples, who represented the completely foreign and threatening enemy of their nation par excellence.

Islam is one of the very few historical examples in which the exact dates and circumstances surrounding the origins of a civilization can be documented with some certainty. It was born during the lifetime of a single individual—that of the Prophet Muhammad (571-632), an Arab from Mecca who managed a caravan business for his wife. Until the age of forty, when God first spoke to him in the month of Ramadan through the Angel Gabriel, Muhammad was known among the tribesmen of the Mecca region not only as a trader but as a respected arbitrator, because of his common sense, intelligence, and proclivity for solitary meditation in the desert. During one of those desert retreats to Mount Arafat, outside Mecca, Gabriel first spoke the message of God to Muhammad—there was only one god, Allah (which happened to be the name given to the tribal deity of the Kuraysh, Muhammad's own tribe), and Muhammad was chosen to be His last and greatest prophet. In a succession of visitations, which lasted throughout the rest of Muhammad's life, the messenger angel continued to relate God's final revelation for the world.

God's will, as proclaimed by Muhammad, was quite simple and straightforward—all humankind must believe in one, absolute, all-powerful God, in God's last and greatest prophet, and in the inevitability of a last judgment by God of all humans who ever lived. This belief was called Islam, meaning "submission" (to the will of God) in Arabic. Those who submitted to God's will were termed Muslims ("those who submitted"). Faith (or submission) carried with it obligations in two further categories beyond faith—in devotional activities and in interpersonal relations—that together encompassed virtually every aspect of human existence. As part of the devotional duties, a Muslim was required to publicly testify to her or his faith in front of at least two witnesses; pray individually five times daily and congregationally on Fridays; fast in daylight hours during the month of Ramadan; give alms to help support the poor; and make a pilgrimage to Mecca at least once during her or his lifetime. There were five levels of activities governing a Muslim's interpersonal relations: mandatory duties, such as marriage contracts, support of families, wearing specific types of clothing, and *jihad* ("holy war")—the duty of all Muslims to fight unbelievers whenever it was legitimately proclaimed (guaranteeing all who died in it the unconditional reward of eternal paradise); recommended duties, such as setting slaves free; permitted actions, such as a male having four wives and simple, fast divorce proceedings; reprobated activities, including gambling, eating pork, drinking wine—all of which were considered hateful; and forbidden actions, such as murdering a Muslim, stealing from a Muslim, mistreating Muslim wives, female infanticide, Muslim males marrying pagans, and Muslim females not marrying Muslim males. All of these precepts were set down by Muhammad and his numerous scribes in the sacred book of divine Islamic revelation called the Koran.

Many of the revelations contained in the Koran were direct or slightly modified stories found in the Jewish Old and Christian New Testaments of the Bible. Most likely, Muhammad had become quite familiar with them from listening to numerous and often lively theological discussions in the various marketplaces of West Asia. The late sixth and early seventh centuries were a time when such matters were mundane topics of conversation among the peoples of the Byzantine Empire, which dominated the commerce of the Eastern Mediterranean region. Once his new religion was set in motion, Muhammad made efforts in the Koran to bring both Christians and Jews living in Arabia into the Islamic fold—he accepted Christ as the next to last prophet of God (second only to himself in greatness), and he related the story of his nocturnal trip to Jerusalem and back. Both efforts eventually failed. Yet Muhammad considered Jews and Christians "People of the Book" (those possessing scriptures that represented divine revelation) who had once known true belief in God but who had drifted away from it and God's precepts over time.

Besides Jewish and Christian components, the revelation in the Koran included native Arabic paganisms. There can be little doubt that Muhammad, a man renowned for his personal intelligence, realized that, so long as the Arabs remained tribally divided, they would continue to play an inferior role to the Byzantines and Persians in West Asian commercial and political life. His insight told him that the key to power in those states lay in the unifying force among their various peoples of an all-encompassing religious belief; Christianity strengthened Byzantium and Zoroastrianism did Persia. To attract Arabs to Islam, Muhammad was not above incorporating certain of the native pagan beliefs, such as the spirituality of the black meteorite—the Kaaba—in Mecca (traditionally considered sent to earth by the gods), and the existence of good and evil spirits (*jins*). In his efforts to convert his tribe and others to the new faith by any means, it was said that Muhammad, in a speech made at the Kaaba, once seemed to give the old pagan local gods the right to intercede between humans and Allah. He later disavowed those statements as being forced from him by the devil, and they were not included in the official compilation of the Koran. (These were the famous *Satanic Verses,* concerning which Salman Rushdie has had to fear for his life.)

Although Muhammad's original revelations constituted the birth of a new religion, they quickly were transformed into something much more comprehensive. For three years following the beginning of Gabriel's visitations, Muhammad unsuccessfully attempted to convert his family and other Mecca tribes to the faith of submission. The Kaaba was considered a holy pagan shrine, from which his family had grown wealthy selling goods to the pilgrims who annually flocked into Mecca to worship. Muhammad, with his constant public attacks on paganism, was bad for family business. In 622 he was forced to flee Mecca with a few devoted disciples to escape murder by the Arabs of the city. He arrived in Medina, a commercial town to the northeast, where his reputation as an arbitrator and holy man led to his swift installation as political leader by the Arab tribes of that city. His flight from Mecca to Medina—the *hijra,* meaning "the journey"—proved such a decisively crucial turning point in his life, and in the fate of Islamic civilization, that the year 622 was eventually designated the year one in the Islamic calendar. From Medina, the Prophet victoriously led his newly converted tribal forces against Mecca (630), after which the *jihad* precept of his proclaimed faith drew an ever-increasing number of Arab tribes to his banners. By the time of his death in 632, the Muslim forces under his command controlled virtually all of the Arabian Peninsula.

Muhammad was both a prophet and a political-military leader, so that, in his person, church and state were indivisibly merged. From the time of the *hijra,* Islam was both a religion and a state. Muhammad declared that Islam constituted a united community of true believers (an *umma*), in which all Muslims were members. That community was governed by the Islamic precepts spelled out in the direct revelations of God through His Prophet. The Koran was not merely the revealed will of God, it was the divinely sanctioned state legal system for the universal community of Muslims. Thus from its very origins, the Islamic state was theocratic. (It is a misnomer, because it is so biased by Western cultural perceptions, to brand as "fundamentalist" today's Muslim political movements that seek the reestablishment of religious governments within Islamic civilization. Unlike the Christian fundamentalists in the United States, who push a radical religious agenda on a government that they nevertheless consider institutionally separate—and necessarily so—the so-called radical Islamic movement simply wishes to reestablish the traditional Islamic political culture that operated among Muslim societies until forms of Western European political culture were imposed on them by the victorious powers of the West following World War I.) The Islamic state was welded together by a common religious belief, a common language—Arabic—forged by Muhammad to write down the revelations of God, and by a common set of laws.

When Muhammad died, the divine revelations ceased and Islam was deemed complete. But he left behind a large and dynamic Islamic state for which many areas of law remained ill defined or were completely untouched by the Koran. Because Islamic religious law was a matter crucial to the state, the legal profession, which comprised the most literate and skilled religious leadership, was forced to find ways of filling the gaps. They turned to examining the stories of Muhammad's life—his words and actions—to extrapolate how he might have ruled in a given situation not specifically covered in the Koran. Eventually six collections of such stories, termed the traditions (*sunna*) of the Prophet, were accepted as canonical (*sunni*) by the Islamic community, and a school of legal thought grew up around each of the collections. Every individual item covered by the traditions was called a *hadith* ("saying"). The Koran and the books of collected sayings together came to constitute the main sources for both Islamic theology and Islamic state jurisprudence. They were collectively termed the *sheriat* ("sacred law").

In examining the life and significance of Muhammad, one might be tempted to view him as a cross between Christ and Emperor Constantine I, but the analogy really does not hold up under close scrutiny—Christ was considered a god by his followers, a divinity to which neither Muhammad nor his followers ever laid claim; and although Constantine played an important role in the Christian church, he was never considered an integral part of the church hierarchy. In a truly telling analogy, one cannot help but be struck with the similarities Muhammad shared with the far more legendary Jewish prophet Moses, whom we think lived around 1400-1200 B.C. Both men directly received divine revelations informing them of God's will for humankind after spending extended periods alone in the desert. (The overwhelmingly vast and desolate nature of the desert environment goes a long way in helping to explain why all of the world's great monotheistic religions—Judaism, Christianity, and Islam— were born in one general area of West Asia.) Both were products of disunited, nomadic and seminomadic West Asian tribal societies, to whom they both brought political and legal unity through the imposition of a set of divinely decreed sacred laws. Both thus forged dynamic theocratic states, whose borders reflected the territories in which their respective church-state held sway and whose governments claimed divine will for their forcible expansion. And, unlike the Christian European worlds, in both of which the separation of church and state ultimately led to the identification of different human societies in nonreligious terms—ethnic or national groups—the Jewish and Islamic worlds persisted in recognizing as fundamental only religious differences among peoples.

The internal unity and innate dynamism of the religious state forged by Muhammad were instrumental in creating one of the most explosively expansive empires known to history. United in faith and eager to spread it and its divinely ordered state throughout the known world, the militant Arab tribes joined together under the green banner of the Prophet and swept out of the Arabian desert wastes into the territories of the Byzantine and Persian empires. Within little more than a decade of Muhammad's death, the Muslim Arabs had conquered all of Iraq and Iran, destroying a Persian Empire that had been fatally weakened by a crushing defeat suffered at the hands of the Byzantines in 628. During the same period of time, the Arabs had wrested the Syrian, Palestinian, and Egyptian provinces away from a Byzantine Empire that had found itself nearly as exhausted by the late Persian wars as its defeated enemy, and which was then also wracked by internal Christian heresy. The majority in the population of the lost provinces held to the Monophysite belief that Christ was not truly human but a divine apparition who only looked human. The Byzantine government in Constantinople, which was Nicæan in belief, tended to discriminate against and even to persecute the heretics to such an extent that the conquering Arabs were often welcomed as liberators by the population, many of whom rapidly converted to Islam since its simple and categorical monotheism made more sense to them than the complexities of the Christian Trinity. Moreover, as "People of the Book," those heretics who did not convert found their Muslim conquerors far more tolerant of their beliefs than their former Byzantine Orthodox governors.

By the middle of the eighth century, the Arabs had swept over all of North Africa and entered Europe, capturing nearly all of the Spanish Peninsula and threatening the heart of France. Only the defenses of Constantinople stopped a similar European incursion by way of the Balkans. In the East by the mid-eighth century, the Muslim warriors had carried their banners into Central Asia—today's Turkmenistan, Uzbekistan, Tajikistan, and Pakistan—and into the Punjab and Kashmir regions of India. These eastern conquests, combined with those in the West, created one of the largest, most ethnically diverse imperial states in the world at the time. It was cemented together by common religious belief, sacred law, and the sacred Arabic literary language. Most of those within its borders who did not convert to Islam found their Muslim masters relatively tolerant of their beliefs because of the Koranic concepts of "Peoples of the Book" and interpersonal hospitality and fairness.

One might glance at a map showing the extent of the Islamic Empire of the eighth and ninth centuries and come away with a false sense of its political realities. The empire seems so vast and so unified that one wonders how the Europeans were able to withstand the militant Muslim pressures on their territories. In this case (and in many cases, one might add), the map is deceiving.

Almost from its inception, the Islamic state suffered from a number of innate weaknesses. First and foremost was its origins in the life of a man who was both prophet and king ruling through divine revelation. At Muhammad's death, his followers were faced with the sticky problem of determining who would serve as his successor. How did one legitimately succeed a leader who ruled as the last Prophet of God? The Arabs' attempts to solve this problem demonstrated an obvious vulnerability in a society that was totally theocratic—any political differences must, of necessity, find a religious expression, and vice versa. Within twenty years of Muhammad's death, the Islamic world experienced its first civil war over the succession question, and the split between the two warring sides has remained to the present day.

The first two successors (*khalifs*) of Muhammad were members of his Hashimite family clan, related to him by either birth or marriage. When the position became open for the third time, in 644, Ali, Muhammad's cousin and son-in-law, was pitted against Osman, member of the Umayyad family clan and husband to two of Muhammad's daughters. Osman was elected but was eventually assassinated by Ali's supporters (656), upon which Ali assumed the khalifate. A blood feud erupted between Ali's faction and the Umayyads that lasted throughout his five-year rule. He was assassinated in his turn by a disaffected follower in 661, and the position of *khalif* passed firmly into Umayyad hands. Ali's party refused to accept this decision and instead held to a belief in the legitimate succession through Ali and his son, Husayn, who was killed by Umayyad forces in 680. In those events were born the two major political-religious branches of Islam—the Sunnis (accepters of the Umayyad succession to the khalifate, who constitute the majority within the Islamic world) and the Shi'ites (upholders of the succession through Ali and Husayn, who have built a religious cult around the bloody events of their lives).

Internal political-religious strife was complicated by another source of divisiveness that the Islamic world never succeeded in overcoming. Despite the unifying overlay of the Islamic concept of a single community, Arab society remained essentially tribal at the grass-roots level. The victorious Arab Islamic armies were tribal in organization and led by traditional tribal leaders. As the empire they created grew larger, the tribal commanders developed into local governors ever more removed geographically from the capital city of the *khalifs,* whether that lay in Mecca, Damascus, or, later, in Baghdad. They assumed growing political autonomy within the regions they controlled, their authority reinforced by the long distances separating them from the recognized center of Islamic power. Regional government basically became divided along tribal lines. Thus, traditional Arabic tribalism, even clothed in the mantle of Islam, prevented the vast Islamic Empire from developing a highly centralized state system. Furthermore, it proved a continual basis for local rebellions against the khalifate, for interregional conflicts, and for the formation of religious splinter movements within Islam, whether Sunni or Shi'ite. There arose within the Islamic Empire a number of essentially independent tribal states, such as the Umayyad Moorish state of Spain and the Fatimid state of Egypt and North Africa. Even today divisions among the various Islamic countries are, at their roots, more fundamentally tribal than national in nature (for instance, the Iraqi-Kuwaiti conflict, the late Lebanese civil war, or the inability of the West Asian and North African Muslim states to coordinate political and economic activities).

Although Islam did not officially recognize nonreligious differences among peoples, another problem was caused by the tendency of the original Arab leadership to favor Arab Muslims over non-Arab Muslim converts by granting the former tax privileges and priority in government and military service. During the early years of the conquests, the Arabs who settled within the newly won lands remained apart from the indigenous populations, in a manner similar to that of the original Germanic invaders in the Western Roman Empire. It took decades for this attempted ethnic isolation to break down through a slow process of intermarriage and active opposition on the part of indigenous converts. But once the ethnic barriers began to collapse, the Islamic ruling class underwent a rapid process of cultural assimilation. In 660 the Umayyads transferred their capital from Mecca to Damascus, located in the heart of former Byzantine territory in West Asia. Faced with the problems of governing a vast empire and possessing little of the necessary bureaucratic experience, the Islamic rulers soon adapted Byzantine systems. Under the "People of the Book" precept, protection (*zimma*) against persecution was offered the Christian and Jewish populations in Syria, many of whom were permitted to enter Umayyad government service. Through Damascus, Arabic Islamic culture received a welcome transfusion of Hellenic culture.

Such a situation caused a reaction within the ranks of the more zealous Muslim Arabs in the empire, which was exacerbated by declining military fortunes against their Byzantine Christian enemies. In the mid-eighth century, the Abbasid Arab family in Iraq raised a successful rebellion against the Umayyads of Damascus, assisted by Shi'ites who were given, as it turned out, empty promises of toleration by the Sunni rebel leaders. In 762 the Abbasid *khalifs* established their new capital at Baghdad, with the result that, despite the ethnic Arab ideology of the rebels, the new seat of government experienced a cultural assimilation similar to that of Damascus before it, only in this case the adapted culture and new government personnel were Persian. The influx of Hellenic and Persian cultures into the Islamic world raised the level of the Arabs' originally Semitic culture to that of a civilization. Fortunately for Islam, the essential ingredients of the original Muhammadan culture were able to assimilate the powerful influences of Hellenism and Persianism to emerge from the process strengthened and still dominant. But by the close of the eighth century, it was obvious that Arab ethnic leadership in the Islamic world was mostly nominal in the face of the empire's non-Arab majority in population and culture.

This fact hit home in the mid-eleventh century when Arab leadership in the Islamic Empire was completely overthrown by relatively new converts to Islam—the Turks. They originally entered the Islamic world as slaves (an accepted fate for pagans or other "unbelievers" captured in battle by Muslim forces) acquired by the Muslims during the constant border warfare along the empire's Central Asian frontiers. Renowned for their military prowess, the captured Turks were converted to Islam and then formed into highly effective slave armies and guard units by their Arab masters, who used the Turks' natural combativeness first to supplement and then to supplant the Arab tribal forces, the members of which were steadily growing sedentary and complacent with their privileges and wealth. There evolved within the Islamic Empire a large praetorian force of powerful and increasingly wealthy Turkish slave forces who, by the eleventh century, realized that they, and not the Arabs, were the true strength of the Islamic state. In 1055 the Arab *khalif* of Baghdad was removed and a Turkish sultan, Tuğrul Bey, installed, who assumed the traditional authority of the *khalif* within the portion of the Islamic world that the Turkish rebels, known as the Selcuks, succeeded in controlling. The Islamic Empire was shattered by the event, with the peripheries dividing into component Arabic tribal states while the Turks commanded the important core territories of West Asia.

The fervently devout Selcuk Turks reinvigorated Islamic militancy. Their incursions into the Byzantine Empire and their more stringent dealings with the Christians of Syria and Palestine helped spark the unsuccessful Crusading movement in Europe. So completely did they transform the ethnic demography of Anatolia, which they wrested from Byzantium after the Battle of Manzikert (1071), from Greek to Turkish that the area has borne the name Turkey to the present day. But the Selcuks too grew sedentary and complacent in turn. They were replaced as leaders of the West Asian Islamic world during the fourteenth century by a new Turkish force recently brought into Anatolia to serve as the principal border guards against declining Byzantium—the Ottoman Turks.

The name Ottoman is a Western corruption of the Turkish, which derived from that of their original tribal leader (*emir*), Osman I (1281-1324). He ruled the principality closest to Byzantium and Europe in the Selcuk state, and he pursued unrelenting warfare against the Christians directly across his borders. This soon attracted to his standard a swelling number of warriors from all parts of the Selcuk world eager to fight for expanding the territories of Islam in the tradition of the *jihad*. (Such men were known as *gazis* and came from numerous Turkish tribes, so that Osman's state quickly acquired a multi- or nontribal character, with loyalty to the house of Osman replacing any strictly tribal allegiances.) By his death, the Byzantines were completely expelled from Anatolia, and under his son and immediate successor, Orhan I (1324-60), the Ottomans (as we collectively may call the assorted warriors and allies of the house of Osman) permanently established themselves in Southeastern Europe. Their military successes against the European Christians stretched in an unbroken string through two and a half centuries under the leadership of an unprecedented succession of ten consecutive rulers, each exceptionally endowed with superb military and political talents. Unfortunately for the Ottomans, with the death of the last, and greatest, of those sultans, Süleyman I the Magnificent (1520-66), and the succession by his son, whose character aptly fit his descriptive title, Selim II the Sot (1566-74), their empire experienced an equally dramatic three hundred years of decline. Under the misguidance of rulers who often equaled their illustrious, able ancestors in the opposite characteristic of incompetence, the Ottoman Empire sank to the level of the "sick man of Europe" by the middle of the nineteenth century.

During most of the period of Ottoman ascension (the fourteenth through the fifteenth centuries), the empire was predominantly non-Muslim in the religious belief of its subjects and non-Turkish in its subjects' ethnic composition. Except for its Anatolian homelands, the territory controlled by the Ottomans until the beginning of the sixteenth century lay in Southeastern Europe, and its population was predominantly Christian. Even with the conquest of Muslim Syria, Palestine, Egypt, and parts of North Africa by Sultan Selim I the Grim (1512-20), the empire's European provinces remained politically and economically important, and their Christian population constituted some 40 percent of all Ottoman subjects. Such a situation presented the Muslim rulers with certain problems related to their ability to govern the European territories, since the law of the land was Islamic sacred law, and that was considered valid for Muslims alone. Even when the Ottoman Empire continued to expand into the predominantly Muslim regions of Iraq and western North Africa during the rest of the sixteenth century, thus increasing the Muslim subject population of the empire, the problem of governing non-Muslims remained.

The Ottomans could draw on past tradition dating back to the time of the Prophet in attempting to deal with the problem of non-Muslim subjects. The precepts of "People of the Book" and the extension to them of "protection" (so long as they recognized the political supremacy of the Islamic rulers and did nothing to impinge upon the glory of the true faith) had been maintained by Umayyad, Abbasid, and Selcuk regimes. The "protected ones" (*zimmis*), as Christian and Jewish subjects were known under the precepts, were forced to pay certain special taxes to the government that Muslim subjects did not, such as the head tax (*cizye*) levied on the male heads of all households and the land-use tax (*haraç*), which under the Ottomans came to be extended to all peasant subjects no matter their religion. Certain social and legal restrictions were placed on the "protected" peoples, such as regulations on the types, textiles, and colors of clothing; the size and height of religious buildings; the ownership of horses and weapons; and ability to give testimony in legal proceedings involving Muslims.

In addition to the traditional restrictions affiliated with "protected" status, the Balkan Christian subjects of the Ottoman Empire were made liable to a child levy (*devşirme*), which was a periodic collection of Christian male children between the ages of seven and fourteen, conducted at intervals of one to seven years, depending on the manpower needs of the Ottoman central government. Only youths demonstrating physical or intellectual promise were chosen. They were then marched off to Anatolia, where they were converted into fanatical Muslims and given the best possible available training to fill posts in all levels of the government bureaucracy or to serve either in the ranks of the famous Ottoman standing infantry force—the Janissaries—or in the sultan's guard cavalry—the Sipahis of the Porte. All of the children collected by *devşirme* were considered enslaved, owned by the office of the Ottoman sultan.

A unique facet of Ottoman government was the fact that, while the empire was in its ascendancy, all of the personnel in the bureaucracy, from the highest administrative office to the lowest, were the household slaves of the sultan, who held over them the absolute power of life and death. This made the government of the Ottoman Empire the most centralized and efficient state administration known from the fourteenth through the mid-sixteenth century. Since Islamic sacred law forbade the enslavement of fellow Muslims, the Ottoman government was overwhelmingly staffed by slaves who originally were Christians. Lest a too prejudicial image be made, however, it should be borne in mind that slavery in the Ottoman context little resembled that of the American South—there were no whips, chains, or other degrading aspects involved. Entry into the sultan's slave household opened the door to immense power, wealth, social position, and public honor for any slave with the natural abilities and dedication to rise through the bureaucratic or military ranks. Every government and standing military office was filled strictly on the basis of individual merit, with no regard whatsoever given to birth status or social position, as was the case among the European societies at the time. Only slaves of the sultan were entrusted with the workings of the government and the highest military commands. To be a slave of the sultan was to possess the opportunity to rise as far as skill and ability would permit. For as long as the sultans were capable rulers and generals able and willing to exert their absolute authority over their slave household, the empire thrived. When the system began to break down in the mid-sixteenth century, with jealous born-Muslims forcing or bribing their way into government and military offices, thus loosening the absolute authority of increasingly inept or disinterested sultans and escalating internal corruption, the Ottoman Empire slipped into irredeemable decline, and the situation of its non-Muslim subjects deteriorated.

During the fourteenth-century period of Ottoman expansion into the Balkans, the Christians of the region were plagued by internecine wars among the various Christian states of Byzantium, Serbia, and Bulgaria. Their populations were burdened with rising semifeudal oppression, economic disruption, and unstable living conditions caused by nearly a century of constant warfare. As the territories captured by the Turks expanded, and it became clear that they were in Europe to stay, many Christian rulers and their subordinate warrior nobility joined the Ottomans as allies, in efforts to retain their political and social positions. Christian Bulgarians and Serbs fought loyally in the Ottoman ranks during most of the military campaigns that won control of the Balkans for the Turks, including that which resulted in the famous Battle of Kosovo (1389), when Serbia definitively was broken as an independent state. Bulgaria and Serbia were incorporated directly into the empire only after certain of their rulers and nobles had reneged on avowed alliances with the Turks.

The administrative system that the Ottomans imposed on their European territories was that of a statewide military compound, in line with the Turks' Islamic perception of their empire as God's military machine for expanding the domains of the "true believers" at the expense of the "infidels" of the world. Istanbul (the former capital of Byzantium, Constantinople), captured in 1453, served as capital and military headquarters for the supreme commander, the sultan. The provinces of the empire were structured as encampments reflecting the Ottoman military organization, with civil and military authority concentrated in the hands of the commanders on the various levels. The European and Asian lands constituted two separate wings (or corps) of the army, and their military commanders were the chief provincial administrators. Under their authority were a number of banners (*sancaks*), analogous to large regiments in Western military terminology, which, in turn, were comprised of a number of companies (*kazas*). Both also were governed by subordinate officers who possessed military and civil authority. Each provincial military-administrative district was required to provide a set number of cavalrymen (*sipahis*) when the sultan declared a campaign. While the provincial cavalry formed the bulk of the Turkish military force, the slave Janissary and guard cavalry of the sultan served as its disciplined, and tactically decisive, shock units. The provincial cavalry was supported by a pseudofeudal system of land tenure. Unlike the medieval Western feudal system that entailed ownership of the land and of its peasant serfs by the knight warriors, the Ottoman provincial support system did not grant any ownership rights to the Turkish warriors. All land conquered by the Turkish forces was considered the personal property of the sultan. To maintain the numerous troops under his supreme command with little recourse to the state treasury (which, in actuality, constituted his personal coffers), the sultan granted his provincial authorities and warriors the rights to collect all or a share, dependent on their military rank, of the taxes due from the inhabitants on parcels of most of the land, distributed throughout the empire, in return for military service. The amount of income granted was set down in a document issued by the sultan's central government. If a recipient did not meet the military requirements, the government was free to revoke the grant and give it to another warrior. An Ottoman military "fief" was thus strictly financial in nature and involved no direct ownership of land or peasants (except for a rather small parcel intended to be used for the holder's personal sustenance). The peasants included under this arrangement, the majority of whom in the European provinces were Christians, retained their personal freedom and, for all practical purposes, ownership of their personal plots.

For as long as the sultans and the slave administration remained strong, this system ensured that the lot of the non-Muslim population of the empire was far better than that enjoyed by their Western European counterparts. In return for tilling their fields and paying their taxes, they were left fairly unmolested by their Muslim overlords. They possessed a considerable amount of local autonomy in regulating the mundane affairs of their lives, and, as protected "People of the Book," they were permitted to worship in the Christian faith of their forefathers. The Ottoman Turks were originally known for their commonsense approach toward building and governing their empire. They realized that the economic and military strength of the state depended on the ability of their conquered subjects to produce the necessary agricultural, craft, and monetary resources. The non-Muslims needed to be protected and husbanded so they could be shorn of revenues and goods on a regular basis to maintain the well-being of Ottoman Islamic society in general. The Turks referred to their peasant population as *reaya,* which means a flock of sheep with this very connotation. Sheep they may have been, but their personal freedom and less burdensome tax and labor obligations to the state and local authorities proved a magnetic draw upon hundreds of serfs who flocked into the Ottoman Empire during the fifteenth and sixteenth centuries from Hungary, Croatia, Austria, and Poland to escape the onerous burdens of peasant life in Western Europe.

The problem of administratively integrating this important non-Muslim segment of the empire's subject population into the theocratic Islamic Ottoman state was definitively solved by Sultan Mehmed I the Conqueror shortly after his conquest of Constantinople in 1453. If the Islamic sacred law of the state could be applied only to Muslims, then Mehmed reasoned that the religious laws of the non-Muslims would serve well to govern legally those respective groups. Using the "People of the Book" precept as his justification, Mehmed's solution to the problem was to institutionalize further the theocratic nature of Islamic political culture by dividing his subject population into *millets* ("nations"), based solely on religious affiliation, and administered by the highest religious authorities of each. All non-Muslims in the empire were officially distributed among three *millets,* representing the three most important non-Muslim faiths existing among the subject population: the Orthodox Christians, headed by the patriarch of Constantinople and representing the single largest, and therefore most important, group of non-Muslims; the Jews, who were of great commercial significance for the Turks, headed by an elected representative of the rabbinical council in Istanbul; and the Armenians, headed by an Armenian patriarch of Istanbul appointed by the sultan, who also came to represent any Roman Catholic subjects of the Turks. The first *millet* officially founded was that of the Orthodox Christians in 1454, one year after the fall of Constantinople. The Armenian *millet* was recognized in 1461, while the Jewish *millet* did not officially come into being until 1839, although a Jewish representative to the Ottoman court was chosen by Mehmed himself in 1453 and the practice was continued by the Istanbul Jewish community thereafter.

Each *millet* was responsible for representing its membership before the Ottoman court and for its own internal administration. They all were granted the rights to tax, judge, and order the lives of their respective members insofar as those rights did not conflict with Islamic sacred law and the sensibilities of the Muslim ruling establishment. The religious hierarchies of the *millets* were thus endowed by the Turkish central authorities with civil responsibilities beyond their ecclesiastical duties, and their head prelate was held accountable by the Turks for the proper functioning of their internal affairs. In effect, each *millet,* personified by its religious administrators, became an integral part of the empire's domestic administration, functioning as a veritable department of the Ottoman central government. In return for ensuring the smooth administration of its non-Muslim subjects, the sultan's government granted each *millet* a considerable amount of autonomy in the spheres of religious devotion and cultural activity, judicial affairs not involving Muslims, and in local self-government.

Although the term *millet* involved the idea of "nation" in the Turkish language, it shared little in common with the Western concept of nationality. In the first place, it identified people solely on the basis of their religion; ethnicity played no role. Both the Armenian and Jewish *millets* were defined by belief, despite their names' apparent modern ethnic connotations. As far as the Ottomans were concerned, Armenians were those non-Muslims who adhered to a form of the Monophysite Christian heresy that had arisen centuries earlier in an Armenian state that no longer existed. It was the religion, not the ethnicity, that was important in the Turks' definition of the *millet*. The same could be said for the Jews. With respect to the Orthodox Christians, the Turks made no distinctions among Greek, Bulgarian, Serbian, or Romanian Orthodox believers. They all were lumped together in a single *millet*, even though it is certain that the Turks were aware that ethnic differences did exist among them. Given the theocratic nature of Islam and the Islamic state, ethnicity was thought to be relatively unimportant in the fundamental scheme of reality for the Muslim Turkish rulers. It made little difference to them that the head of the Orthodox *millet* was, and would remain, a Greek. In the second place, by eliminating all consideration of ethnicity, the *millet* identification entirely lacked the territoriality associated with the Western concept of the nation. No matter where one lived within the empire, no matter how mixed the population, *millet* affiliation governed one's life. Neighbors could be Muslims, Orthodox Christians, Jews, or Armenians, and that fact did not lead to national animosity and territorial disputes among them because all were members of their own self-contained administrative systems, complete unto themselves, with no claims whatsoever on the others. For all the subjects of the Ottomans, their homeland was anywhere within the borders of the empire. This fact led to increasingly mixed ethnic populations throughout the Balkans, especially in regions where the traditional homelands of different ethnic groups lay side by side (for instance, in northern Macedonia, where Bulgarians and Serbs rubbed elbows, or in southern Macedonia, where Greeks and Bulgarians met).

By the seventeenth century, the absolute authority of the sultan, on which the entire stability of the state structure was dependent, had begun to decline with the onset of successively inept holders of the office. The effects of this loss of authority at the center were magnified by disruptive external and internal pressures. Western European technologies played havoc on the tradition-bound Islamic approach to state reality. Naval developments in the West ushered in the Age of Discovery, beginning in the sixteenth century, which opened sea routes to the necessary and lucrative spice trade with Far East Asia, circumventing the Ottoman middlemen who had controlled such commerce in the past. Gold and silver from the Americas flooded the eastern Mediterranean markets of the empire, causing rapid inflation, higher taxes, and an explosive rush for cash on all levels of Ottoman society. Moreover, in the seventeenth century, Western military gunpowder technologies transformed the weaponry and tactics of warfare, to which the Ottomans, holding fast to the traditional military approaches that had served them so well in the past, were slow to respond. The result was the end of Ottoman military dominance in Eastern Europe and the onset of ever-greater ignominious defeats in battles with "infidel" Christian enemies. Western European states, such as France and England, were able to force on the Turks treaties—the nature of which was reflected in their titles: capitulations—that placed nearly all of the empire's trade relations and profits in their own hands. Militarily antiquated and economically strangled, the empire ceased to expand, and, following the disastrous second Ottoman siege of Vienna in 1683, it was forced into gradual, but perpetual, contraction in Southeastern Europe.

Lacking the bedrock of the sultan's strong central authority, the declining economic and military fortunes of the empire led to the breakdown of internal order. The slave household government was disbanded in favor of selling offices to the highest bidders in efforts to bring more increasingly valueless currency into the central treasury. The need for additional state revenues resulted in the resort to tax-farming, with its heinous financial oppression of the lowly taxpayers. State lands, formerly not bestowed as military fiefs, were sold off as private property to high-ranking administrators and commanders, who converted their holdings into income-producing estates. In addition, a growing number of provincial cavalrymen took advantage of the increasing ineffectiveness of the central government to cast off their military obligations and illegally transform their conditional holdings into private estates. This situation, in turn, resulted in the rise of provincial banditry among those troops who either lost their lands to more powerful warriors or could no longer expect to win holdings from newly conquered regions. The central government was forced to depend on its paid standing Janissary forces, which meant drastically increasing their strength. The ranks of the Janissaries swelled with the influx of born-Muslims, who bribed their way into the ranks and who possessed little inclination for military discipline, often making or breaking sultans at their whim. The state treasury thus was forced to pay the salaries of an increasing number of worthless troops. And so the fiscal conditions of the empire were caught in a constant downward spiral.

The non-Muslim population was forced to foot the lion's share of the bill through exorbitant taxes. Many Muslims considered their Western Christian enemies to be the cause of the problems, so, during the eighteenth and early nineteenth centuries, disgruntled Janissaries, bandit troopers, and local Turkish authorities were not above venting their frustrations over the worsening state of the empire on the Christian subjects close at hand. Banditry and local anarchy grew commonplace, and the Christian subjects were exposed to rising bouts of violence. The pretexts for the adoption of Western European national concepts by the Ottomans' subject Christian populations lay in the burgeoning chaos within the empire during the eighteenth century, and in the inability to overcome the anarchy and effectively to modernize in the Western mold during the nineteenth.

The nationalist contentions of all the Balkan Christian peoples (Bulgarians, Serbs, Greeks, Macedonians, Montenegrins, and Romanians) paint a picture of Ottoman rule in Southeastern Europe as one long period of oppression, degradation, and enslavement—they call it the "Ottoman yoke." But the five hundred-year "yoke" was mostly myth. Until the West definitively gained the military and economic upper hand over the Turks at the end of the seventeenth century, the lot of the Balkan Christians within the empire was better than that enjoyed by most of the general populations in Western European states. Certain of them, especially the Greeks, enjoyed lucrative privileged political and commercial status—they controlled the Orthodox *millet,* played a dominant role in foreign trade, and monopolized most Ottoman diplomatic and foreign affairs offices of state. While the very ideas of a child levy and state slavery strike Westerners and Westernized Europeans as repugnant, it should be noted that many Christian mothers begged the local Ottoman authorities to take their sons because they realized it was the only avenue open to non-Muslims to social and political advancement and the attendant possibilities of untold wealth, prestige, and power. (Many levied children later remembered their families and regions of origin by extending to them preferential treatment.) Although every Balkan Christian national myth includes frightening images of conversions to Islam forced on them by the Turks, in reality thousands of Christians voluntarily made the decision to change faith to gain local economic or social benefits, such as reduced taxes or acquisition of careers not normally open to Christians, such as law. Certainly there existed scattered local cases of forced conversions, especially during the period of decline, but those same conditions also contributed to increased voluntary conversions as well. Converts to Islam removed themselves from their *millets;* therefore they were lost to the only mechanism available for expressing non-Muslim group self-identity. As far as their former *millet* compatriots were concerned, the converts became "Turks."

It was, after all, the *millet* system of Ottoman administration that permitted non-Muslims in the empire to retain and develop their individual sense of ethnic self-awareness. Free to practice their faiths and cultivate their religious cultures, they naturally came to identify with their religion and the form of language used in their devotions. As early as the seventeenth century, the Slavic Orthodox Christians (Bulgarians and Serbs) were aware that, although they were Orthodox, they did not speak the same language as did the Greek church hierarchy that controlled the *millet.*

As the empire declined and the lot of the non-Muslims deteriorated, the Western nationalist concepts that seeped into the Balkans from across the frontiers with Austria and Russia were first digested within the context of the *millet*. When the Serbs rose in revolt (1804-13), they were reacting against local atrocities perpetrated on the Christians of the Belgrade region by that city's undisciplined Janissary garrison. The Serbs claimed to be acting in the interests of the Ottoman sultan when their rebel forces defeated his unruly and anarchistic provincial governor, who was terrorizing faithful members of the Orthodox *millet,* and thus acting to restore central control over the region. Only when the weak central government proved unable to reassert its direct authority in the region and local Turkish anarchy again prevailed did the Serbs, now infected by Western nationalist ideas spread to them by fellow Serbs north of the Danube, resurrect their rebellion as an ultimately successful national struggle (1815-30) for autonomy, and finally complete independence (1878) from the Turks.

As for the Greeks, though their War of Independence (1821-31) was instigated by nationalist firebrands in Russian military service, the masses of the Greek population who fought the war were reacting against rising local Turkish anarchy. Their goal was to win self-rule for the Greek speakers of the Orthodox *millet*. Rising Greek nationalism, brought to mainland Greece by expatriates living in merchant communities in the West and in Russia, and reinforced by numerous romantic Western philhellenes who poured into Greece as rebel volunteers, laid claim to all regions in the Balkans existing under the *millet* authority of the Greek patriarch of Constantinople. Later the Greek nationalists came to claim the reestablishment of a Greek-dominated Byzantine Empire as their primary aim, but their tactical approach toward its attainment leaned heavily on the *millet* argument.

The Bulgarian example was the purest case of a Balkan nationalist movement operating within the *millet* context. Latecomers to the Balkan nationalist scene, the Bulgarians were influenced by ideals acquired from Russia, Serbia, and Greece. But when the Bulgarians began their push for national recognition in 1860, they did so by campaigning for recognition of a separate Bulgarian *millet* by the Ottoman central government, which would entail the creation of a Bulgarian Orthodox church independent of the Greek patriarchate. They succeeded in this goal in 1870, causing immediate troubles to arise with their now-autonomous neighbors, Serbia and Greece. In the eyes of all three peoples, the geographic extent of the independent Bulgarian church would be synonymous with the geographical borders of some future independent Bulgarian state. The now highly nationalist Serbs and Greeks could not permit regions they claimed for themselves to be swallowed by Bulgarians simply because the majority of the Orthodox population in them adhered to the

Bulgarian church. This dispute between nationalism and national *millet* continued long after Bulgaria succeeded in winning political autonomy in 1878 (and complete independence from the Ottoman Empire in 1908), and lay at the root of the violent conflicts over Macedonia that raged until the Balkan Wars (1912-13), after which the struggles among the three contenders became nationalistic in the strictly Western sense.

Events in the Balkans over the past decade have demonstrated that the curious intertwining of national and *millet* identities is a continuing legacy for the peoples of Southeastern Europe. The triumph of Western European nationalist concepts among the modern, post-Ottoman Balkan Christian states could not help but affect the Muslim populations living within the borders of those states.

In Bulgaria, for instance, until the 1950s, the Muslims, who constituted about 10 percent of the total population, were considered second-class but economically necessary citizens. They were virtually ignored by the government and resented by the Slavic population, who had been fed the standard "Turkish yoke" nationalist line in their schools. Most of the Muslims in Bulgaria talked, dressed, and acted like Turks, and were considered as such by the Slavic Bulgarians, by the Turks in Turkey, and by themselves. A small percentage of Muslims, however, may have dressed like Turks but spoke Bulgarian. Most of these were recognized as descendants of Orthodox Bulgarians who had converted (or, according to the Bulgarian nationalist line, were forced to convert) to Islam during the period of Ottoman rule. They were not considered Turks by either Bulgarians or Turks. Yet both Muslim groups were effectively treated in the same perfunctory manner by the government and people of the country—a Muslim was a Muslim and could never be a Bulgarian national; it was a *millet* approach. In the 1980s the Communist government reversed this policy, claiming that most of the Muslims who were identified as Turks were actually descendants of converted ethnic Bulgarians (which is probably a historically accurate claim). So, by rejecting the *millet* identity of the Muslims, the government set about forcibly "Slavifying" or deporting the Turks in Bulgaria, in a misguided attempt to create an ethnically pure Bulgarian nation-state. The Muslims responded by fortifying their *millet* identity with claims to group rights within the country couched in traditional Western nationalist terms. The authorities' misguided policy was one of the main factors leading to the downfall of the Bulgarian Communist government in 1989, since Turkish human rights (a concept born of Western nationalist struggles) became the umbrella under which all Bulgarian anti-Communist oppositional movements were first able to unite. The question of the Turks in Bulgaria—whether they are *millet* or ethnic in identity—remains a burning issue in the post-Communist period and poses a continuing problem for the new Bulgarian coalition government, which finds itself posing as a representative of a Christian Slavic nation-state dependent on the support of a crucial Muslim (non-Bulgarian, in *millet* terms) political party.

A similar problem plagued the former Yugoslavia, with its numerous Muslim populations in Bosnia-Hercegovina, Macedonia, and the Serbian regions of Kosovo and Sandjak. Except for the Muslims of Kosovo and many in Macedonia, who were ethnically Albanian, most were ethnic descendants of Slavs who had converted to Islam during the Ottoman period. Like the Muslims in Bulgaria, they were largely ignored by the Serb-dominated government until following World War II and Tito's attempt to hold together a country that had shown signs of disintegrating along ethnic lines in the years just prior to the war. Under Tito Yugoslavia was divided into a federation of six republics and two autonomous Serbian provinces. Each republic supposedly represented the state of an officially recognized "nation." The demographic majorities in the two autonomous Serbian provinces were ethnically non-Serbian (Kosovo's population was predominantly Albanian and Vojvodina possessed a mixed Hungarian, Slovak, and Romanian majority). Tito's system attempted to incorporate the Muslim populations by recognizing the rights of "nationalities" within all of the national republics for groups not belonging to the so-called nation, among whom a category of Muslims, primarily in Bosnia-Hercegovina, was listed at one time as "Undefined Yugoslavs." Although neither the Communists nor, it seems, Western specialists appeared to realize it, this organization officially re-created the traditional *millet* as far as Yugoslav Muslims were concerned, while simultaneously dealing with them in Western ethnic-national terms.

When Yugoslavia collapsed as a state in 1991, the splinter successor states spun off by its demise attempted to make nation-state reality of the Tito republic system. All of the newly independent ex-Yugoslav countries—Slovenia, Croatia, Macedonia, and Bosnia-Hercegovina—as well as the new, Serb-dominated "Yugoslav" state, composed of Serbia (without autonomous regions, which had been absorbed directly into Serbia proper) and Montenegro, issued new state constitutions declaring their respective national programs. In every case except one, the strict precepts of the Western-style nation-state were proclaimed as the law of the land. Each defined the state in terms of its dominant ethnic nation, and each, though avowing legal equality for all within its borders, structured its governing authority in a way to guarantee that ethnic minorities—frequently referred to as "nationalities," à la the old Titoesque jargon—were relegated to an inferior political and social position, thus enhancing the risk of interethnic conflicts soon after independence was declared.

The single exception to the nation-state approach were proposed constitutions for ethnically and religiously mixed Bosnia-Hercegovina issued in 1992. While the state was declared sovereign within its borders, no single ethnic group—Croat or Serb—or single religious group—Muslim, Catholic, or Orthodox—was proclaimed dominant. Attempts were made to reconcile the national and the *millet* approaches that these considerations raised to some compromise political-social organization for the country. The first considered dividing Bosnia-Hercegovina into a federation of seven to ten districts, each with a particular ethnic or religious majority in its population, governed by a presidency that was rotated among the Croats, Serbs, and Muslims. This same idea later emerged as the Vance-Owen peace initiative sponsored by the United Nations in a failed attempt to stop the bloodshed in the Bosnian war. It, like its original predecessor, failed because it was unworkable. It was unworkable because it mixed the proverbial apples and oranges—nation-state, territorial ethnic nationalism with *millet* religious, nonterritorial self-identity. The members of the three different cultures in Bosnia-Hercegovina —more accurately, three different civilizations—were so territorially intermixed that partition into enclaves truly representative of each would have fractured the country into hundreds of little parcels, making effective government impossible. In deliberations leading up to the original constitutional proposal, the delegates of the Serb population in Bosnia walked out because they refused to accept anything less than complete ethnic-national autonomy and more territory than the planned partition granted them.

When the original partition plan proved unacceptable, the Muslim party, headed by Alija Izetbegović, put forth a new proposed constitution that sprang directly from the Ottoman Islamic *millet* tradition. In it Bosnian and Hercegovinian citizens were not recognized officially by ethnicity but by religious affiliation. All religions were considered equal under law. The central government was to be elected democratically on a proportional basis relative to the strength of the three main religions. The Croats, with the least numbers in the total population, reluctantly agreed to cooperate with the Izetbegović Islamic approach, if only because it dampened the Serb ultra-nationalist claims. If the Croats, who had little experience of Ottoman rule, were wary in their response to the Muslim constitution, the Orthodox Serbs, with their inflamed and long-standing anti-Turk national mythology, were positively enraged. Claiming that the Bosnia-Hercegovinian government was "fundamentalist" and attempting to reinstate Islamic dominance over the Christians, and encouraged by the nationalist Milošević Serb government, the Serb nationalists in Bosnia-Hercegovina immediately took up arms and precipitated the Bosnian war.

The *millet* traditions of the Bosnia-Hercegovinian, predominantly Muslim, government made it difficult for it to accept the various peace proposals made by Western and United Nations mediators. Not once during the excruciating process of innumerable agreed-upon but broken cease-fires and so-called peace negotiations did the European and American diplomats involved give serious consideration to the Izetbegović plan, which was more attuned to the human realities of Bosnia-Hercegovina than were Western state concepts. Its lack of a nation-state mentality was too foreign—too Islamic—for them to have perceived its possibilities. Despite its public display of sympathy for the sufferings of the Muslims in Bosnia-Hercegovina, the West tolerated the atrocities committed in the name of conquering "national" territories by Serbs and Croats, and of self-defense by Muslims, all the while wringing its hands over the difficulties in finding a Western-style nation-state solution to a problem that could never be solved conclusively by that method. Perhaps the West's open concern for the Bosnia-Hercegovinian Muslims was a diplomatic ploy to retain some sort of credibility in the general Islamic world, while its historical inner cultural antagonism toward Islamic civilization would not permit it to effectively help the Muslims fend off the Serb and, later, Croat nationalist onslaughts. Be that as it may, with no concrete military or diplomatic support from the West, the Izetbegović government was forced to consider a new, less complicated tripartition plan advanced by the Serbs and Croats and embraced by the Western powers, resulting in even further bloodshed as the Muslims' former Croat allies turned on them to secure as much territory as possible for themselves.

The various Christian nationalities of the Balkans are dangerously befuddled when dealing with Muslim populations in their midst because of the nebulous merging of the two concepts of nation and *millet*. They persist on treating Muslims as a distinct group apart, no matter their ethnic character (the *millet* approach), while projecting on them a sort of national character as the traditional enemy of Balkan Christian nations—the Turks. The Balkan Muslims, in their turn, being a mixed bag in ethnic composition and surrounded by highly nationalistic and hostile neighbors, have been forced to adapt a certain amount of the Western nationalist program to their essentially *millet* character. Many Western analysts see this as a growing "Muslim nationalism" (historically, a contradiction in terms!). Given the chance by their nationalist Christian neighbors, Bosnian or Albanian Muslims would probably choose to emulate the Turks of Turkey, who managed to merge Western nationalist concepts with their Islamic traditions, although the merger was (and remains) disruptive and far from stable. But the Turks were fortunate enough to have succeeded in expelling most of the non-Turks from their territories right at the beginning (1921-23). They did not have to face the problem of dealing with significant numbers of ethnic-national minorities enjoying potent national support from relatives just across their borders, as do both the Albanian and Bosnian Muslims today. The Bosnian Muslims have given the world a preview of how a modern Muslim state in Europe might deal with its multicultural population—an updated version of the traditional Islamic institution of toleration, the *millet*. The Serbs have demonstrated how the post-Communist, nationalist Balkan Christian world would react. Their perception of the new Balkan political reality is a near-carbon copy of the old nineteenth-century view, summarized in the words of a Bosnian Serb *četnik* officer in a television interview given on the front lines somewhere near Srebrenica: "The *Turks* are just over that hill. I am fighting to drive the *Turks* out of my village, out of my land. I am fighting for my Orthodox faith. I am fighting because I am a Serb and this land is mine." (He was, in fact, fighting brother ethnic Serbs whose faith was Islam and whose ancestors had lived in that region for as long as his own.)

No analyst could create a more telling expression of the cultural conflict that permeates today's Southeast European political conditions.

BY WAY OF CONCLUSION:

SOME THOUGHTS

● ○ ●

Attempting to gain an initial and workable understanding of Eastern Europe is no easy task. Every college undergraduate who attends a survey course of the region for the first time experiences the confusion that invariably arises over the innate complexity of the subject. The term "Eastern Europe" itself defies simple, unambiguous definition because of the human diversity that it represents. Sorting through the variegated identities and interrelationships of some seventeen major ethnic groups, three different civilizations, at least seven forms of religion, two separate alphabets, nineteen states, and four empires that have existed in the area over the span of some fifteen hundred years—and then making useful sense of it all—can be a daunting task indeed. Very little about Eastern Europe readily lends itself to simple explanation. In the classroom, this difficulty poses a problem that, while important for the overall grade point average of individual students, has minor import on day-to-day human existence. In the post–cold war world outside the classroom, however, where decisions must be (and are being) made regarding East European developments that will have lasting impact on millions of human lives, a comprehensive and fundamental understanding of the region is imperative. We cannot afford to take actions that are not well informed.

The West has taken a number of approaches in its efforts to gain the insight needed for dealing with Eastern Europe since the fall of European communism. Most commonly these approaches essentially are couched in Western political and economic terms. They emphasize the failure of Marxist philosophy in constructing thriving, viable modern societies in the region and its inordinately obstructive legacy to the former socialist states that must come to terms with Marxism's collapse. Such approaches measure East European events, situations, and developments as to how effectively liberal-democratic and industrial capitalistic standards have been established among the societies wrecked by the mistakes of communism. Problems, ranging to outright conflicts, among the East European populations are attributed to irrational ethnic and religious differences fueled by undemocratic political growth and economic underdevelopment. Solutions are presumed to lie in the swift, unfettered implementation of Western political and economic standards in place of what are considered "outmoded" or "failed" traditional ideals and despite the disruption their enactment may cause among the societies involved. The thrust of nearly all Western approaches toward Eastern Europe and its troubles is to transform the region into an extension of Western Europe.

Since European communism's demise in 1989-91, the successor governments throughout Eastern Europe have made efforts to initiate liberal-democratic and capitalist industrial economic policies in the image of the West. Some East European states, especially Poland, have sought out direct aid from the West in developing blueprints for westernized political and economic transformation and are attempting to abide faithfully by the plans created for them by Westerners. All have established at least the semblance of Western-style liberal-democratic political institutions, such as elected government officials and national assemblies, and have passed laws encouraging a certain amount of private property ownership and market commodity exchange.

This willingness to embrace quickly Western political and economic models stems from a pronounced predisposition for things Western that had grown within Eastern Europe during the final decade of communism. Many of the East European states had been unwilling Soviet puppet satellites from the beginning and had never completely come to terms with their subordinate situations within the East Bloc, as the disturbances in Poland and Hungary during the 1950s, in Czechoslovakia in 1968, and in Ceauşescu's Romania in the 1970s and 1980s demonstrated. So long as the world was locked into a near-universal ideological confrontation between two overwhelmingly strong military superpowers—the United States and the Soviet Union—there was little room for East European deviation from the order established by, and in the interests of, the Soviet Union, which maintained a large military presence among its subordinate allied/satellite states.

From its start in the late 1940s, the cold war was ahistorical for most of the states involved on both sides. The traditional foreign policy of the United

States until its entry into World War II had been isolationist (acquisitions in the Pacific resulting from the 1898 Spanish-American War, and their consequent Asian economic ties, constituted a noted exception), primarily confined to securing the oceanic shores of the country and preserving its dominant political and economic monopoly in the Western Hemisphere. Most of its important Western European allies in the cold war—France, England, and Germany—themselves had been powerful political and economic forces in the world for centuries prior to the war and found their post-1948 subordinate positions difficult to accept completely, despite the naked economic and military reality of American predominance. Beginning in the 1960s with Charles de Gaulle's expulsion of American military forces from France and his espousal of European common market ideals in French foreign policy, the Western European states gradually gave vent to growing frustrations over being relegated to a subsidiary position in world affairs through the evolution of the European Union (EU) movement. If successful, the EU could place a united Western Europe on an economic par with the United States and Japan, and perhaps lead to authentic world political punch as well. Given the ideals for which they and the United States had taken their stand in the cold war—political and economic freedom within the framework of liberalism and capitalism—the United States did not actively resist this move on the part of Western European states to reclaim a measure of independence on their own terms.

In the opposing cold war camp, only the Soviet Union itself operated in historically traditional fashion. It was the direct child of the former tsarist Russian Empire in territory and mentality, upholding centuries-old imperialist conceptions, albeit clothed in Western socialist garb. Traditional involvements in general East European affairs, especially in Poland and in the Balkans, in which Russia played the role of mighty foreign imperial power, were nothing new. But with the possible exceptions of the Bulgarians and the Serbs, the native populations perceived Russia's historical presence in Eastern Europe in a mostly negative light. Most peoples of the region had enjoyed strong and continuing contacts with Western Europe prior to the outbreak of World War II and could not help but be emphatically influenced by those associations. Poles, Hungarians, and Romanians had nationalist reasons to view Russians with distrust and even animosity, given the imperialist role played by Russia in their history. Czechs, Croats, and Slovaks found little they shared in common with Russians beyond Slavic ethnicity, and their brief idealization of Russia during their Panslavic period of national awakening in the nineteenth century was definitively dispelled by Russian Slavophile imperialist policies. Albanians had virtually no contact with Russia prior to 1945; their brief exposure to Russians in the Ionian theater of the Napoleonic Wars made little positive impact on them.

A number of East European peoples—Hungarians, Czechs, Poles, Bulgarians, and Serbs—had possessed in the past states of their own that had played important roles in European affairs. That these had been dismantled by powerful foreign empires and their populations reduced to subservient subjects served to intensify nationalist pretensions among many East Europeans that were antithetical to strict Soviet domination, which was maintained primarily through blatant military intimidation. By the time Soviet-style communism began showing its internal economic weaknesses in the 1980s, forcing Gorbachev to instigate his perestroika and glasnost policies in an attempt to salvage the situation for the party, the East European satellites were restless with Soviet rule. Glasnost, which opened the Communist world to direct contact with the West on a level and frequency not known since before 1948, tended to reinforce the East Europeans' uneasiness with a continued direct Soviet presence and to reinforce their predisposition for adopting Western concepts, either to proclaim their anti-Russian sentiments or to demonstrate their "Europeanness." Thus, when the opportunity arose in 1989-91, perestroika in Eastern Europe rapidly became a successful movement to end Soviet-style communism rather than an agent of its reform.

Nowhere in Eastern Europe and Eurasia has the attempt to overcome the political, economic, and human stultification of discredited communism been without its problems. Balanced power between newly elected heads of state and representative assemblies has not fully emerged as yet, inflation and unemployment have generally increased, social programs (including health care) are suffering, and environmental problems, never before adequately addressed, are looming as catastrophic future concerns. On top of these predictable, one might say expected, difficulties of the post-Communist transition now under way, the renewed outbreak of national, ethnic, and religious conflicts among certain of the populations of Eastern Europe and Eurasia pose a dangerous additional threat to peaceful stability in the regions for which the West and the westernizers in the former European Communist world failed to account sufficiently in advance in their somewhat idealistic plans for life after communism. In their least threatening aspect, such conflicts have led to the division of larger states into smaller ones through mostly political means —Czechoslovakia into separate Czech and Slovak republics and the Soviet Union into the Commonwealth of Independent States. In their most dangerous aspect, they have led to the disintegration of Yugoslavia into atrocious, bloody chaos and to rampant warfare, both civil and national, in the Caucasus and in Central Asia, all of which threaten the very existence of political and economic security in their regions for years to come.

There appears to be a pattern to the extent and in the nature of the problems associated with the attempt to institute Western political and economic models in post-Communist Eastern Europe and Eurasia. Variations in the speed, effectiveness, and efficiency with which Western liberal-democratic political and capitalist market economic institutions have been adopted, and in the extent and intensity of the resistance to them, have been pronounced among the various former Communist states and cannot be adequately explained by standard Western political and economic models. All of the former Communist states were oppressed equally by Marxist-Leninist political totalitarianism, and all suffered similar economic repression at the hands of socialist central planning. It follows that, if the two problems are solved along accepted Western lines, a measure of transitional turmoil can be expected in the short term, but, in the long, all should be well.

But all is not well throughout Eastern Europe and Eurasia, nor can conditions realistically be expected to improve dramatically in the foreseeable future. Only in Hungary, the Czech Republic, Slovakia, Poland, and Slovenia (the former East Germany is omitted from consideration here on the historical technicality of its being a recognized Western European state) have liberal-democratic and capitalist reforms made noticeable and relatively peaceful headway. Similar attempts in Bulgaria and Albania have left them both effectively adrift politically and economically, with the old Communist order nominally overthrown but no new institutions as yet able to fill the vacuum. Romania has managed to adopt an outward veneer of democracy to mask the continued rule of a powerful political oligarchy, which hopes to manipulate market economic growth in its own interests. Much the same might be said of the former Soviet republics, including the Russian Federation, where the situation is often complicated by conflicts stemming from a powerful older Western influence imported over a century ago and suppressed, but not eradicated, by communism—that is, nationalism. Nowhere have the dangers of long pent up nationalism been more dramatically apparent than in the violent dissolution of Yugoslavia.

It should be noticed that the most peaceful and effective steps toward implementing liberal democracy and market capitalism have been concentrated among states located in Northeastern and Central-Eastern Europe, while the least are found in states having a long history of non-European (especially, Islamic) preponderance—western and central Southeastern Europe, the Caucasus, and Central Asia. Those states whose transitional democratic-capitalist situation currently lies somewhere in between—trying to implement certain of the required reforms (without obvious success to date) and experiencing an assortment of persistent resistance—are found in the eastern Balkans and in Western Eurasia.

The reasons advanced by Western thinkers for such a varied and uneven distribution of successful integration of Western political and economic models are commonly grounded in concepts of modernization. According to this theory of socioeconomic reality, modern society possesses a core region— roughly, the United States, Canada, England, France, Belgium, the Netherlands, Germany, and Northern Italy—that represents modernization in its most advanced state. This core, which represents the geographical heart of Western European civilization, shapes and develops the nature of modern existence for all others. It is surrounded by geographically concentric rings of less developed peripheral societies, whose level of modernization is determined by their proximity to and direct relations with the societies of the core. Thus, the states of Northeastern and Central-Eastern Europe, being located closer to the core states of Western Europe, will logically attain a level of Western-like development more readily than those further removed, such as in Southeastern Europe, Western Eurasia, Central Asia, and the Caucasus. While modernization theory offers an explanation for the uneven distribution of development along Western lines in Eastern Europe and Eurasia, it is geographically deterministic in its conclusions. By giving short shrift to the human factor in social organization, modernization theory provides very little in the way of useful insight for dealing with the problems in those regions. Thus, modernization has few practical solutions to the national, ethnic, and religious conflicts that have broken out in those areas. It simply considers them the by-products of regional underdevelopment.

The Western modernization approach has been augmented by further economic theories that attempt to explain such problems in a more universal human fashion. These tend to reduce all conflicts among and within societies, from local squabbles among villagers to warfare among whole societies, to a Malthusian struggle for land and its resources, whether they are food, minerals, energy sources, or any number of other useful assets the earth provides. Thus, for example, Muslims, Croats, and Serbs are killing each other in Bosnia-Hercegovina over land acquisition. So too are Armenians and Azerbaijanis, as well as Georgians and Abkhazis, in the Caucasus, and Romanians and Russians in Moldova, to mention a few examples. According to these Malthusian theories, since the West has developed to the point where the elemental cause of such conflicts—competition over territorial assets—has been institutionally and technologically overcome through effective liberal politics and sophisticated market relationships satisfying most human resource needs, it has come to experience political and economic stability. Once effective liberal governments and profitable market relationships are established in the former Communist world, the resource needs of the populations ultimately will be satisfied and the conflicts logically will end.

Liberal democracy, market-oriented industrial capitalism, modernization, Malthusian relationships—all of these approaches toward understanding and acting upon developments in post-Communist Eastern Europe and Eurasia make a great deal of sense to the Western mind. They are sophisticated, logical, and amenable to quantitative analyses. In short, they fit perfectly the Western mentality. They should because they are all distinct products of the Western mind—they are expressions of the West's perception of reality, of Western civilization itself. And therein lies the crux of the problem over gaining a useful understanding of events in Eastern Europe and Eurasia. We Westerners usually see and understand the world only in our own terms. We engage in countless discussions and advance innumerable analyses of such problem areas as Bosnia-Hercegovina and Russia that are couched exclusively in concepts that we ourselves impose on the situations under consideration in the belief that they alone are true reflections of the realities. We have grown conditioned to such a self-centered perception of the world—that it exists on our own terms—by centuries of Western colonialism and imperialism, in which most of the world was bent to the West's political and economic will through the use of its indisputably superior technologies.

Perhaps it is only a natural human failing for Westerners to believe that Western European technological superiority, especially when it has forced virtually every human society on the face of the globe to adapt to it in some way or another, translates into absolute Western European cultural superiority. After all, highly effective technology is the practical application of an intrinsic Western cultural development—sophisticated mathematics-based science. It follows logically that, given the proven success of scientifically spawned technologies, the Western European precepts of human "sciences"—political, economic, and social (we study them as such in our schools)—must also be superior. Having reached this conclusion, it requires little imagination to take the ultimate step and claim superiority for even the West's nonscientific, intellectually creative endeavors, such as fine arts and literature. As Westerners, most of us tacitly accept our sense of world superiority without so much as a second thought on the matter. We tend to take it for granted. Our obvious dominance in world affairs won and maintained by our technologies serves to constantly reinforce our elevated perception of ourselves. We actively educate our young in this perception by upholding school curricula that emphasize "Western Civilization" as a primary component subject at the expense of "World Civilizations." The West tends to live in a world assumed to be created in its own image and likeness.

While such Western cultural self-centeredness may be natural, given historical developments since the beginning of the late fifteenth century European Age of Discovery, it is not absolute global reality. Four other civilizations are also alive among the human inhabitants of this earth, and they all hold a similar outlook regarding themselves in relation to the rest of the world. Although all of their populations have been forced to make certain, at times wholesale, compromises to Western concepts over the years, each retains a large, intact reservoir of its own native cultural heritage that precludes any possibility of its total capitulation to that of the West. Western "forms" adapted by these non-Western societies are significantly modified by their adapters' "natures." The extent to which Western forms are adapted outside the West ranges from the minimal, as among certain African and South American societies, to the maximum, as in Japan.

The Japanese provide us with a telling example of how Western forms are significantly modified in non-Western human environments. In both the political and economic spheres, the Japanese have espoused Western forms that have been superimposed on centuries-old Japanese traditions. These traditions spring from a Shinto culture that accepts the family as the fundamental model for shaping all human social organization, from the existence of the individual to the nature of the state as a whole. All traditional human interrelationships are predicated on and related to those found in the family, refined and ritualized to emphasize recognizable lines of authority running from the father figure, through the various family members, to those outside of the family. Western parliamentary liberalism has been grafted onto a Far East Asian monarchy, in which the emperor (the "Son of Heaven"), though politically powerless, is still generally considered divine by the population. Although constitutional monarchies are understandable to the West, it is in the economic sphere that Western misunderstanding of Japanese realities is most pronounced. The Japanese have adapted all of the outward forms of Western industrial capitalism, from high technology in the plants down to the suits and ties of corporate managers, and they have deftly integrated them into the traditional family culture that has shaped Japanese business organization for the past four hundred years. Some of today's Japanese corporate giants have been family-run businesses for centuries, in which all operations and all suppliers have been undertaken through enterprises controlled by members of one large extended family. Mitsubishi, for example, was established in 1620 as a family business of the Mitsuis and has been dealing with a specific set of suppliers ever since in a traditional familial relationship. Such family-oriented business relationships are accepted as natural in Japan but they run against the grain of Western corporate culture, as the current charges of "unfair" and "monopolistic" supply practices leveled against Japanese corporations by frustrated Western businesses demonstrates. The importance to the Japanese of their family business culture also helps explain their tariff policies. In the traditional Japanese cultural reality, Westerners, after all, are foreigners and thus on the periphery of any family-oriented relationship.

As the Japanese example demonstrates, Western forms ostensibly adapted by societies outside the West are never truly Western below the surface. The reason for that lies in the nature of the forms themselves. They are creations of a particular, unique civilization—Western European—and are shaped to express the Western perception of reality, its culture. Non-Western societies possess their own perceptions of what is real—their own cultures—and when they adapt Western forms, they do so within the framework of their native conceptions. Just how well the two are able to be reconciled determines how stable Western forms will become in those societies and how effectively they will operate. The Japanese discovered that Western industrial capitalism fit rather comfortably within the traditional family culture in the area of business, so that the differences between form and nature in their adaptation is outwardly subtle (but inwardly overt). Such relatively harmonious adaptations of Western forms are not always the case.

Because the continued existence of non-Western civilizations precludes any one of them from realistically claiming an absolute lock on "true," universal reality, it is logical that Western attempts to acquire a useful understanding of post-Communist Eastern Europe and Eurasia should include serious consideration of the cultural dimensions of those regions' societies. It will be those societies that will make the adaptations of Western forms that will determine the future of the regions and the nature of their continued relationships to the West.

For a Westerner to raise the issue of examining non-Western civilizations on their own terms, and thus essentially granting them validity equal to that of Western European civilization, is culturally dangerous. The West cherishes and defends the superior self-image it has crafted and tends to pejoratively label any deviation from it by its members as "relativism." Relativism puts Western civilization into a world cultural community of peers in which all members have unique value. It is much more comfortable for the West to believe that its culture constitutes world reality than it is to accept that Western civilization is merely one of a number of such approaches toward perceiving life held by millions of non-Western human beings. We Westerners should realize that if a "true," absolute reality exists for all humankind, that reality must, of necessity, be "relativistic" in nature. We need to come to grips with this reality. Only then can we attain useful and workable understandings of human events in Eastern Europe and Western Eurasia (let alone the world).

As we have seen, there are three distinct civilizations existing within Eastern Europe and Western Eurasia—Western European, Eastern European, and Islamic. The Western European is espoused by the populations inhabiting Northeastern, Central-Eastern, and the northwest corner of Southeastern Europe. They are essentially Roman Catholic or Protestant Christian in religious belief, and they have historically experienced and contributed to all of the various stages in Western European civilization's development—Renaissance, Reformation, Scientific Revolution, Enlightenment, Liberalism, Industrial Revolution, and Romantic Nationalism. Their cultural kindred to the states of Western Europe was never lost sight of in the West, even during the Communist period, where discussions of "Eastern Europe" often concentrated almost exclusively on Poland, Hungary, and the former Czechoslovakia. (This tendency continues at present.) It is precisely among these Western societies in Eastern Europe that post-1989 liberal-democratic and market-capitalist reforms are currently progressing with the least resistance or modification. It is also upon these societies that most current Western developmental attention, in terms of foreign aid, state and private investment, joint ventures, consultative services, and the like, is focused. They are being welcomed back into the Western European family of nations after a four-decade, highly disruptive forced separation.

Among the remaining societies of the regions, those who are not members of Western European civilization, adaptation of Western forms is a different matter. Both East European and Muslim societies in Eastern Europe and Eurasia possess their own unique perceptions of reality that have enjoyed centuries of native development. Both have been in direct contact with and influenced (to varying extents) by Western European civilization. It is among these societies that post-1989 Western-like reforms are experiencing resistance and noticeable modification, especially in the political sphere.

The member societies of Eastern European civilization are Orthodox Christian in religious belief (guaranteeing them a European self-identity), but their historical traditions are linked to developmental stages in their civilization springing from the culture of the Byzantine Empire and filtered through an Islamic (either Ottoman Turkish or Tatar-Mongolian) cultural sieve. They possess no native cultural traditions equivalent to those spawned in the West by the Renaissance (they did not need it as such), the Reformation, the Enlightenment, or Liberalism, which led to the formation of modern Western political and economic structures. Rather, historically they have espoused Byzantine imperialist ideals, cultivated a staunch tradition of resistance to perceived threats from both the Christian West and Islamic East, and today continue to retain strong proclivities for centralized, autocratic authority that regulates all aspects of society to ensure strength against outside dangers. Adaptations of Western political forms by Eastern Europeans can be characterized as possessing a distinct tinge of authoritarianism that is lacking in the Western originals. Whereas Polish President Wałęsa is politically a figurehead and most authority rests in the elected Polish Assembly, Serb President Milošević virtually controls the Serb parliament as would an autocratic ruler his assembly of notables. President Iliescu of Romania now enjoys governing the country because of his blatant willingness to use muscle on his opposition when he deems it necessary. And in the classic, well-publicized case of the Russian Federated Republic, President Yeltsin has shown himself to be a direct cultural descendant of the Russian tsars and Soviet secretary-generals in his public decrees, his smashing of the parliament in Moscow, and his postparliament emergency measures. Lest we Westerners wax too angrily over his apparent deviations from Western-style liberal democracy, we should heed the words of two native Russian journalists, now working in New York, when asked by American analysts their opinions of the assault on the Russian White House. They both supported Yeltsin completely, praising him for his "strong" leadership. (One even went so far as to admit that Russians are "comfortable" only with political leaders who can give an "autocratic" sense of direction to the country!)

Societies forming part of the Islamic civilization are, by definition, Muslim in their religious beliefs. As in Eastern European civilization, Islamic societies possess an autocratic perception of political reality, but while the East Europeans root their political autocracy in the office of Byzantine emperor, who was considered God's representative on earth and "Thirteenth Apostle of Christ" ruling in partnership with the Orthodox church, Muslims traditionally view their political leadership as being synonymous with their religious leadership—in other words, a theocracy. The traditional Islamic supreme head of state is also the direct descendant of the Prophet Muhammad. Regional rulers are usually traditional tribal leaders. While East Europeans are able to adapt Western political forms to their traditional political culture with a modicum of disruption and modification, Western political precepts, with their insistence on separating the church from the state, have proven highly disruptive in the Islamic world ever since their essentially forced imposition on the Muslim Arabic societies of West Asia following World War I and the dismantling of the Ottoman Empire. Even in Turkey, where westernization is the result of a native nationalist movement in the 1920s, the cultural tensions caused by the adaptation of Western political forms continue to bubble just below the surface. In other parts of the Islamic world, the Western-Islamic cultural tensions have exploded into the open, with the Ayatollah-led Shi'ite revolution in Iran and the current Islamic bugaboo in the West—the Islamic "fundamentalists." Interestingly, the Muslims of Southeastern Europe, those most closely involved in the post-1989 transitional process in Eastern Europe, have shown themselves most willing to adapt Western political forms, à la the Turks of Turkey. They express their cultural uniqueness in their adaptations more subtlely.

The point about Balkan Muslim political subtlety raises a question about an important Western cultural expression that enjoys the longest, most widespread, and accepted influence among the non-Western societies of Eastern Europe and Western Eurasia. Nationalism began filtering into Eastern European civilization among the Greeks and the Serbs starting in the late eighteenth century. By the end of the nineteenth, it had been embraced by every East European society. Its adaptation was less an expression of nationalism's intrinsic, universal political reality than it was a handy device to further specific political agendas. In the Russian Empire, it was used by the Russians to refine the nature of tsarist rule in accepted "European" terms and to validate imperialist aims in both Europe and Asia. Among the Balkan East European societies, it was the tool used to throw off Islamic Ottoman rule and to carve out states of their own along the lines of their powerful Western European neighbors. Lacking the sort of cultural development that naturally supported nationalistic concepts in their Western homelands, the East European adaptation stressed the ethnic and nation-state aspects wedded to the traditional native autocratic-imperialistic approach to state-building. In a confined geographical region such as the Balkans, which possesses limited and unevenly distributed resources and is inhabited by a number of different peoples in competition for those resources, nationalism exploded like a bomb. Innately aggressive and a source of conflict in its Western homelands, nationalism in the Balkans attained the height of endemic violence among the states of the region by the opening of the twentieth century. It, and the wars it spawned, lies at the root of such past human tragedies as the "Macedonian Question" among the Bulgarians, the Serbs, and the Greeks and the Croat- and Serb-perpetrated atrocities associated with the World War II Croatian *Ustaše* regime and its demise. On a streetcorner in Sarajevo one June day in 1914, it sparked World War I. Nationalism is at the heart of the current catastrophe in Bosnia-Hercegovina. Once the Serbs and Croats of the region realized that the predominantly Muslim government was set on establishing an essentially *millet,* rather than a national, state, they rebelled against a perceived threat to their very existence as peoples ("nations"). To do so, they were forced to brand the Muslims of Bosnia-Hercegovina as either "fundamentalists" (which did not catch on among the Westerners sitting on the sidelines) or as Muslim "nationals" (a contradiction in terms that, however, has been accepted by interested Western parties because it makes sense within their own cultural perspectives).

It is nationalism, uprooted from its native Western cultural environment and adapted as a tool by non-Western East Europeans for justifying their small-scale, local imperialist pretensions, that poses the most burning threat to political and economic stability in the post-1989-91 European world. Since the West insists on claiming its cultural superiority in the world and on determining the future of world development, it has a clear responsibility to intervene in ending the chaos and bloodshed that its adapted nationalist political culture has propagated among the non-Western societies of Eastern Europe and Eurasia. But its role cannot and must not be limited merely to crisis intervention. If conflicts in Eastern Europe and Eurasia born of mutually exclusive national agendas are to be settled without recourse to weapons and violence, an alternative to nationalism as a source of group ethnic-political pride and measure of group value must be offered to those regions' societies along with the liberal and capitalistic models. Given the role of institutional model that the West has played, plays today, and most likely will continue to play into the future, it is up to the West to provide the necessary alternative. In fact, this substitute is already at hand, although it is still in its somewhat unsteady infancy—the European Union.

The EU has appeared all things to all people at various times, ranging from a mere economic free trade common market (its original label) to a potential future united European political superpower. But whatever the EU now is or will become, one singularly important cultural development is involved in its very idea: that it transcends nationalism in favor of an all-Western European sense of identity (in a way, having a certain analogy to the traditional Islamic *millet* approach, with ethnicity substituted for religion). Even without the still-murky political unification that the Maastricht Treaty only begins to define, the imposition of common "European" standards throughout all the member states illustrates a certain willingness on their part to forgo minor marks of nationalist distinction, although it has not been arrived at easily. (For instance, new EU plumbing standards require indoor hot and cold water lines to be run so as to permit their flow into a common mixing valve and faucet. Traditional English plumbing standards required that the two water lines remain such a distance apart that a common mixer and faucet were impractical, hence, the separate hot and cold water taps found in virtually every English home, which almost unconsciously became an expression of "Englishness." The English put up quite a defense of their double faucets before finally bowing to EU consensus.) The Danish and French votes on Maastricht have demonstrated just how difficult it is for a civilization to make a fundamental change in a single important component of its culture. The fact that the logical conclusion of the EU should be a new developmental stage in Western European civilization that moves it beyond nationalism and the nation-state to a new level of human organization is a frightening prospect for societies so determinedly attached to their old political order. The road will not be without its pitfalls and conflicts, and the process will require much time, energy, and dedication on the part of those Westerners whose vision of the future is a fully developed integrated, multinational Europe.

An EU that is strong, both politically and economically, can provide the sort of Western model that may ultimately bring peace and stability to Eastern Europe and Eurasia. A functioning EU would demonstrate to those fractured and conflicting societies that strength and prosperity can be attained despite multicultural diversity in a given region through the forging of common interests resting on a level higher than the regional nation-state. It would permit them to continue expressing their diverse native cultures unhindered while encouraging them to stop fighting among themselves and to start concentrating on constructing such multinational communities of their own if they hope to enjoy a viable political-economic future in a world that will rapidly become dominated by large competing regional political free-trade blocs similar to the EU of Western Europe. (The very fact that the EU was not functioning at an optimal level in 1989 to serve as a true model led to the dissolution of Comecon, the socialist trading bloc, which, in post-Communist circumstances, could have served as an established framework for a beneficially revised Eastern European and Western Eurasian sister organization.)

The EU (or, at least, what it represents) is the hope for continued dynamism in Western European civilization. As a model, it is the best prospect currently available for reversing the ill effects of past Western nationalist influences on Eastern Europe and Western Eurasia and for lighting the road to their peaceful and stable futures.

◙ On Further Readings ◙

The essays found in this collection are not the products of dedicated, specific research. Rather, they are syntheses of personal perceptions formulated over nearly two decades of teaching, research, discussion, travel, and living in Eastern Europe. They represent one individual's attempt to apply broadly a body of academic experience in Eastern Europe and Western Eurasia to the dramatic events that have occurred in those regions in an effort to make some sort of understandable sense of them for others—especially for nonspecialists, for students, and for specialists willing to consider alternative approaches of analysis. They were written while sitting in front of a computer at home and letting the ideas flow, without the use of research notes or specialized texts. For this reason, a formal bibliography, as is common for scholarly writings, is impossible. But given the nature and intent of the essays, a guide to further readings that will assist those interested in delving into the complex worlds of Eastern Europe and Western Eurasia in greater detail or in discovering just where the author's ideas may have originated—or both—is highly appropriate.

The following overview of literature is not comprehensive. To be so, a rather thick bibliographic tome would be necessary rather than a brief essay. Nor is it highly selective. For the most part, the titles given are those with which the author of the essays is most familiar. Because the intended audience is assumed to be English-speaking from the start, the more specialized works discussed are exclusively written in English. While this might seem too arbitrarily limited in scope, it is not. Those who possess the ability to read non-English languages will find plenty of additional titles to explore in the bibliographies and notes to the works cited. In most cases, the citations noted are bibliographically standard. In some cases, they represent those editions of works that have been most readily available and, thus, not necessarily bibliographically original or first editions (such as paperback editions).

Every academic discipline has its own jargon that nonspecialists may not find familiar. Terminology that has common meaning in the general vocabulary often may possess a very specific, narrow definition when used in any given scholarly field. History is no exception. The essays in this collection take a historical and cultural approach to Eastern Europe and Western Eurasia, so a precise understanding of the two key words—history and culture—is necessary. Despite their apparently obvious meanings, these terms are philosophically complex. One way to grasp their historical meanings is to take the road of simplicity, which has been done by Edward M. Anson in his *A Civilization Primer,* 3rd ed. (San Diego: Harcourt Brace Jovanovich, 1993), in which he presents definitions for standard historical terminology in the simplest terms possible. Care should be taken, however, in accepting some of his explanations, since Anson obviously displays in his historical approach the common West-centric perceptions clothed in objectivity found in many Western historians. A representative cross section of more sophisticated but essentially straightforward Western interpretations of the nature and uses of history might include: Marc Bloch, *The Historian's Craft,* trans. Peter Putnam (New York: Vintage Books, 1953); Robert V. Daniels, *Studying History: How and Why* (Englewood Cliffs, NJ: Prentice-Hall, 1966); Christopher Dawson, *The Dynamics of World History* (New York: Mentor Books, 1962); or Brian Tierney, Donald Kagan, and L. Pearce Williams, eds., *What Is History—Fact or Fancy?,* 3rd ed. (New York: Random House, 1977). For some beneficial intellectual amusement regarding approaches to history, there are W. C. Sellar and R. J. Yeatman, *1066 and All That* (New York: Barnes & Noble, 1993), and Robin W. Winks, *The Historian as Detective: Essays on Evidence* (New York: Harper & Row, 1969).

Another way to understand the meanings of history and culture is to treat with them on a sophisticated level. No more useful scholarly treatment can be found in English than that produced over the 1940s and 1950s by Arnold J. Toynbee in his mammoth, multivolume analysis, *A Study of History.* Wordy, rambling, and difficult to work through, Toynbee's monstrous study does manage to present a most comprehensive, cohesive, and valuable philosophy of history based on human culture. Luckily, the core of his thinking has been preserved in a masterful two-volume abridgment by D. C. Somervell (New York: Oxford University Press, 1947-57 [with additional editions since]), which succeeds in making Toynbee both readable and useful. Prior to World War II, Toynbee's cultural philosophy of history received much attention in the West, but the advent of the cold war left him relatively ignored, as the West turned from cultural to socioeconomic approaches toward history in an effort to combat a seemingly convincing Marxist historical materialism more on its own terms. The fall of European and Western Eurasian communism after 1989 and the consequent national, ethnic, and religious problems in the regions have returned the historical importance of culture to center stage, along with politics and economics, in our general considerations of driving human forces. While one might disagree with some of Toynbee's specific points (especially with his conclusion that future development in Western European civilization probably will be molded by Roman Catholicism), no better set of definitions for historical and cultural terminology, and no more intellectually intelligible analysis of the importance of human culture in shaping world developments, can be had than in Toynbee. His definition of civilization as the only logical, primary unit of study for history, the theory of "challenge and response" within human societies as the fundamental driving force behind history, and the idea that all civilizations potentially experience a common life cycle somewhat analogous to that of living creatures are interesting, insightful, and of continued value.

Toynbee wrote his epic study in part out of a desire to counter an earlier, somewhat pessimistic twentieth-century Western philosophy of history advanced by the German schoolteacher Oswald Spengler. His two-volume *Decline of the West,* which has recently appeared in a single-volume abridgment by Helmut Werner, translated by Charles F. Atkinson (New York: Oxford University Press, 1991), originally appeared in the 1920s and 1930s and reflected in tone the German mentality of national humiliation resulting from defeat in World War I. An adherent of Nietzschean philosophy, Spengler Romantically defined culture as the natural expression of a nation's soul and civilization as its fossilized, empty corruption. In treating with Western European culture, which he considered superior to all others, Spengler considered it to be in dramatic decline, falling into meaningless civilization and redeemable only by the advent of a strong German leader who would force the reversal of the process by reinvigorating Western core cultural values. Hitler confused Spengler's Nietzschean "strong-man" elements with the Nazi "superman" Aryan ideology and made him required reading throughout the Third Reich, which, of course, ultimately linked the demise of Spengler's philosophy with that of his own. (Spengler himself died a decade before Hitler.) Despite the essentially misguided overall German bias of his work and its subsequent ill-fated Nazi perversion, Spengler's analyses of the nature of culture and of the unity of its manifestation over the diverse gamut of human expression (religion, philosophy, science, literature, music, architecture, painting, sculpture, politics, economics, or any of the other means) still provide intellectually stimulating food for thought.

Some useful specific studies of various stages in the development of Western European civilization are: Robert Anchor, *The Enlightenment Tradition* (New York: Harper & Row, 1967); Angus Armitage, *The World of Copernicus* (New York: Signet Science Library, 1963); Roland H. Bainton, comp. and ed., *The Age of the Reformation* (Princeton, NJ: D. Van Nostrand Co., 1956); John G. Gagliardo, *Enlightened Despotism* (New York: Thomas

Y. Crowell Co., 1967); Frank E. Manuel, *The Age of Reason* (Ithaca, NY: Cornell University Press, 1968); and W. E. Knowles Middleton, *The Scientific Revolution* (Cambridge, MA: Schenkman Publishing Co., 1963). An interesting popular work positing that Western scientific reality is actually a purely cultural phenomenon is James Burke, *The Day the Universe Changed* (Boston: Little, Brown, 1985).

Other Western historians take a less West-centric approach in their studies, which, unfortunately, are usually restricted to general studies of world history and rarely projected into more specific area treatments. Three good examples are Fernand Braudel, *The Mediterranean and the Mediterranean World in the Age of Philip II*, 2 vols., translated by Siân Reynolds (New York: Harper & Row, 1972-73), William H. McNeill, *A World History,* 3rd ed. (New York: Oxford University Press, 1979), and J. M. Roberts, *The Pelican History of the World,* rev. ed. (New York: Penguin Books, 1988 [also a 1993 ed., retitled *The Penguin History of the World*]). Two other useful works providing a global overview of history, thus emphasizing multicivilizational historical reality, are Bernard Grun, comp., *The Timetables of History: A Horizontal Linkage of People and Events* (New York: Touchstone Books, 1982), and William L. Langer, comp. and ed., *An Encyclopedia of World History: Ancient, Medieval, and Modern, Chronologically Arranged,* rev. ed. (Boston: Houghton Mifflin, 1948 [and subsequent later editions]).

The idea that fault lines exist among civilizations is not new. A number of history teachers have used the analogy in the classroom to simplify understanding of complex historical situations throughout the world. More recently, we have grown accustomed to hearing or reading about "faults" in discussions of events in the Balkans and elsewhere. Most such references are used purely as convenient literary metaphors to help describe particular conflict situations. The idea that cultural fault lines constitute true human reality (as the essays in this collection posit) is not widely accepted as yet. A noted exception is the political scientist Samuel P. Huntington, "The Clash of Civilizations?," *Foreign Affairs,* 72, no. 3 (Summer 1993): 22-49. Huntington is an influential policymaker in the United States who has concluded that the world does not operate strictly by Western standards. His article, while seemingly on the right track with regard to global human realities, suffers from a flawed conclusion that appears to justify a "do-nothing" American foreign policy in Bosnia-Hercegovina (thus condoning genocidal conduct), the Balkans in general, and Western Eurasia.

The classic conceptual study of European and Eastern European boundaries is Oscar Halecki, *The Limits and Divisions of European History* (Notre Dame, IN: University of Notre Dame Press, 1962). A more recent treatment is that of the Hungarian scholar Jenő Szűcs, *The Three Historical Regions of Europe* (Budapest: Hungarian Academy of Sciences, 1983). A general geographical study of Eastern Europe can be found in R. H. Osborne, *East-Central Europe: An Introductory Geography* (New York: Praeger, 1967), which does not include Greece. One might also usefully refer to Monica and Robert Beckinsale, *Southern Europe: A Systematic Geographical Study* (New York: Holmes & Meier Publishers, 1975), concerning Greece, Albania, and the former Yugoslavia. For a rudimentary treatment of the ethnic definition of Eastern Europe, see R. V. Burks, *East European History: An Ethnic Approach* (Washington, D.C.: American Historical Association, 1973). As to Slavs in general, there are a number of studies, including: Samuel H. Cross, *Slavic Civilization Through the Ages* (New York: Russell & Russell, 1963); Marija A. Gimbutas, *The Slavs* (New York: Praeger, 1971); Roger Portal, *The Slavs: A Cultural and Historical Survey of the Slavonic Peoples* (New York: Harper & Row, 1969); and Hermann Schreiber, *Teuton and Slav: The Struggle for Central Europe* (New York: Alfred A. Knopf, 1965). Hans Kohn, *Pan-Slavism: Its History and Ideology,* 2nd rev. ed. (New York: Vintage, 1960), provides a clear overview of that nineteenth-century Slavo-centric intellectual ethnic movement among East European and Russian Slavs. For the Hungarian viewpoint on Panslavism, see Sándor Kostya, *Pan-Slavism* (Astor, FL: Danubian Press, 1981). The question as to whether there is an "Eastern Europe" is addressed by Timothy G. Ashe, "Does Central Europe Exist?" *New York Review of Books,* (9 October 1986), 45-52.

Although there have been many studies dealing with Eastern Europe in general over the years, it is rare when a significant number of them are in print at any particular time since the period immediately following the onset of the cold war in the late 1940s-1950s. The recent and current developments in the region following 1989 have sparked a new gush of publications, not all of which are of particular value. Among general studies worth perusing are: Henry Bogdan, *From Warsaw to Sofia: A History of Eastern Europe,* trans. Jeanie P. Fleming (Santa Fe, NM: Pro Libertate Publishing Co., 1989); Oscar Halecki, *Borderlands of Western Civilization: A History of East Central Europe* (New York: Ronald Press Co., 1952); Robin Okey, *Eastern Europe 1740-1985: Feudalism to Communism,* 2nd ed. (Minneapolis: University of Minnesota Press, 1986), who uses the modernizational approach; and E. Garrison Walters, *The Other Europe: Eastern Europe to 1945* (Syracuse, NY: Syracuse University Press, 1988). Most all of them ignore Greece.

Medieval Eastern Europe was largely shaped by its populations' relationships with the Byzantine Empire and the German Holy Roman Empire. Regarding the former, a number of interesting and worthwhile general studies are commonly available. Good general histories of Byzantium include: Norman H. Baynes and H. St. L. B. Moss, eds., *Byzantium: An Introduction to East Roman Civilization* (Oxford: Clarendon Press, 1961); Robert Browning, *The Byzantine Empire* (New York: Scribner, 1980); Charles Diehl, *Byzantium: Greatness and Decline*, trans. Naomi Walford (New Brunswick, NJ: Rutgers University Press, 1957); Joan M. Hussey, *The Byzantine World*, 3rd ed. (London: Hutchinson & Co., 1967); Romilly J. H. Jenkins, *Byzantium: The Imperial Centuries, A.D. 610-1071* (New York: Vantage Books, 1969); Cyril Mango, *Byzantium, the Empire of New Rome* (New York: Scribner, 1980); George Ostrogorsky, *History of the Byzantine State*, trans. Joan M. Hussey (New Brunswick, NJ: Rutgers University Press, 1957); A. A. Vasiliev, *History of the Byzantine Empire*, 2 vols. (Madison: University of Wisconsin Press, 1928-29); Philip Whitting, ed., *Byzantium: An Introduction* (New York: Harper & Row, 1973); and, for the sheer pleasure of his prose more than for historicity, Robert Byron, *The Byzantine Achievement: An Historical Perspective, A.D. 330-1453* (London: Routledge & Kegan Paul, 1987 [reprint]). Edward Gibbon, *The Decline and Fall of the Roman Empire*, abridgment by D. M. Low, 3 vols. (New York: Washington Square Press, 1962 [and subsequent editions]), while a masterful work of literature, is culturally biased. Two volumes of a planned three-volume popular history of Byzantium by John J. Norwich have appeared to date: *Byzantium: The Early Centuries* (New York: Alfred A. Knopf, 1992); and *Byzantium: The Apogee* (New York: Alfred A. Knopf, 1993).

Comprehensive studies of Byzantine culture can be found in H. W. Haussig, *A History of Byzantine Civilization*, trans. Joan M. Hussey (New York: Praeger, 1971), and in Steven Runciman, *Byzantine Civilization* (Cleveland: World Publishing Co., 1961). The standard work on Byzantine art and architecture is David T. Rice, *Byzantine Art*, rev. and expanded ed. (Baltimore, MD: Pelican Books, 1968). Rice's *Byzantine Painting: The Last Phase* (New York: Dial Press, 1968) treats with the period in which Byzantine art made its most lasting impact on the Orthodox populations of the Balkans. Also of interest with regard to Byzantine art are: John Beckwith, *The Art of Constantinople: An Introduction to Byzantine Art, 330-1453*, 2nd ed. (London: Phaidon, 1968); Cyril Mango, *The Art of the Byzantine Empire, 312-1453: Sources and Documents* (Englewood Cliffs, NJ: Prentice-Hall, 1972); and Gervase Mathew, *Byzantine Aesthetics* (New York: Harper & Row, 1971). For general histories of the Orthodox church, see Ernst Benz, *The Eastern Orthodox Church: Its Thought and Life*, trans. Richard and Clara Winston (Chicago: Aldine Publishing Co.,

1963), and Alexander Schmemann, *The Historical Road of Eastern Orthodoxy,* trans. Lydia W. Kesich (New York: Holt, Rinehart & Winston, 1963). Joan M. Hussey, *The Orthodox Church in the Byzantine Empire* (Oxford: Clarendon Press, 1990), Harry J. Magoulias, *Byzantine Christianity: Emperor, Church and the West* (Chicago: Rand McNally & Co., 1970), and Steven Runciman, *The Byzantine Theocracy* (Cambridge: Cambridge University Press, 1977), deal with the essential cultural roles of the emperor and the Orthodox church in Byzantium and their consequent impact on Byzantine-Western relations. Those often stormy connections are treated in greater detail by: Ernle Bradford, *The Great Betrayal: Constantinople, 1204* (London: Hodder and Stoughton, 1967); Charles M. Brand, *Byzantium Confronts the West, 1180-1204* (Cambridge, MA: Harvard University Press, 1968); two studies of Deno J. Geanakoplos, *Byzantine East and Latin West: Two Worlds of Christendom in Middle Ages and Renaissance. Studies in Ecclesiastical and Cultural History* (New York: Harper & Row, 1966), and *Interaction of the "Sibling" Byzantine and Western Cultures in the Middle Ages and Italian Renaissance* (New Haven, CT: Yale University Press, 1976); Joseph Gill, *Byzantium and the Papacy, 1198-1400* (New Brunswick, NJ: Rutgers University Press, 1979); Angeliki E. Laiou, *Constantinople and the Latins: The Foreign Policy of Andronicus II, 1282-1328* (Cambridge, MA: Harvard University Press, 1972); William Miller, *The Latins in the Levant: A History of Frankish Greece (1204-1566)* (Cambridge: Speculum Historiale, 1964); Donald E. Queller, ed., *The Latin Conquest of Constantinople* (New York: John Wiley & Sons, 1971); Steven Runciman, *The Eastern Schism: A Study of the Papacy and the Eastern Churches during the 11th and 12th Centuries* (London: Panther Books, 1970); and Speros Vryonis, Jr., *Byzantium and Europe* (New York: Harcourt, Brace & World, 1967).

Studies of the two seminal Byzantine emperors—Constantine I and Justinian I—are readily available. For Constantine, see A. H. M. Jones, *Constantine and the Conversion of Europe* (Toronto: University of Toronto Press, 1993 [reprint]), and Ramsay MacMullen, *Constantine* (New York: Harper Torchbooks, 1971). Among the more interesting biographies of Justinian (as well as his wife, Theodora) are: John W. Barker, *Justinian and the Later Roman Empire* (Madison: University of Wisconsin Press, 1966); Robert Browning, *Justinian and Theodora* (New York: Praeger, 1971); J. B. Bury, *History of the Later Roman Empire from the Death of Theodosius I to the Death of Justinian,* 2 vols. (New York: Dover Publications, 1958); and Glanville Downey, *Constantinople in the Age of Justinian* (New York: Dorset, 1991 [reprint]). One of the more fascinating historical primary sources from the European Middle Ages is Procopius, *The Secret History,* trans. G. A.

Williamson (Baltimore, MD: Penguin Books, 1966), which might be equated to a Byzantine *National Enquirer* article on the secret personal lives of Justinian and Theodora.

The historical and cultural impact of Byzantium on Eastern Europe and Russia is excellently presented by Dimitri Obolensky, *The Byzantine Commonwealth: Eastern Europe, 500-1453* (New York: Praeger, 1971). Also see: Lowell Clucas, ed., *The Byzantine Legacy in Eastern Europe* (Boulder, CO: East European Monographs, 1988); Gyula Moravcsik, *Byzantium and the Magyars,* 2nd ed., trans. Samuel R. Rosenbaum (Budapest: Hungarian Academy of Sciences, 1970); and Andrew B. Urbansky, *Byzantium and the Danube Frontier: A Study of the Relations Between Byzantium, Hungary, and the Balkans during the Period of the Comneni* (New York: Twayne Publishers, 1968).

Also influential in the early development of Eastern Europe was the medieval West. There are relatively few good general histories of the period in English, and among the more interesting are: Geoffrey Barraclough, *The Crucible of Europe: The Ninth and Tenth Centuries in European History* (Berkeley: University of California Press, 1976); William J. Brandt, *The Shape of Medieval History: Studies in Modes of Perception* (New York: Schocken Books, 1973); Norman F. Cantor, *Medieval History: The Life and Death of a Civilization,* 2nd ed. (London: Macmillan, 1969); Christopher Dawson, *The Making of Europe: An Introduction to the History of European Unity* (Cleveland: Meridian, 1962); H. St. L. B. Moss, *The Birth of the Middle Ages, 395-814* (London: Oxford University Press, 1963); and, of course, the important study by Charles H. Haskins, *The Renaissance of the Twelfth Century* (Cambridge, MA: Harvard University Press, 1933).

One of the most significant historians of medieval Europe was the Belgian scholar Henri Pirenne. In *Mohammed and Charlemagne,* trans. Bernard Miall (New York: Barnes & Noble, 1992 [reprint]), originally published posthumously in the 1930s, he theorized that Western Europe was conclusively forced down the road toward developing its own civilization not by the consequences of the Germanic barbarian invasions but by the rise of the Islamic civilization and its rapid geographical expansion into, and control over, the eastern Mediterranean. His thesis has been consistently subjected to questioning since its appearance by traditional Western scholars, who refuse to acknowledge that forces outside the West could play such an important deterministic role inside the West itself. See Alfred F. Havighurst, ed., *The Pirenne Thesis: Analysis, Criticism, and Revision* (Lexington, MA: D. C. Heath, 1969), for a sampling of their arguments. Other important works by Pirenne are: *Economic and Social History of Medieval Europe,* trans. I. E. Clegg (New York: Harcourt Brace & World, 1937); *A History of Europe,* vol. 1, *From the End of the Roman*

World in the West to the Beginnings of the Western States, trans. Bernard Miall (Garden City, NY: Doubleday, 1956); and *Medieval Cities: Their Origins and the Revival of Trade,* trans. Frank D. Halsey (Garden City, NY: Doubleday, 1956). For the medieval German Holy Roman Empire, see James Bryce, *The Holy Roman Empire,* 5th ed. (New York: Macmillan, 1928), and Friedrich Heer, *The Holy Roman Empire,* trans. Janet Sondheimer (New York: Praeger, 1968). Also of interest in this context is James W. Thompson, *Feudal Germany,* 2 vols. (New York: Frederick Ungar, 1969). In the fifteenth century, the Habsburg family came to dominate the imperial throne of Germany and also became a force within Eastern Europe in their own right. There are a number of general works on the Habsburgs. These include: R. J. W. Evans, *The Making of the Habsburg Monarchy, 1550-1700: An Interpretation* (Oxford: Clarendon Press, 1991); David F. Good, *The Economic Rise of the Habsburg Empire, 1750-1914* (Berkeley: University of California Press, 1984); two works by Robert A. Kann, *The Habsburg Empire: A Study in Integration and Disintegration* (New York: Octagon, 1973), and *A History of the Habsburg Empire, 1526-1918* (Berkeley: University of California Press, 1974); C. A. Macartney, comp. and ed., *The Habsburg and Hohenzollern Dynasties in the Seventeenth and Eighteenth Centuries* (New York: Harper & Row, 1970); Henry W. Steed, *The Habsburg Monarchy,* 2nd ed. (New York: H. Fertig, 1969); Victor-L. Tapié, *The Rise and Fall of the Habsburg Monarchy,* trans. Stephen Hardman (New York: Praeger, 1971); and A. J. P. Taylor, *The Habsburg Monarchy, 1809-1918: A History of the Austrian Empire and Austria-Hungary* (New York: Harper & Row, 1965).

There are even fewer general works in English on medieval Eastern Europe than there are for the West. Of primary importance are two studies by Francis Dvornik: *The Slavs: Their Early History and Civilization* (Boston: American Academy of Arts and Sciences, 1956); and *The Slavs in European History and Civilization* (New Brunswick, NJ: Rutgers University Press, 1962). Also see Imré Boba, *Nomads, Northmen and Slavs: Eastern Europe in the Ninth Century* (The Hague: Mouton, 1967).

Postmedieval periods enjoy much more coverage in English. A useful general study is Alan Palmer, *The Lands Between: A History of East-Central Europe since the Congress of Vienna* (New York: Macmillan, 1970). For the rise and impact of nationalism in Eastern Europe, see such works as: Robert A. Kann, *The Multinational Empire: Nationalism and National Reform in the Habsburg Monarchy, 1848-1918* (New York: Columbia University Press, 1950); Walter Kolarz, *Myths and Realities in Eastern Europe* (London: Lindsay Drummond, 1946), which bursts many an East European nationalist bubble; and the important collection edited by Peter F. Sugar and Ivo J. Lederer, *Nationalism in*

Eastern Europe (Seattle: University of Washington Press, 1969), of which both a revised edition and a separate twentieth-century update are due to appear in 1994. In considering nationalism, one must also treat with the problem of national minorities. Among such studies are Edward Chaszar, *The International Problem of National Minorities* (Indiana, PA: Indiana University of Pennsylvania Minority Rights Research Program, 1988), and Elemér Illyés, *Ethnic Continuity in the Carpatho-Danubian Area* (Boulder, CO: East European Monographs, 1988).

Eastern Europe during the period between World Wars I and II is studied by: Stephen Borsody, *The Tragedy of Central Europe: The Nazi and Soviet Conquest of Central Europe* (New York: Collier Books, 1962); C. A. Macartney and A. W. Palmer, *Independent Eastern Europe: A History* (London: Macmillan, 1966); Joseph Rothschild, *East Central Europe Between the Two World Wars* (Seattle: University of Washington Press, 1974); and Hugh Seton-Watson, *Eastern Europe Between the Wars, 1918-1941*, 3rd ed. (New York: Harper & Row, 1967 [reprint]).

The post-World War II Communist period in East European history understandably has received the most coverage in English-language studies. A great many of these suffer from explicit or hidden ideological bias, but a number remain informative. Among these can be listed: Stephen Fischer-Galati, ed., *Eastern Europe in the Sixties* (New York: Praeger, 1963); Ghita Ionescu, *The Break-up of the Soviet Empire in Eastern Europe* (Baltimore, MD: Penguin Books, 1965); Joseph Rothschild, *Return to Diversity: A Political History of East Central Europe Since World War II*, 2nd ed. (New York: Oxford University Press, 1993); Hugh Seton-Watson, *The East European Revolution*, 3rd ed. (New York: Praeger, 1956); Thomas W. Simons, Jr., *Eastern Europe in the Postwar World*, 2nd ed. (New York: St. Martin's Press, 1993); and Geoffrey and Nigel Swain, *Eastern Europe Since 1945* (New York: St. Martin's Press, 1993). One of the latest studies to appear on the end of communism in Eastern Europe is that by Gale Stokes, *The Walls Came Tumbling Down: The Collapse of Communism in Eastern Europe* (New York: Oxford University Press, 1993). Misha Glenny, *The Fall of Yugoslavia: The Third Balkan War* (New York: Penguin Books, 1992), is a less-than-adequate attempt to make sense of the warfare that has erupted in the former Yugoslavia since 1991.

Besides Western Europe and Byzantium, the Ottoman Empire and its Islamic civilization have made a lasting impact on Eastern Europe, especially on the Balkans. Some general studies of Islam might include: Wilson B. Bishai, *Islamic History of the Middle East: Backgrounds, Development, and Fall of the Arab Empire* (Boston: Allyn & Bacon, 1968); Philip Hitti, comp.

and ed., *Islam and the West: A Historical Cultural Survey* (Princeton, NJ: D. Van Nostrand Co., 1962); Arthur Jeffery, ed., *Islam: Muhammad and His Religion* (New York: Liberal Arts Press, 1958); Bernard Lewis, ed. and trans., *Islam: From the Prophet Muhammad to the Capture of Constantinople,* 2 vols. (New York: Harper & Row, 1974); Glenn E. Perry, *The Middle East: Fourteen Islamic Centuries,* 2nd ed. (Englewood Cliffs, NJ: Prentice Hall, 1992); and Fazlur Rahman, *Islam* (New York: Holt, Rinehart & Winston, 1966). A most important work is H. A. R. Gibb, and Harold Bowen, *Islamic Society and the West: A Study of the Impact of Western Civilization on Moslem Culture in the Near East,* vol. I, *Islamic Society in the Eighteenth Century,* 2 pts. (London: Oxford University Press, 1967). Of great importance is Bernard Lewis, *et. al.,* eds., *The Encyclopaedia of Islam,* rev. ed. (Leiden: E. J. Brill, 1960-).

Regarding the Ottoman Empire, a number of valuable general studies are available in English. These include: Paul Coles, *The Ottoman Impact on Europe* (New York: Harcourt Brace & World, 1968); Halil Inalcik, *The Ottoman Empire: The Classical Age, 1300-1600* (London: Weidenfeld & Nicolson, 1973); Norman Itzkowitz, *Ottoman Empire and Islamic Tradition* (Chicago: University of Chicago Press, 1980); Lord [John P. D. B.] Kinross, *The Ottoman Centuries: The Rise and Fall of the Turkish Empire* (New York: Quill, 1977); C. M. Kortepeter, *Ottoman Imperialism During the Reformation: Europe and the Caucasus* (New York: New York University Press, 1972); Albert H. Lybyer, *The Government of the Ottoman Empire in the Time of Suleiman the Magnificent* (Cambridge, MA: Harvard University Press, 1913); William H. McNeill, *Europe's Steppe Frontier, 1500-1800* (Chicago: University of Chicago Press, 1964); Stanford J. Shaw, *History of the Ottoman Empire and Modern Turkey,* 2 vols. (Cambridge: Cambridge University Press, 1976-77); L. S. Stavrianos, *The Ottoman Empire: Was It the Sick Man of Europe?* (New York: Holt, Rinehart & Winston, 1957); Dorothy M. Vaughan, *Europe and the Turk: A Pattern of Alliances, 1350-1700* (New York: AMS, 1976); Wayne S. Vucinich, *The Ottoman Empire: Its Record and Legacy* (Huntington, NY: Robert E. Krieger, 1979 [reprint]); and Paul Wittek, *The Rise of the Ottoman Empire* (London: Royal Asiatic Society, 1966).

For the *millet* system and the Orthodox Christians under the rule of the Ottomans, see: Franz Babinger, *Mehmed the Conqueror and His Time,* trans. Ralph Manheim (Princeton, NJ: Princeton University Press, 1978 [orig. Ger. ed., 1953]); Charles A. Frazee, *Catholics and Sultans: The Church and the Ottoman Empire, 1453-1923* (London: Cambridge University Press, 1983); N. J. Pantazopoulos, *Church and Law in the Balkan Peninsula During the Ottoman Rule* (Thessaloniki: Institute for Balkan Studies, 1967); T. H. Papadopoullos, *Studies and Documents Relating to the History of the Greek*

Church and People under Turkish Domination (Brussels: Wetteren, 1952); B. G. Spiridonakis, *Essays on the Historical Geography of the Greek World in the Balkans during the Turkokratia* (Thessaloniki: Institute for Balkan Studies, 1977); and Peter F. Sugar, *Southeastern Europe under Ottoman Rule, 1354-1804* (Seattle: University of Washington Press, 1977). Studies of Eastern Europe often take a subregional approach. For example, for the Northeastern and Central-Eastern subregions, there is Piotr S. Wandycz, *The Price of Freedom: A History of East Central Europe from the Middle Ages to the Present* (London: Routledge, 1992). Central-Eastern Europe is usually covered by works treating generally with the Habsburg Empire, many of which have been noted above. Southeastern Europe is addressed generally by a number of interesting studies. General histories include: Barbara Jelavich, *History of the Balkans,* 2 vols. (Cambridge: Cambridge University Press, 1985); Charles Jelavich, *The Balkans in Transition: Essays on the Development of Balkan Life and Politics Since the Eighteenth Century* (Berkeley: University of California Press, 1963); John Lampe and Marvin R. Jackson, *Balkan Economic History, 1550-1950: From Imperial Borderlands to Developing Nations* (Bloomington: Indiana University Press, 1982), advancing another modernizational approach; Ferdinand Schevill, *The History of the Balkan Peninsula from the Earliest Times to the Present Day* (New York: Harcourt Brace and Co., 1922), now somewhat dated; L. S. Stavrianos, *The Balkans Since 1453* (New York: Holt, Rinehart & Winston, 1958), still the "bible" of general Balkan textbooks; Traian Stoianovich, *A Study in Balkan Civilization* (New York: Alfred A. Knopf, 1967 [a new rev. ed., with modified title, is due out in 1994]); Nikolai Todorov, *The Balkan City, 1400-1900* (Seattle: University of Washington Press, 1983); and Robert L. Wolff, *The Balkans in Our Time* (Cambridge, MA: Harvard University Press, 1956), which excludes Greece from consideration.

John V. A. Fine, Jr., has published an impressive two-volume history of the medieval Balkans: *The Early Medieval Balkans: A Critical Survey From the Sixth to the Late Twelfth Century* (Ann Arbor: University of Michigan Press, 1983), and *The Late Medieval Balkans: A Critical Survey from the Late Twelfth Century to the Ottoman Conquest* (Ann Arbor: University of Michigan Press, 1987). The nineteenth- and twentieth-century period of nationalism in the Balkans is treated in: Wesley M. Gewehr, *The Rise of Nationalism in the Balkans, 1800-1930* (Hamden, CT: Archon Books, 1967); Charles and Barbara Jelavich, *The Establishment of the Balkan National States, 1804-1920* (Seattle: University of Washington Press, 1977); Paul Lendvai, *Eagles in Cobwebs: Nationalism and Communism in the Balkans* (Garden City, NY: Doubleday, 1969); William S. Murray, *The Making of the Balkan States* (New

York: AMS, 1967); Leo Pasvolsky, *Economic Nationalism of the Danubian States* (New York: Macmillan, 1928); R. W. Seton-Watson, *The Rise of Nationality in the Balkans* (New York: H. Fertig, 1966); and L. S. Stavrianos, *The Balkans, 1815-1914* (New York: Holt, Rinehart & Winston, 1963).

We now must turn to a brief notice of East European national histories. Albania is sparsely represented in English-language works. There are the general studies of Stefanaq Pollo and Arben Puto, *The History of Albania: From Its Origins to the Present Day* (London: Routledge & Kegan Paul, 1981), and of Joseph Swire, *Albania: The Rise of a Kingdom* (New York: Arno Press, 1971 [reprint]). The beginnings of Albanian nationalism are treated in Stavro Skendi, *The Albanian National Awakening, 1878-1912* (Princeton, NJ: Princeton University Press, 1967). Communist Albania is dealt with by: William E. Griffith, *Albania and the Sino-Soviet Rift* (Boston: MIT Press, 1963); Harry Hamm, *Albania —China's Beachhead in Europe,* trans. Victor Andersen (New York: Praeger, 1963); Nicholas C. Pano, *The People's Republic of Albania* (Baltimore, MD: Johns Hopkins University Press, 1968); and Stavro Skendi, ed., *Albania: East-Central Europe under the Communists* (New York: Praeger, 1956). Edith Durham, *High Albania* (Boston: Beacon Press, 1987 [reprint]), provides an interesting early twentieth-century travel account of the land and people.

Until 1992, Bosnia-Hecegovina was usually dealt with in works dedicated to Yugoslavia. There are no good general histories in English available to date. Among the smattering of more specialized studies are: Vladimir Dedijer, *The Road to Sarajevo* (New York: Simon & Schuster, 1966), addressing the role played by Bosnian Serb nationalism in sparking World War I; John V. A. Fine, Jr., *The Bosnian Church: A New Interpretation. A Study of the Bosnian Church and Its Place in State and Society from the 13th to the 15th Centuries* (Boulder, CO: East European Monographs, 1975), concerning the so-called Bogomil heretics; Bernadotte E. Schmitt, *The Annexation of Bosnia, 1908-1909* (New York: H. Fertig, 1970); and Peter F. Sugar, *Industrialization of Bosnia-Herzegovina, 1878-1918* (Seattle: University of Washington Press, 1963), on the economic changes wrought by Austro-Hungarian occupation and annexation.

Bulgaria fares slightly better than Albania in available English-language texts. General studies include: two works by Richard J. Crampton, *A Short History of Modern Bulgaria* (Cambridge: Cambridge University Press, 1987), and *Bulgaria, 1878-1918: A History* (Boulder, CO: East European Monographs, 1983); David M. Lang, *The Bulgarians: From Pagan Times to the Ottoman Conquest* (Boulder, CO: Westview Press, 1976); and Mercia MacDermott, *A History of Bulgaria, 1393-1885* (New York: Praeger, 1962). Medieval Bulgaria is studied by: Robert Browning, *Byzantium and Bulgaria: A Comparative Study Across the Early Medieval Frontier* (Berkeley: University of California Press, 1975); Assen Nicoloff, *Samuel's Bulgaria* (Cleveland: Author, 1969); and Steven Runciman, *A History of the First Bulgarian Empire* (London: G. Bell & Sons, 1930). The Ottoman period is treated in Dennis P. Hupchick, *The Bulgarians in the Seventeenth Century: Slavic Orthodox Society and Culture under Ottoman Rule* (Jefferson, NC: McFarland and Co., 1993), and in Machiel Kiel, *Art and Society of Bulgaria in the Turkish Period: A Sketch of the Economic, Juridical and Artistic Preconditions of Bulgarian Post-Byzantine Art and Its Place in the Development of the Art of the Christian Balkans, 1360/70-1700. A New Interpretation* (Maastricht: Van Gorcum, 1985). The Bulgarian national revival period is covered in two works by James F. Clarke, *Bible Societies, American Missionaries and the National Revival of Bulgaria* (New York: Arno Press, 1971 [reprint]), and *The Pen and the Sword: Studies in Bulgarian History,* ed. Dennis P. Hupchick (Boulder, CO: East European Monographs, 1988), and by Thomas A. Meininger, *The Formation of a Nationalist Bulgarian Intelligentsia, 1835-1878* (New York: Garland, 1987). Cyril E. Black, *The Establishment of Constitutional Government in Bulgaria* (Princeton, NJ: Princeton University Press, 1943), analyzes the liberal democratic state of Bulgaria founded in 1878. The country's history from 1878 through World War II is treated in: Frederick B. Chary, *The Bulgarian Jews and the Final Solution, 1940-1944* (Pittsburgh: University of Pittsburgh Press, 1972); Stephan Constant, *Foxy Ferdinand, 1861-1948, Tsar of Bulgaria* (London: Sidgwick & Jackson, 1979); and Stephane Groueff, *Crown of Thorns: The Reign of King Boris III of Bulgaria, 1918-1943* (Lanham, MD: Madison Books, 1987). The Communist period has been studied by: John Bell, *The Bulgarian Communist Party From Blagoev to Zhivkov* (Stanford, CA: Hoover Institute Press, 1985); L. A. D. Dellin, *Bulgaria: East-Central Europe under the Communists* (New York: Praeger, 1957); Nissan Oren, *Bulgarian Communism: The Road to Power, 1934-1944* (New York: Columbia University Press, 1971); and Joseph Rothschild, *The Communist Party of Bulgaria* (New York: Columbia University Press, 1959).

While Croatia receives treatment in general studies of the former Yugoslavia, it has enjoyed a certain amount of independent attention. A good collection of general studies can be found in Francis H. Eterovich and Christopher Spalatin, eds., *Croatia: Land, People and Culture,* 2 vols.

(Toronto: University of Toronto Press, 1964-70). Stephen Gazi, *A History of Croatia* (New York: Philosophical Library, 1973), provides an elementary overview. Croatia's early history is examined in two works by Stanko Guldescu: *History of Medieval Croatia* (The Hague: Mouton, 1964), and *The Croatian-Slavonian Kingdom, 1526-1792* (The Hague: Mouton, 1970). For the period in which Croatia was transformed into the Habsburgs' Balkan military buffer against the Ottoman Turks, see the two studies by Gunther E. Rothenberg: *The Austrian Military Border in Croatia, 1522-1747* (Urbana: University of Illinois Press, 1960), and *The Military Border in Croatia, 1740-1881: A Study of an Imperial Institution* (Chicago: University of Chicago Press, 1966). For the French Illyrian Provinces period, see George J. Prpić, *French Rule in Croatia: 1806-1813* (Thessaloniki: Institute for Balkan Studies, 1964). Elinor M. Despalatović, *Ljudevit Gaj and the Illyrian Movement* (Boulder, CO: East European Monographs, 1975), deals with the emergence of the Croatian nationalist South-Slav movement. Also see Ante Kadić, *From Croatian Renaissance to Yugoslav Socialism* (The Hague: Mouton, 1969). Ivo Omrčanin, *Economic Wealth of Croatia* (Philadelphia: Dorrance, 1973), treats with socialist Croatia, and a collection edited by Antun Bonifačić and Clement S. Mihanovich, *The Croatian Nation in Its Struggle for Freedom and Independence: A Symposium by Seventeen Croatian Writers* (Chicago: "Croatia" Cultural Center, 1955), demonstrates the continuation of the Croats' anti-Serb nationalist movement in the early years of Tito's Communist rule.

Czech history is commonly treated in studies of Czechoslovakia. Some general studies of the Czechs and Bohemia include: Reginald R. Betts, *Essays in Czech History* (London: Athlone, 1969); Frederick G. Heymann, *Poland and Czechoslovakia* (Englewood Cliffs, NJ: Prentice-Hall, 1966); Robert J. Kerner, *Bohemia in the Eighteenth Century: A Study in Political, Economic, and Social History* (Orono, ME: Academic International, 1969), and Kerner, ed., *Czechoslovakia* (Berkeley: University of California Press, 1945); R. W. Seton-Watson, *A History of the Czechs and Slovaks* (Hamden, CT: Archon Books, 1965); Elizabeth Wiskemann, *Czechs and Germans: A Study of the Struggles in the Historic Provinces of Bohemia and Moravia* (London: Oxford University Press, 1938); and William E. Wright, *Serf, Seigneur, and Sovereign: Agrarian Reform in Eighteenth-Century Bohemia* (Minneapolis: University of Minnesota Press, 1966). Early Czech history is addressed by: Jaroslav Böhm, et. al., eds., *The Great Moravian Empire: Thousand Years of Tradition of State and Culture* (Prague: Czechoslovak Academy of Sciences, 1963); Thomas J. Drobena, *Heritage of the Slavs: The Christianization of the Slavs and the Great Moravian Empire* (Columbus, OH: Kosovo, 1979); and Péter Püspöki-Nagy, *On the Location of Great Moravia: A Reassessment* (Pittsburgh: Duquesne

University Studies in History, East Central and Southeast European Series, 1982). Studies of Czech nationalism and Czech-controlled Czechoslovakia can be found in: Tomas G. Masaryk, *The Making of a State* (New York: Frederick A. Stokes, 1927); Paul H. Segal, *The French State and French Private Investment in Czechoslovakia, 1918-1938: A Study of Economic Diplomacy* (New York: Garland Publishers, 1987); S. Harrison Thomson, *Czechoslovakia in European History* (Hamden, CT: Archon Books, 1965); Felix J. Vondraček, *The Foreign Policy of Czechoslovakia, 1918-1935* (New York: AMS, 1968); Paul Vysny, *Neo-Slavism and the Czechs, 1898-1914* (Cambridge: Cambridge University Press, 1977); and Zbynek A. B. Zeman, *The Masaryks: The Making of Czechoslovakia* (New York: Barnes & Noble, 1976).

The period from the Munich Crisis to the Communist takeover in 1948 is dealt with in: Edvard Beneš, *Memoirs: From Munich to New War and Victory* (New York: Arno Press, 1972 [reprint]); Vojta Beneš and R. A. Ginsburg, *Ten Million Prisoners (Protectorate Bohemia and Moravia)* (Chicago: Czech-American National Alliance, 1940); George F. Kennan, *From Prague After Munich: Diplomatic Papers, 1938-1940* (Princeton, NJ: Princeton University Press, 1968); Josef Korbel, *The Communist Subversion of Czechoslovakia, 1938-1948: The Failure of Coexistence* (Princeton, NJ: Princeton University Press, 1959); Radomir Luza, *The Transfer of the Sudeten Germans: A Study of Czech-German Relations, 1933-1962* (New York: New York University Press, 1964); Hubert Ripka, *Munich: Before and After. A Fully Documented Czechoslovak Account of the Crises of September 1938 and March 1939* (New York: H. Fertig, 1969); and Laurence Thompson, *The Greatest Treason: The Untold Story of Munich* (New York: Morrow & Co., 1968).

General studies of socialist Czechoslovakia include: Judy Batt, *Economic Reform and Political Change in Eastern Europe: A Comparison of the Czechoslovak and Hungarian Experiences* (New York: St. Martin's Press, 1988); Eugen Loebl, *Stalinism in Prague: The Loebl Story,* trans. Maurice Michael (New York: Grove Press, 1969); Jiri Mucha, *Living and Partly Living,* trans. Ewald Osers (New York: McGraw-Hill, 1967); Jiri Pelikan, *Socialist Opposition in Eastern Europe: The Czechoslovak Example* (New York: St. Martin's Press, 1976); Zdenek Suda, *The Czechoslovak Socialist Republic* (Baltimore, MD: Johns Hopkins University Press, 1969); and Tad Szulc, *Czechoslovakia Since World War II* (New York: Viking Press, 1971). No other event in the history of socialist Czechoslovakia receives as much attention as the 1968 Soviet invasion. Among the more interesting works are: Edward Czerwinski and Jaroslaw Piekalkiewicz, eds., *The Soviet Invasion of Czechoslovakia: Its Effects on Eastern Europe* (New York: Praeger, 1972); Vladimir V. Kusin, *The Intellectual Origins of the Prague Spring: The*

Development of Reformist Ideas in Czechoslovakia (Cambridge: Cambridge University Press, 1971); Robert Littell, ed., *The Czech Black Book* (New York: Praeger, 1969); Harry Schwartz, *Prague's 200 Days: The Struggle for Democracy in Czechoslovakia* (New York: Praeger, 1969); Philip Windsor and Adam Roberts, *Czechoslovakia 1968: Reform, Repression and Resistance* (New York: Columbia University Press, 1969); and Zbynek A. B. Zeman, *Prague Spring* (New York: Hill and Wang, 1969).

We can discard works dealing with classical Greek history and concentrate on those covering Greece starting with the Byzantine period, although some general histories include the ancient era. Some useful general studies are: Robert Browning, ed., *The Greeks: Classical, Byzantine and Modern* (New York: Portland House, 1985); Richard Clogg, *A Short History of Modern Greece* (Cambridge: Cambridge University Press, 1979); David Holden, *Greece Without Columns: The Making of Modern Greece* (Philadelphia: J. B. Lippincott, 1972); two works by Apostolos E. Vakalopoulos, *Origins of the Greek Nation: The Byzantine Period, 1204-1461,* trans. Ian Moles (New Brunswick, NJ: Rutgers University Press, 1970), and *The Greek Nation, 1453-1669: The Cultural and Economic Background of Modern Greek Society* (New Brunswick, NJ: Rutgers University Press, 1976); C. M. Woodhouse, *A Short History of Modern Greece* (New York: Praeger, 1968); and D. A. Zakythinos, *The Making of Modern Greece: From Byzantium to Independence* (Totowa, NJ: Rowman & Littlefield, 1976). *Medieval Greece* (Hartford, CT: Yale University Press, 1981), by N. Cheetham, is also of interest. So, too, is Eric Forbes-Boyd, *Aegean Quest: A Search for Venetian Greece* (London: J. M. Dent & Sons, 1970).

The rise of Greek nationalism, the Greek War of Independence, and developments into World War II can be surveyed in: Richard Clogg, ed., *The Struggle for Greek Independence: Essays to Mark the 150th Anniversary of the Greek War of Independence* (Hamden, CT: Archon Books, 1973); C. W. Crawley, *The Question of Greek Independence: A Study of British Policy in the Near East, 1821-1833* (Cambridge: Cambridge University Press, 1930); Charles G. Cruickshank, *Greece, 1940-1941* (Newark, DE: University of Delaware Press, 1979); Domna Dontas, *The Last Phase of the War of Independence in Western Greece (December 1827 to May 1829)* (Thessaloniki: Institute for Balkan Studies, 1966); G.P. Henderson, *The Revival of Greek Thought, 1620-1830* (Albany: State University of New York Press, 1970); John L. Hondros, *Occupation and Resistance: The Greek Agony, 1941-44* (New York: Pella, 1983); William H. McNeill, *The Greek Dilemma: War and Aftermath* (Philadelphia: J. B. Lippincott, 1947); René Puaux, *The Sorrows of Epirus* (Chicago: Argonaut Publishers, 1963 [reprint]); and Arnold

J. Toynbee, *The Western Question in Greece and Turkey* (London: Constable & Co., 1922). For post-World War II Greece, including the Greek Civil War and the dictatorship of the Colonels, see: T. Bahcheli, *Greek-Turkish Relations Since 1955* (Boulder, CO: Westview Press, 1990); Wray D. Candilis, *The Economy of Greece, 1944-66: Efforts for Stability and Development* (New York: Praeger, 1968); Jane P. Carey, *The Web of Modern Greek Politics* (New York: Columbia University Press, 1968); Richard Clogg and George Yannnopoulos, eds., *Greece under Military Rule* (New York: Basic Books, 1972); Dominique Eudes, *The Kapetanios: Partisans and Civil War in Greece, 1943-1949* (New York: Monthly Review, 1973); William H. McNeill, *The Metamorphosis of Greece Since World War II* (Chicago: University of Chicago Press, 1978); Edgar O'Ballance, *The Greek Civil War, 1944-1949* (New York: Praeger, 1966); and C. M. Woodhouse, *The Rise and Fall of the Greek Colonels* (New York: Franklin Watts, 1985).

Because of its large emigré population, Hungary has received an impressive amount of consideration in English-language studies. Some useful general works include: Jorg K. Hoensch, *A History of Modern Hungary* (London: Longman, 1988); Dominic G. Kosáry and S. Béla Várdy, *History of the Hungarian Nation* (Astor Park, FL: Danubian Press, 1969); Emil Lengyel, *1,000 Years of Hungary* (New York: John Day Co., 1958); C.A. Macartney, *Hungary: A Short History* (Chicago: Aldine, 1962); Denis Sinor, *History of Hungary* (London: Allen & Unwin, 1959); and Francis S. Wagner, *Hungarian Contributions to World Civilization* (Center Square, PA: Alpha Publications, Inc., 1977). Hungary prior to its incorporation into the Habsburg Empire is examined in C. A. Macartney, *The Magyars in the Ninth Century* (Cambridge: Cambridge University Press, 1968), and in Domokos Varga, *Hungary in Greatness and Decline: The 14th and 15th Centuries,* trans. Martha Szacsvay Lipták (Atlanta: Hungarian Cultural Foundation, 1982).

For Habsburg Hungary through 1918, including the national revival and the revolution of 1848-49, see: István Deák, *The Lawful Revolution: Louis Kossuth and the Hungarians, 1848-1849* (New York: Columbia University Press, 1979); Phineas C. Headley, *The Life of Louis Kossuth, Governor of Hungary* (Freeport, NY: Books for Libraries, 1971); Béla K. Király, *Hungary in the Late Eighteenth Century: The Decline of Enlightened Despotism* (New York: Columbia University Press, 1969); Henrik Marczali, *Hungary in the Eighteenth Century* (New York: Arno Press, 1971 [reprint]); and Edsel Stroup, *Hungary in Early 1848: The Constitutional Struggle Against Absolutism in Contemporary Eyes* (Buffalo, NY: Hungarian Cultural Foundation, 1977). The period between the close of World War I and that of World War II, including

Hungarian irredentism, especially regarding Transylvania, can be examined in: Gabor Baross, *History of Hungary: Hungary and Hitler* (Los Angeles: University of Southern California Press, 1964); Stephen Borsody, ed., *The Hungarians: A Divided Nation* (New Haven, CT: Yale Center for International and Area Studies, 1988), which continues the examination of Hungarian irredentism into the 1980s; Randolf L. Braham and Béla Vago, eds., *The Holocaust in Hungary: Forty Years Later* (New York: Social Science Monographs, 1985); Andrew C. Janos, *The Politics of Backwardness in Hungary, 1825-1945* (Princeton, NJ, Princeton University Press, 1982), and Janos and William B. Slottman, eds., *Revolution in Perspective: Essays on the Hungarian Soviet Republic of 1919* (Berkeley: University of California Press, 1971); C. A. Macartney, *A History of Hungary, 1929-1945*, 2 vols. (New York: Praeger, 1956); Mark I. Major, *American Hungarian Relations, 1918-1944* (Astor Park, FL: Danubian Press, 1974); Nicholas M. Nagy-Talavera, *The Green Shirts and the Others: A History of Fascism in Hungary and Rumania* (Stanford, CA: Hoover Institute Press, 1970); Peter Pastor, *Hungary Between Wilson and Lenin: The Hungarian Revolution of 1918-1919 and the Big Three* (Boulder, CO: East European Monographs, 1976); Thomas L. Sakmyster, *Hungary, the Great Powers, and the Danubian Crisis, 1936-1939* (Athens: University of Georgia Press, 1980); Rudolf L. Tokes, *Béla Kun and the Hungarian Soviet Republic: The Origins and Role of the Communist Party of Hungary in the Revolutions of 1918-1919* (New York: Hoover Institute Press, 1967); and Ivan Volgyes, *The Hungarian Soviet Republic, 1919: An Evaluation and a Bibliography* (Stanford, CA: Hoover Institute Press, 1970).

General studies of socialist Hungary include: Douglas M. Brown, *Towards a Radical Democracy: The Political Economy of the Budapest School* (London: Unwin Hyman, 1988); C. Gati, *Hungary and the Soviet Bloc* (Durham, NC: Duke University Press, 1986); Bennett Kovrig, *The Hungarian People's Republic* (Baltimore, MD: Johns Hopkins University Press, 1970), and *Communism in Hungary: From Kun to Kadar* (Stanford, CA: Hoover Institute Press, 1979); Paul Lendvai, *Hungary: The Art of Survival* (London: I.B. Tauris, 1988); Peter A. Toma and Ivan Volgyes, *Politics in Hungary* (San Francisco: W.H. Freeman, 1977); and Laszlo Zsoldos, *The Economic Integration of Hungary into the Soviet Bloc: Foreign Trade Experience* (Columbus: Ohio State University Press, 1963). The 1956 Hungarian Uprising has attracted numerous studies, among which the following are of some interest: Leslie B. Bain, *The Reluctant Satellites: An Eyewitness Report on East Europe and the Hungarian Revolution* (New York: Macmillan, 1960); Richard Lettis and William E. Morris, *The Hungarian Revolt, October 23-November 4, 1956* (New York: Scribner, 1961); Bill Lomax, *Hungary 1956* (New York:

St. Martin's Press, 1976); Endre Marton, *The Forbidden Sky* (Boston: Little, Brown, 1971); and Ferenc A. Vali, *Rift and Revolt in Hungary: Nationalism Versus Communism* (Cambridge, MA: Harvard University Press, 1961). Macedonia is a new country with a very long history. Although it was renowned in classical Greek times because of its father and son kings, Philip II and Alexander the Great, we need not deal directly with that period in our overview of readings. Macedonia became an Eastern European entity during medieval times. Most literature on Macedonia either treats with it in the Yugoslav context or in that of the famous nineteenth-early twentieth century international question. There are few satisfactory studies of the area in English. Two commonly available works are Ivan Mihailoff, *Macedonia: A Switzerland of the Balkans,* trans. Christ Anastasoff (St. Louis: Pearlstone Publishing Co., 1950), written by a Macedonian revolutionary leader fighting for an independent Macedonia, and Stoyan Pribichevich, *Macedonia: Its People and History* (University Park, PA: Pennsylvania State University Press, 1982). The medieval and Ottoman periods in Macedonian history usually are addressed in general Balkan, Byzantine, Bulgarian, Serbian, and Ottoman works.

It is the "Macedonian Question" that has received most notice by scholars, but here again, works written in English are few. One might usefully, but carefully, peruse: Christ Anastasoff, *The Tragic Peninsula: A History of the Macedonian Movement for Independence Since 1878* (St. Louis: Blackwell Wielandy Co., 1938); Elisabeth Barker, *Macedonia: Its Place in Balkan Power Politics* (London: Royal Institute of International Affairs, 1950); Ivan Ilcheff, *The Truth About "The Macedonians" According to the "Harvard Encyclopedia of American Ethnic Groups in America" Published in October, 1980* (Indianapolis: Macedonian Tribune, 1982); and Mercia MacDermott, *Freedom or Death: The Life of Gotsé Delchev* (London: Journeyman Press, 1978). One of the most enlightening demonstrations of the utterly arbitrary and unreal nature of Romantic nationalism and its nation-state efforts to draw borders emerged from studies treating with the Macedonian dilemma. If anyone doubts the inability of maps and mapmaking to accurately express human nationalist reality in the Balkans, she or he need only refer to H. R. Wilkinson, *Maps and Politics: A Review of the Ethnographic Cartography of Macedonia* (Liverpool: University of Liverpool Press, 1951). The lessons of the work need to be learned by present Western diplomats, who think the maps generated by the various plans for solving the violence in Bosnia-Hercegovina truly reflect human realities on the ground.

There is a plethora of works treating with Poland. Like the Hungarian emigration to the West, the Poles have populated Western countries in great numbers. Some good general histories include: Norman Davies, *Heart of*

Europe: A Short History of Poland (Oxford: Oxford University Press, 1986), and his *God's Playground, A History of Poland,* 2 vols. (New York: Columbia University Press, 1982); Oscar Halecki, *A History of Poland,* trans. Monica M. Gardner and Mary Corbridge-Patkaniowska (New York: Roy Publishers, 1943 [and subsequent editions]), as well as his editorship of *Poland* (New York: Praeger, 1957) and his *Poland and Christendom* (Houston: University of St. Thomas Press, 1964); W. F. Reddaway, *et. al.,* eds., *Cambridge History of Poland,* 2 vols. (Cambridge: Cambridge University Press, 1941-50); Samuel L. Sharp, *Poland: White Eagle on a Red Field* (Cambridge, MA: Harvard University Press, 1953); and Adam Zamoyski, *The Polish Way: A Thousand-Year History of the Poles and Their Culture* (New York: F. Watts, 1988).

Poland from medieval times through the partitions is addressed by: Robert N. Bain, *The Last King of Poland and His Contemporaries* (New York: Arno Press, 1971 [reprint]); Witold Dzieciol, *The Origins of Poland* (London: Veritas, 1966); Linda Gordon, *Cossack Rebellions: Social Turmoil in the Sixteenth-Century Ukraine* (Albany: State University of New York Press, 1983); Pawel Jasienica, *Jagiellonian Poland* (Miami: American Institute of Polish Culture, 1978), and his *Piast Poland* (New York: Hippocrene Books, 1985); Herbert H. Kaplan, *The First Partition of Poland* (New York: Columbia University Press, 1962); Charlotte Kellogg, *Jadwiga, Poland's Great Queen* (New York: Macmillan, 1931); Paul W. Knoll, *The Rise of the Polish Monarchy: Piast Poland in East Central Europe, 1320-1370* (Chicago: University of Chicago Press, 1972); Witold Kula, *An Economic Theory of the Feudal System: Towards a Model of the Polish Economy, 1500-1800* (London: NLB, 1976); Robert H. Lord, *The Second Partition of Poland: A Study in Diplomatic History* (New York: AMS, 1969); Albert Sorel, *The Eastern Question in the Eighteenth Century: The Partition of Poland and the Treaty of Kainardji* (New York: H. Fertig, 1969); and Daniel Stone, *Polish Politics and National Reform, 1775-1788* (Boulder, CO: East European Monographs, 1976).

For Poland from the partitions through World War II, see: Bohdan B. Budurowycz, *Polish-Soviet Relations, 1932-1939* (New York: Columbia University Press, 1963); Edward Chmielewski, *The Polish Question in the Russian State Duma* (Knoxville: University of Tennessee Press, 1970); Anna M. Cienciala, *Poland and the Western Powers 1938-1939: A Study in the Interdependence of Eastern and Western Europe* (London: Routledge & Kegan Paul, 1968); J. K. Fedorowicz, ed. and trans., *A Republic of Nobles: Studies in Polish History to 1864* (Cambridge: Cambridge University Press, 1982); Jan Karski, *The Great Powers & Poland, 1919-1945: From Versailles to Yalta* (Lanham, MD: University Press of America, 1985); Titus Komarnicki, *Rebirth of the Polish Republic: A Study in the Diplomatic History of Europe, 1914-1920*

(London: W. Heinemann, 1957); Josef Korbel, *Poland Between East and West: Soviet and German Diplomacy Toward Poland, 1919-1933* (Princeton, NJ: Princeton University Press, 1963); Roy F. Leslie, *Polish Politics and the Revolution of November 1830* (Westport, CT: Greenwood, 1969), as well as Leslie, ed., *The History of Poland since 1863* (Cambridge: Cambridge University Press, 1980); Antony Polansky, *Politics in Independent Poland 1921-1939: The Crisis of Constitutional Government* (Oxford: Clarendon Press, 1972); Harold von Riekhoff, *German-Polish Relations, 1918-1933* (Baltimore, MD: Johns Hopkins University Press, 1971); James T. Shotwell and Max M. Laserson, *Poland and Russia, 1919-1945* (New York: King's Crown, 1945); Frank W. Thackeray, *Antecedents of Revolution: Alexander I and the Polish Kingdom, 1815-1825* (Boulder, CO: East European Monographs, 1980); and Piotr S. Wandycz, *The Lands of Partitioned Poland, 1795-1918,* rev. ed. (Seattle: University of Washington Press, 1984).

Studies on socialist Poland include: Michael Checinski, *Poland, Communism, Nationalism, Anti-Semitism* (New York: Karz-Cohl, 1982); Tadeusz N. Cieplak, ed., *Poland Since 1956: Readings and Essays on Polish Government and Politics* (New York: Twayne Publishers, 1972); Ajit Jain, ed., *Solidarity: The Origins and Implications of Polish Trade Unions* (Baton Rouge, LA: Oracle Press, 1983); George Kolankiewicz, *Poland: Politics, Economics, and Society* (London: Pinter, 1988); James F. Morrison, *The Polish People's Republic* (Baltimore, MD: Johns Hopkins University Press, 1968); Arthur Rachwald, *In Search of Poland: The Superpowers' Response to Solidarity, 1980-1989* (Stanford, CA: Hoover Institute Press, 1990); Hansjakob Stehle, *The Independent Satellite: Society and Politics in Poland Since 1945* (New York: Praeger, 1965); Konrad Syrop, *Spring in October: The Story of the Polish Revolution, 1956* (New York: Praeger, 1957); Jan Szczepanski, *Polish Society* (New York: Random House, 1970); and Jerzy Wiatr, *The Soldier and the Nation: The Role of the Military in Polish Politics, 1918-1985* (Boulder, CO: Westview Press, 1988).

Romania, like most Balkan states other than Greece, is not well represented in English-language literature. Among the few available general studies are: Denise Basdevant, *Against Tide and Tempest: The Story of Rumania* (New York: R. Speller, 1966); D. Berciu, *Ancient Peoples and Places: Romania* (New York: Praeger, 1967); Charles U. Clark, *Greater Roumania* (London: Dodd, Mead, 1922); Stephen Fischer-Galati, *et. al.,* eds., *Romania Between East and West: Historical Essays in Memory of Constantin C. Giurescu* (Boulder, CO: East European Monographs, 1982); Andrei Oţetea, ed., *The History of the Romanian People,* trans. Eugenia Farca (New York: Twayne Publishers, 1970); and R. W. Seton-Watson, *A History of the Roumanians* (New York: Shoe String Press, 1934).

Studies of Ottoman and early national Romania to 1878 include: William G. East, *The Union of Moldavia and Wallachia, 1859: An Episode in Diplomatic History* (New York: Octagon Books, 1973); Radu Florescu and Raymond T. McNally, *Dracula, Prince of Many Faces: His Life and His Times* (Boston: Little, Brown, 1989); Keith Hitchins, *The Rumanian National Movement in Transylvania, 1780-1849* (Cambridge, MA: Harvard University Press, 1969); Beatrice Marinescu, *Romanian-British Political Relations, 1848-1877*, trans. Liliana Teodoreanu (Bucharest: The Academy, 1983); and Paul E. Michelson, *Conflict and Crisis: Romanian Political Development, 1861-1871* (New York: Garland Press, 1987).

Post-1878 Romania through World War II, including Romania's side in the "Transylvanian Question," is examined in: Cornelia Bodea, *Transylvania in the History of the Romanians* (Boulder, CO: East European Monographs, 1982); John M. Cabot, *The Racial Conflict in Transylvania: A Discussion of the Conflicting Claims of Rumania and Hungary to Transylvania, the Banat, and the Eastern Section of the Hungarian Plain* (Boston: Beacon Press, 1926); Ludanyi Cadzow, ed., *Transylvania: The Roots of Ethnic Conflict* (Kent, OH: Kent State University Press, 1983); Miron Constantinescu and Ştefan Pascu, eds., *Unification of the Romanian National State: The Union of Transylvania with Old Romania* (Bucharest: The Academy, 1971); Constantin C. Giurescu, *Transylvania in the History of the Romanian People* (Bucharest: Meridiane, 1968); Elemer Illyes, *National Minorities in Romania: Change in Transylvania* (Boulder, CO: East European Monographs, 1982); Mircea Muşat and Ion Ardeleanu, *Political Life in Romania, 1918-1921*, trans. Sanda Mihailescu (Bucharest: The Academy, 1982); Ştefan Pascu, *A History of Transylvania*, trans. D. Robert Ladd (New York: Dorset, 1982); Pavel Pavel, *Transylvania and Danubian Peace* (London: New Europe Publishing Co., 1943); and R. W. Seton-Watson, *Transylvania: A Key-Problem* (Oxford: Classic Press, 1943).

Romania under communism is addressed by: Nicholas Dima, *Bessarabia and Bukovina: The Soviet-Romanian Territorial Dispute* (Boulder, CO: East European Monographs, 1982); Stephen Fischer-Galati, *The Socialist Republic of Rumania* (Baltimore, MD: Johns Hopkins University Press, 1969), and his *The New Rumania: From People's Democracy to Socialist Republic* (Cambridge, MA: MIT Press, 1967); David Floyd, *Rumania: Russia's Dissident Ally* (New York: Praeger, 1965); Ronald H. Linden, *Communist States and International Change: Romania and Yugoslavia in Comparative Perspective* (Boston: Allen & Unwin, 1987); Ian M. Matley, *Romania: A Profile* (New York: Praeger, 1970); John M. Montias, *Economic Development in Communist Rumania* (Cambridge, MA: MIT Press, 1967); and Corneliu Vasilescu, *Romania in International Life* (Bucharest: Meridiane, 1969).

Slovakia has been dealt with mostly in studies of the former Czechoslovakia. There are, however, some works dedicated to the Slovaks in particular. These include: Emanuel Bohm, ed., *Human Rights Violations: Sixty Documents From the Occupied Territories of Southern and Eastern Slovakia in Years 1938-1940* (Cleveland: Slovak Institute, 1986); Thomas Čapek, *The Slovaks of Hungary, Slavs and Panslavism* (New York: Knickerbocker, 1906); Joseph A. Mikuš, *Slovakia: A Political History, 1918-1950* (Milwaukee: Marquette University Press, 1963); Gilbert L. Oddo, *Slovakia and Its People* (New York: Robert Speller & Sons, 1960); Stephen J. Palickar, *Slovakian Culture in the Light of History, Ancient, Medieval and Modern* (Cambridge, MA: Hampshire, 1954); Eugen Steiner, *The Slovak Dilemma* (Cambridge: Cambridge University Press, 1973); and Peter P. Yurchak, *The Slovaks: Their History and Traditions* (Whiting, IN: John J. Lach, 1946).

There now are two meanings to the proper term "Yugoslavia." One refers to the former, pre-1991 state that was formed in 1918; the other now consists of Serbia and Montenegro. Regarding the former (in more ways than one!), some general studies treating with the country through World War II are: Charles A. Beard and George Radin, *The Balkan Pivot: Yugoslavia. A Study in Government and Administration* (New York: Macmillan, 1929); Stephen Clissold, ed., *A Short History of Yugoslavia: From Early Times to 1966* (Cambridge: Cambridge University Press, 1966); Dimitrije Djordjević, ed., *The Creation of Yugoslavia* (Santa Barbara, CA: Clio, 1980); J. B. Hoptner, *Yugoslavia in Crisis, 1934-1941* (New York: Columbia University Press, 1962); Robert J. Kerner, ed., *Yugoslavia* (Berkeley: University of California Press, 1949); Matteo J. Milazzo, *The Chetnik Movement & the Yugoslav Resistance* (Baltimore, MD: Johns Hopkins University Press, 1975); Dragisa N. Ristić, *Yugoslavia's Revolution of 1941* (University Park, PA: Pennsylvania State University Press, 1966); Allen Roberts, *The Turning Point: The Assassination of Louis Barthou and King Alexander I of Yugoslavia* (New York: St. Martin's Press, 1970); Carlo Sforza, *Fifty Years of War and Diplomacy in the Balkans: Pashich and the Union of the Yugoslavs* (New York: Columbia University Press, 1940); and Jozo Tomasevich, *The Chetniks: War and Revolution in Yugoslavia* (Stanford, CA: Stanford University Press, 1975). Rebecca West, *Black Lamb and Grey Falcon: A Journey Through Yugoslavia* (New York: Penguin Books, 1982), provides one of the most insightful glimpses into the cultural and national problems that, just prior to World War II, were threatening to dissolve Yugoslavia into the sort of bloody chaos that exists in the area today.

Socialist Yugoslavia is examined in two incisive works by Milovan Djilas: *The New Class* (New York: Praeger, 1957, and *The Unperfect Society: Beyond the New Class*, trans. Dorian Cooke (New York: Harcourt Brace & World, 1969). Other studies include: Hamilton F. Armstrong, *Tito and Goliath* (New York: Macmillan, 1951), for the Tito-Stalin split; John C. Campbell, *Tito's Separate Road: America and Yugoslavia in World Politics* (New York: Harper & Row, 1967); Jack C. Fisher, *Yugoslavia, A Multinational State: Regional Difference and Administrative Response* (San Francisco: Chandler, 1966); Bruce J. McFarlane, *Yugoslavia: Politics, Economics, and Society* (London: Pinter, 1988); Christopher Prout, *Market Socialism in Yugoslavia* (New York: Oxford University Press, 1985); Pedro Ramet, *Nationalism and Federalism in Yugoslavia, 1963-1983* (Bloomington: Indiana University Press, 1984); Alvin Z. Rubinstein, *Yugoslavia and the Unaligned World* (Princeton, NJ: Princeton University Press, 1970); Wayne S. Vucinich, ed., *At the Brink of War and Peace: The Tito-Stalin Split in a Historic Perspective* (New York: Brooklyn College Press, 1982); Duncan Wilson, *Tito's Yugoslavia* (Cambridge: Cambridge University Press, 1979); and M. George Zaninovich, *The Development of Socialist Yugoslavia* (Baltimore, MD: Johns Hopkins University Press, 1968).

The present Serb-Montenegrin Yugoslavia is a Serb-dominated state. The Serbs were the first Balkan people to win autonomy, then independence, from the rule of the Ottoman Turks. Some general studies of Serbia include: R. G. D. Laffan, *The Serbs: The Guardians of the Gate* (New York: Dorset, 1989 [reprint]); David MacKenzie, *The Serbs and Russian Pan-Slavism, 1875-1878* (Ithaca, NY: Cornell University Press, 1967); Michael B. Petrovich, *A History of Modern Serbia, 1804-1918,* 2 vols. (New York: Harcourt Brace Jovanovich, 1976); Harold W. V. Temperley, *History of Serbia* (New York: H. Fertig, 1969 [reprint]); and Wayne S. Vucinich, *Serbia Between East and West: The Events of 1903-1908* (New York: AMS, 1968). For Montenegro in English, there are: Christopher Boehm, *Blood Revenge: The Anthropology of Feuding in Montenegro and Other Tribal Societies* (Lawrence: University of Kansas Press, 1984); Milovan Djilas, *Njegoš: Poet, Prince, Bishop* (New York: Harcourt Brace & World, 1966); and John D. Treadway, *The Falcon and the Eagle: Montenegro and Austria-Hungary, 1908-1914* (West Lafayette, IN: Purdue University Press, 1983).

Just as it is impossible to provide a truly comprehensive bibliography for Eastern Europe within the confines of a single essay, the same holds true for the former Russian/Soviet Empire. That which follows is merely a representative sampling of English-language works available.

General histories of Russia abound. Not all, however, are of high quality. Those works published prior to the onset of the cold war tend to be more objective than those that appeared afterward, since they were less tarnished by ideological propaganda. Most Western studies suffer, in greater or lesser degree, from the standard Western biases. Perhaps the best overall survey of Russia and the Soviet Union is David MacKenzie and Michael W. Curran, *A History of Russia and the Soviet Union, and Beyond,* 4th ed. (Belmont, CA: Wadsworth, 1993), an objective text that presents descriptions and samples of the major, controversial problems of interpretation in Russian/Soviet history. Also of interest among the general studies of imperial Russia are: John D. Bergamini, *The Tragic Dynasty: A History of the Romanovs* (New York: G. P. Putnam's Sons, 1969); Jerome Blum, *Lord and Peasant in Russia: From the Ninth to the Nineteenth Century* (New York: Atheneum, 1968); Joel Carmichael, *A Cultural History of Russia* (New York: Weybright & Talley, 1968); Michael Cherniavsky, *Tsar and People: Studies in Russian Myths* (New York: Random House, 1969); Allen F. Chew, *An Atlas of Russian History: Eleven Centuries of Changing Borders* (New Haven, CT: Yale University Press, 1970 [rev. ed., with later eds. available]); Jesse D. Clarkson, *A History of Russia* (New York: Random House, 1962); James Cracraft, ed., *Major Problems in the History of Imperial Russia* (Lexington, MA: D. C. Heath & Co., 1994); Michael T. Florinsky, *Russia: A History and an Interpretation,* 2 vols. (New York: Macmillan, 1955 [and later eds.]); Hans Kohn, ed., *The Mind of Modern Russia: Historical and Political Thought of Russia's Great Age* (New York: Harper & Bros., 1962); Bernard Pares, *A History of Russia* (New York: Alfred A. Knopf, 1953 [and later eds.]); Richard Pipes, *Russia Under the Old Regime* (New York: Charles Scribner's Sons, 1974); Nicholas V. Riasanovsky, *A History of Russia,* 5th ed. (New York: Oxford University Press, 1993); B. H. Sumner, *A Short History of Russia,* rev. ed. (New York: Harcourt Brace & World, 1949); and George Vernadsky, *A History of Russia,* 5th ed. (New Haven, CT: Yale University Press, 1961).

For medieval Russia to the age of Peter the Great, see: Michael Crichton, ed., *Eaters of the Dead: The Manuscript of Ibn Fadlan Relating His Experiences with the Northmen in A.D. 922* (New York: Alfred A. Knopf, 1976), regarding the Viking origins of Kievan Russia; Charles J. Halperin, *Russia and the Golden Horde: The Mongol Impact on Medieval Russian History* (Bloomington: Indiana University Press, 1985); Richard Hellie, *Enserfment and Military Change in Muscovy* (Chicago: University of Chicago Press, 1971); Vasili Klyuchevsky, *A Course in Russian History: The Seventeenth Century,* trans. Natalie Duddington (Chicago: Quadrangle Books, 1968); Arthur Koestler, *The Thirteenth Tribe: The Khazar Empire and Its Heritage*

(New York: Random House, 1976), a controversial theory on the origins of European Ashkenazi Jewry among the steppe Turkic tribes; Jacques Margeret, *The Russian Empire and the Grand Duchy of Muscovy: A 17th-Century French Account,* trans. and ed. Chester S. L. Dunning (Pittsburgh: University of Pittsburgh Press, 1983); Antonio Possevino, *The Moscovia,* trans. Hugh F. Graham (Pittsburgh: University of Pittsburgh Press, 1977); A. E. Presniakov, *The Formation of the Great Russian State: A Study of Russian History in the Thirteenth to Fifteenth Centuries,* trans. A. E. Moorhouse (Chicago: Quadrangle Books, 1970); and two studies by George Vernadsky, *Kievan Russia* (New Haven, CT: Yale University Press, 1948), and *The Mongols and Russia* (New Haven, CT: Yale University Press, 1953).

Among the general works covering the broad period of Peter the Great to the 1917 revolutions, see: E. M. Almedingen, *The Emperor Alexander I* (New York: Vanguard Press, 1964); Paul Avrich, *Russian Rebels, 1600-1800* (New York: Schocken Books, 1972); Aleksandr N. Engelgardt, *Letters from the Country, 1872-1887,* trans. Cathy A. Frierson (New York: Oxford University Press, 1993); Beatrice Farnsworth and Lynne Viola, eds., *Russian Peasant Women* (New York: Oxford University Press, 1992); Vasili Klyuchevsky, *Peter the Great,* trans. Liliana Archibald (New York: Vintage Books, 1958); Robert K. Massie, *Nicholas and Alexandra* (New York: Dell, 1967); John Maynard, *Russia in Flux: Before October* (New York: Collier Books, 1962); Anatole G. Mazour, *The First Russian Revolution, 1825. The Decembrist Movement: Its Origins, Development, and Significance* (Stanford, CA: Stanford University Press, 1971); Allen McConnell, *Tsar Alexander I: Paternalistic Reformer* (Northbrook, IL: AHM Publishing, 1970); W. E. Mosse, *Alexander II and the Modernization of Russia* (London: I.B. Tauris, 1992 [new ed.]); two works by L. Jay Oliva, *Russia in the Era of Peter the Great* (Englewood Cliffs, NJ: Prentice-Hall, 1969), and Oliva, ed., *Russia and the West from Peter to Khrushchev* (Boston: D. C. Heath & Co., 1965); Bernard Pares, *The Fall of the Russian Monarchy: A Study of the Evidence* (New York: Vintage Books, 1961); Hugh Ragsdale, ed., *Paul I: A Reassessment of His Life and Reign* (Pittsburgh: University of Pittsburgh Press, 1979); Geroid T. Robinson, *Rural Russia under the Old Regime: A History of the Landlord-Peasant World and a Prologue to the Peasant Revolution of 1917* (Berkeley: University of California Press, 1969); Ronald Seth, *The Russian Terrorists: The Story of the Narodniki* (London: Barrie & Rockliff, 1966); B. H. Sumner, *Peter the Great and the Emergence of Russia* (New York: Collier Books, 1968); Wayne S. Vucinich, ed., *The Peasant in Nineteenth-Century Russia* (Stanford, CA: Stanford University Press, 1968); and Avrahm Yarmolinsky, *Road to Revolution: A Century of Russian Radicalism* (New York: Collier Books, 1969).

For Russian imperialist foreign policy in Europe, especially in the Balkans, the following may be consulted: Matthew S. Anderson, *The Eastern Question, 1774-1923: A Study in International Relations* (London: Macmillan, 1966); Virginia Cowles, *The Russian Dagger: Cold War in the Days of the Czars* (New York: Harper & Row, 1969); Charles Jelavich, *Tsarist Russia and Balkan Nationalism: Russian Influence in the Internal Affairs of Bulgaria and Serbia, 1879-1886* (Berkeley: University of California Press, 1958); Richard Millman, *Britain and the Eastern Question, 1875-1878* (Oxford: Clarendon Press, 1979); Philip E. Mosely, *Russian Diplomacy and the Opening of the Eastern Question in 1838 and 1839* (Cambridge, MA: Harvard University Press, 1934); Michael B. Petrovich, *The Emergence of Russian Panslavism, 1856-1870* (New York: Columbia University Press, 1966); Ann P. Saab, *The Origins of the Crimean Alliance* (Charlottesville: University of Virginia Press, 1977); B. H. Sumner, *Russia and the Balkans, 1870-1880* (Oxford: Clarendon Press, 1937), still important; and Andrew Rossos, *Russia and the Balkans: Inter-Balkan Rivalries and Russian Foreign Policy, 1908-1914* (Toronto: University of Toronto Press, 1981).

Overviews of the Soviet period in Russian history can be had in: Isaac Deutscher, *The Unfinished Revolution: Russia, 1917-1967* (New York: Oxford University Press, 1967); Harold Fullard, ed., *Soviet Union in Maps* (Chicago: Denoyer-Geppert Co., 1965); Ian Grey, *The First Fifty Years: Soviet Russia, 1917-67* (New York: Coward-McCann, 1967); Georg von Rauch, *A History of Soviet Russia,* 4th rev. ed., trans. Peter and Annette Jacobsohn (New York: Praeger, 1966); Harrison E. Salisbury, ed., *The Soviet Union: The Fifty Years* (New York: Signet, 1968); and Theodore H. Von Laue, *Why Lenin? Why Stalin? Why Gorbachev?: The Rise and Fall of the Soviet System,* 3rd ed. (New York: HarperCollins Publishers, 1993).

A few general studies of the 1917 revolutions, of the civil war, and of Lenin are worth a serious glance: E. H. Carr, *The October Revolution: Before and After* (New York: Alfred A. Knopf, 1969); Robert V. Daniels, *Red October: The Bolshevik Revolution of 1917* (New York: Charles Scribner's Sons, 1967 [and subsequent eds.]); Louis Fischer, *The Life of Lenin* (New York: Harper & Row, 1964); Sheila Fitzpatrick, *The Russian Revolution, 1917-1932* (Oxford: Oxford University Press, 1982); W. Bruce Lincoln, *Red Victory: A History of the Russian Civil War* (New York: Simon & Schuster, 1989); Alan Moorehead, *The Russian Revolution* (New York: Harper & Row, 1965); David Shub, *Lenin: A Biography* (New York: New American Library, 1948 [abridged ed.]); and Leon Trotsky, *The Young Lenin,* trans. Max Eastman (Garden City, NY: Doubleday, 1972).

The period from Stalin through Gorbachev is addressed by: Abraham Brumberg, ed., *Russia Under Khrushchev: An Anthology from* Problems of

Communism (New York: Praeger, 1964); Edward Crankshaw, *The New Cold War: Moscow v. Pekin* (Baltimore, MD: Penguin Books, 1963), the origins of the latest Eastern European-Far East Asian tremor; Isaac Deutscher, *Stalin: A Political Biography* (New York: Vintage, 1960); Daniel C. Diller, ed., *Russia and the Independent States* (Washington, D.C.: Congressional Quarterly, 1993); Walter LaFeber, *America, Russia, and the Cold War, 1945-1990,* 6th ed. (New York: McGraw-Hill, 1991), quite interesting; Moshe Lewin, *The Gorbachev Phenomenon: A Historical Interpretation* (Berkeley: University of California Press, 1989); Michael Mandelbaum, ed., *The Rise of Nations in the Soviet Union: American Foreign Policy and the Disintegration of the USSR* (New York: Council on Foreign Relations, 1991); and John Scott, *Behind the Urals: An American Worker in Russia's City of Steel* (Bloomington: Indiana University Press, 1989 [enlarged ed.]).